ONLY ONE LIFE

Because of Calvary
1 Cor. 4:2

To Bruce, Geraldine and Vicki
In appreciation for our new friendship

Ken Steward
June 17, 2009
kmsteward@gmail.com

+ ONLY ONE LIFE +

The Story of My Life and Ministry

Kenneth N. Steward

Copyright © 2008 by Kenneth N. Steward

ONLY ONE LIFE
By Kenneth N. Steward

Printed in the United States of America

ISBN 978-1-60647-139-5

All rights reserved solely by the author. The author guarantees all contents are original and do not infringe upon the legal rights of any other person or work. No part of this book may be reproduced in any form without the permission of the author. The views expressed in this book are not necessarily those of the publisher.

Unless otherwise indicated, Bible quotations are taken from the King James Version.

www.xulonpress.com

Dedication

To Jesus Christ, Who made a claim on my life as a boy of sixteen and called my wife and me to a life of service in India, Canada and many other places around the world. God marvelously provided our every need when there was nothing in either the pocket or pantry.

To my wife, Wilma, who encouraged me to write my story and willingly allowed me many hours to write in the privacy of my office. She willingly surrendered me to the will of the Lord in this effort. I love her for her dedication to the Lord and for serving Him together with me these many years.

Only one life 'twill soon be past;
Only what's done for Christ will last.

CONTENTS

Preface	i - iv
Part One: My Beginning Years	1 - 44
Part Two: A Changed Life	45 - 56
Part Three: Life At Bob Jones College	57 - 78
Part Four: Uncle Ken And His Gospel Magic	79 - 93
Part Five: The Goal Before Us	94 - 213
Part Six: A Major Change	214 - 269
Part Seven: A Call To Canada	270 - 316
Part Eight: Another Major Chance	317 - 335
Postlogue	336
Addenda	337 - 354

+ Preface +

This is the story of my life. My original purpose in telling it was that my children, their children, their children's children and how many other generations there may be that follow, would come to know what rich spiritual heritage they have. In the meantime, as others came to know of the writing of my life and ministry, I was encouraged to have my story published and made available to the public.

The inspiration for writing this, if that is what you can call it, came from a very dear friend of ours, a member of Central Baptist Church in Memphis, Tennessee, one of our longtime supporting churches. Dawn Amburgey had asked us sometime in 1995 if she could interview us for writing a story about us, which she could use in Sunday School. We agreed to that, not knowing at the time that with a brief narration of our life, Dawn would write four chapters, along with pictures. Those pictures were a result of her artistic abilities, drawn in color. She later sent us a copy of her writing, with a set of the pictures she used, accompanied by a letter of explanation. She related in that letter of her using the story of our lives in devotional talks in the church's Christian academy. In addition, she told the story to the Chums group during AWANA club time. As a result of what Dawn Amburgey had done, I was encouraged to produce this story of my life, and ministry, which I have entitled ***ONLY ONE LIFE***. And so, my first thanks goes to Dawn and the many hours that took her to write the story, which she entitled, "Faithful is He" (1 Thessalonians 5:24 - "Faithful is he that calleth you, who also will do it").

I acknowledge the wise input of Dr. William Smallman, Vice President of Baptist Mid-Missions, who worked with me in the editing and revision of my work. Dr. Smallman must have spent many hours pouring over my writing, page after page and word after word. Without his help I would not have been able to bring the story of my life and ministry to completion and ready for the publishers.

I must not forget to express my sincere appreciation to Laura Poe, who designed the cover to this book. I enjoyed working with Laura as we went over details of what was to be included in the design.

I am also grateful for the advice and input of Jeff Fitzgerald, a staff member at Xulon Press, publishers of this book.

Lastly, I will be ever thankful for my third daughter, Gloria Anslow, for the time and effort she put into formatting the book as it is. She also skillfully arranged pictures at the end of each part of the book. Each picture portrays, in part in pictorial form, the story of my life and ministry. Gloria, you are fantastic and I love you for what you have done for me in helping to bring this book to reality.

There have been many men and women over the course of my life who have had a great influence in my life. They are too numerous to name here, but each one is known to God and shall be rewarded for their part in my becoming who and what I am. I can truly echo the words of the apostle Paul, "I am what I am by the grace of God" (1 Corinthians 15:10). But the one who has had the greatest influence in my life is my wife, Wilma. I praise God for choosing her to be my wife, the mother of my children and to labor with me in the gospel ministry. God called us together to serve Him. I am thankful for her faithfulness to me and that God has kept me faithful to her.

As we have served the Lord together over these many years, one thing that He has expected of me has been to be faithful; faithful to Him and His word; faithful to His calling, faithful in whatever task was assigned to me, however great or small. I have tried to be faithful, though I know that many times I have failed Him. I am thankful for a God Who is merciful and forgiving, for when I have come to know that I have sinned, having been convicted of that sin by the indwelling Holy Spirit and have confessed that sin, God has been "faithful and just to forgive (my) sin and to cleanse (me) from all unrighteousness" (1 John 1:9). One lesson, which was drilled into us by Dr. Bob Jones Sr., when I was a student at Bob Jones College, was, "it is a sin to do less than your best."

All that I am and all that I have is because of God's grace in my life. Even before I was born God had a plan for my life. He chose me unto salvation, even as God, in eternity past, determined that Christ should come in the fullness of time, the sinless Son of God, born of the virgin Mary. He came to suffer and die for me in my place on a cruel cross, for "He who knew no sin was made sin for me that I might be made the righteousness of God in Him" (2 Corinthians 5:21). God chose me to be His servant to take the gospel to those who knew not the gospel. I am humbled by the fact that God chose to "reveal His Son in me…that I might preach Him among the heathen…" (Galatians 1:16).

It is my prayer that any who reads this story of my life and ministry will realize that they too have only one life and, as a Christian, that life is not their own, but belongs to God Who purchased them through the death of Christ on the cross and the shedding of His blood. God gave His best to them. He expects only their best in serving Him in whatever kind of service and wherever in the world it might be.

My years left on this earth, before God takes me home to heaven, are not many; I realize that. If God should take me by way of death and the grave, I do not fear that path He would choose for me. Until the time I meet my Savior face to face, like the apostle Paul, I am willing "to be absent from the body and to be present with the Lord…that whether present or absent…(I) may be accepted of him"

(2 Corinthians 5:8 – 9)

I have only one life; it belongs to God.

Part One: My Beginning Years

December 12, 1925 – January 10, 1942

Everlasting Love

"For God so loved the world that he gave His only begotten Son, that whosoever believeth in Him should not perish, but have everlasting life."
(John 3:16)

Mother was hoping I would be a girl, for she had already been blessed with one son. Because of this, my parents had really not decided on any boys' names, though, as you will soon see, they did have some in mind. I have no idea what girls' names they may have chosen, had I been a girl; they never told me. At any rate, on the 12th day of December 1925, at exactly 10:15 p.m., local time, I made my entrance into this world at the Maternity Hospital in Minneapolis, Minnesota. Sometimes I tell people that I was born in a hospital because I wanted to be near my mother! What a surprise that must have been to my mother! Another boy! Nameless as I was at the time, I am sure of this one thing, I was just as much welcomed and loved by my parents as if I had been a girl. My mother stood only 4' 10" tall at the time and was destined to have three sons; she never did get her girl. I was the middle of those three sons.

Certainly, the most important thing for my parents to take care of, even before my birth was recorded in the county register, was to give me some names. It would have sounded somewhat ridiculous to have me listed on my birth certificate as "The Nameless One." The question before them, therefore, was, "What are we going to name our son?" Ah, someone came up with a plan. I don't know whom to blame for this, but it was as good a plan as any other. Several names were each written on a piece of paper, put into a hat and then two of them would be drawn out of the hat, one at a time. My older brother, Warren, who was not quite two years old at the time, was told to draw out the two pieces of paper from the hat. The first one would be my first name and the second one would be my second name; that simple. And so, Warren reached his little hand into the hat and out came, you guessed it, Kenneth. Again, his hand went into that hat and out came Norman. Thus, my name became officially Kenneth Norman Steward. I came to find out later that my name means "Handsome Warrior." Now, I will leave it to the reader to decide if those were appropriate names for me.

At the time of my birth, my parents lived at 2928 – 36th Avenue South in Minneapolis, not very far from Fort Snelling. That army base will figure in the story of my life over 17 years later. A number of years ago Wilma and I were in Minneapolis to visit some of my relatives and friends of years gone by. I decided to drive down to that part of the city and see if the house was still there; it was and we found that it was actually a single story duplex. I am only sorry that we were not able to go inside to see where I possibly could have slept in my infant's bed.

My birth certificate states that I was "born alive" at 10:15 p.m. on the 12th day of December 1925; but no place was given for recording the birth weight and how long I was. At any rate, I do know that I was a good size baby and my mother, being as small as she was, must have had a difficult time giving birth. My birth announcement was printed in the local newspaper, along with other public announcements, such as marriage licenses, divorces granted deaths, building permits and stolen automobiles.

Someone's Ford roadster was reported stolen. It must have been black and probably a convertible with a rumble seat in the back, similar to the one that my older brother and I jointly bought for $100 when we were in high school; but, again, that is another story that will have to wait until later to be told. For my birth announcement I was listed as a boy; no name. There I am, still the "Nameless One!"

On the back of the newspaper, giving my birth announcement, now yellow with age, printed over 80 years ago at this writing, are some advertisements of men's and women's clothes on sale at Donaldson's Basement Store. One of the ads was for men's broadcloth shirts "that make acceptable gifts." The price given was for $1.95. Ladies' underwear – "Delight every feminine heart." This ad was printed just before Christmas; the ad states further, "You can rest assured she'll be thrilled beyond words if you give her some dainty piece of lingerie for Christmas." Prices for these items ranged from $1.95 to $2.92.

A baby book – Our Baby – was given by a friend of the family and there it is recorded on the first page that I actually weighed in at 8 lbs. 8 oz. at birth and gained nearly 1 lb. 8 oz. by the first month. On my first birthday I weighed just an ounce under 25 pounds. I must have been a contented and happy baby; at least Mother recorded in my baby book that I gave my first real smile at five weeks of age.

As stated earlier, my mother had wanted me to be a girl. Until I was at least one year old, she put me in dresses. I have a picture of my older brother and me, taken when I was six months old. My brother was dressed in what was known as a "Little Lord Fauntleroy" outfit, which were popular little boys' suits in those days, for they were named after a character in a movie, who wore a similar outfit. There I am in that picture, sitting beside my brother on a small table in my lace-trimmed dress. I don't seem to be looking too happy in that picture. Could it have been that even at that tender age of six months I knew that dresses were meant for girls, not boys! Maybe some of the blame falls on my father's oldest sister regarding this matter of my being in a dress, for it is recorded in my baby book that one of the gifts I received at birth was that dress from my aunt.

On January 1, 1926, New Year's Day, my parents took my brother and me to see our Grandfather and Grandmother Steward. We had to go on the streetcar, for we didn't have an automobile. It was a long trip, for we had to go from the southeast end of the city all the way to the northwest end. It must have taken well over an hour, or more; and then there would have to be at least one transfer made to another streetcar. Fares were paid by token, costing 5 cents each; the tokens would be dropped through a slot at the top of a box by the streetcar driver when a passenger got on. That meant that one could ride from one end of the city to the other for just that 5 cent token. In my baby book, Mother recorded that "he slept all the time he was there." Wasn't that an enjoyable time I had at Grandma Steward's house on my first New Year's Day!

I don't think my parents were too happy about what happened when I was seven months old. They did not have many expensive things in their home; but one thing that my mother valued greatly was a glass bowl with some bright red poppies in it. She had put that bowl, with the bright red poppies in it on a table, which was covered with a cloth. One day, as I was trying to walk, I stumbled and began to fall. It was only natural that I should reach out to grab something in order to keep from falling. Well, I grabbed the end of that cloth which hung over the edge of the table. As a result, the tablecloth and the glass bowl, with the bright red poppies in it, came crashing to the floor; the glass bowl smashed to pieces. Why I know that this happened was because Mother just had to record in my baby book what I had done. That baby book reveals many things about me in my first year of life.

Though my mother must have been quite distraught at what happened that day, when the glass bowl, with the bright red poppies in it, came crashing to the floor, she seemed proud of other accomplishments that I was responsible for. I was seven months old when my first tooth broke through. The story of that even is also recorded in my baby book. Maybe that first tooth made up for my having broken her glass bowl with the bright red poppies in it! How proud my parents must have been when I took my first steps all by myself, without having to hold onto anything, or anybody holding onto me. I had just had my first birthday three days before.

I was sick a lot in the first few years of my life. I had whooping cough or pneumonia – I can't remember which, exactly – three times and my parents nearly lost me the third time. Back in those days there were not the wonder drugs we have today. The only remedy then was to cover the bare chest with a warm mustard plaster and hope that it would do the job and cure the patient. It must have worked in my case, because I am still here to attest to its apparent efficacy. One day, when I was learning to walk, I fell onto a hot air register on the floor. In those days our house was heated with coal and there was a large grate right above the furnace, which was in the basement. I had fallen onto the metal grate, which was extremely hot. I must have screamed in terrible pain until someone came and picked me up; but it was too late, for I was burned badly, leaving me with scars on both hands that remain there to this day.

Even though we were poor, we enjoyed doing things together as a family. The simple little things were fun. A few years after my father died on December 11, 1974, I found a small packet of papers, including a copy of his brief memoirs. He wrote the following, which tells of the life we had as a family in our early days:

"While we lived in South Minneapolis, we used to fix a picnic basket and take the boys on the street car to Minnehaha Falls and the boys would ride the ponies. As I look back on those years, when the boys were small and our devotion to them laid the groundwork for their devotion to us. As they grew up, we did not worry who their friends were as they used to bring them home. And we were proud of the boys the way they picked their friends."

When I was growing up my mother used to call me Kenny. I knew that when she used that name, everything was okay; but if she used my full name, Kenneth, I became suspicious and wondered as to what I had done to incur her displeasure. When I was very young, smaller than my mother in size, I would try to run away, rather than be punished for any "crime" I had committed. If I stayed away long enough, maybe Mother would forget and I would be able to escape any punishment due me. Sometimes it worked and sometimes it didn't.

There were five lakes close to downtown Minneapolis, all joined together by beautiful lagoons, or streams. When I was a teenager, I enjoyed paddling in a canoe through those lagoons; that was certainly a fun part of my early life. Minneapolis is called the 'City of Lakes." Minnesota is referred to as 'The Land of Sky Blue Water" and its motto is, 'The Land of 10,000 Lakes," though I have heard it said that there are many more than 10,000.

My Family Heritage

Minnesota was heavily populated with people of Scandinavian descent, especially from Sweden and Norway. If your name did not end with 'son,' you were simply a foreigner to the Scandinavian people; you stood out like the proverbial 'sore thumb.' My heritage is Scottish and Irish, mainly. As a Steward, my father's people came from Scotland, from the Steward, or Stuart clan. On my mother's side, her mother's father, which is, my great grandfather, came from somewhere in what is now Northern Ireland; he was a McDermott, or McDermont. My great grandfather McDermott immigrated to America in the early part of the 19th century and eventually settled in the southern part of Minnesota. My maternal grandfather's people came from County Cork in the Republic of Ireland.

I have a rich heritage on both sides of my family. On my maternal grandmother's side we can go back seventeen generations to Plymouth Colony, to my ancestor William Sabin, who, in 1640 married a woman by the name of Mary Elizabeth Wright; she died some twenty years later, having borne to William twelve children. William Sabin then married again and his second wife, Martha Allen, bore him eight children. That means that my ancestor had fathered twenty children in all, a big family, even for that day. William Sabin went on to become one of the founders of the town of Rehoboth, Massachusetts, but now in the State of Rhode Island. The town is well known in early American New England history. William Sabin apparently operated a grist mill; the mill is gone, but there is a sign there today, showing the spot where the mill had stood beside a small stream.

Through one of my ancestors, our family can be traced back to none other than King Alfred the Great. Was royal blood flowing through my veins? Well, by the time it reached me it has become very, very thin! More important than that kind of royal blood that may be flowing so thinly through my veins is the "royal" line I have belonged to since I was accepted into the family of the King of kings, Jesus Christ. But even that story must wait until later to be told in these memoirs of mine.

As to my maternal grandfather, Azro Dallas Condon, little is known at this point in time, beyond the fact that he was born in the small southern Minnesota town of St. Peter. I do know, as previously mentioned, that his people came from somewhere in County Cork in what is now the Republic of Ireland. I would like to know more about that side of my family.

When I was a small child, I knew very little about my father's family. My Grandmother Steward whose name was Laurie Angeline Carter, was a quiet person and she kept pretty much to herself. It was not until nearly ten years before I began penning these words that I came to know that she was born in the small town of Edgerton, Minnesota, as were my father and all his siblings. Edgerton is located in the southwestern part of the state. It was there that my grandmother's father was a minister in the Congregational church.

As a young boy, Elisha Carter bought his first Bible, when he was only 8 years of age, with pennies he had saved over a number of years. The Bible was published by the British and Foreign Bible Society in 1838 and he preached from that Bible. Needless to say, Bibles didn't cost anywhere as much as they do today; but neither did anything else. My great grandfather Carter's Bible is in the possession of a cousin of mine, the elder daughter of my father's oldest sister. While Wilma and I were visiting in the home of my cousin, Audrey Mielke, I was able to hold that Bible in my hands and read the note that our great grandfather had written, telling the story of how he had bought that Bible as a young lad; that note was in the fly leaf of the Bible. The thrilling part of the story is of how he had gone on to become a minister of the gospel and preach from that very Bible. I am awed to this very day by the whole matter. The congregational denomination preached the gospel in those early days; but that was not true by the time I was born. Our family attended the Congregational church in Robbinsdale, a suburb of Minneapolis on the north side of the city, near where I lived in my early teen years. The minister didn't believe the Bible to be the very Word of God and that it was without error of any kind. In fact, he openly denied the truths of the Bible and the very deity of Christ. We heard him say at one time that Jesus was born of an illicit relationship between Mary and a blond, blue-eyed Roman soldier. How times have changed.

My father's father, William Steward, was born in Kendall County in Illinois, which is southwest of Chicago about 40 miles. His grandfather had moved west with the family from Pennsylvania in a covered wagon. The Illinois River Valley is a rich agricultural region and in time, my ancestor was able to acquire a vast amount of land and became a well-to-do farmer. He had a part in the founding of Plano, Illinois. There is another town just west of Plano that is named Steward, which was begun by a member of that family. Shortly after my mother died, as we were going through many things she had saved, we found a newspaper article, now turned yellow with age, which told the amazing story of how my ancestor had helped an inventor by the name of Charles W. Marsh, begin a company for the purpose of manufacturing a farming implement that Marsh had invented.

In time, my ancestor sold his interest in the company. The company, joined with others, each one of them also small in size, to begin a new company that eventually came to be known as the International Harvester Company. A mural in the entrance to Plano High School attests to the fact that Plano, Illinois was the home of International Harvester Company.

One time, while we were back in the States on furlough from India, I had occasion to be in that area. I made a special trip to Plano, sought out the mayor of the town in order to garner from him some information about the town, the Steward families that still lived in the area, along with other information. After talking with the mayor, I went out to the town cemetery and there found row after row of Stewards, who had been buried in the cemetery, all ancestors of mine. Well, speaking of the supposed wealth of my great-great-grandfather and of what eventually became the largest farm implement company in the world, which also produces large trucks, none of that wealth trickled on down to our family. As I look at it now, it was probably a good thing. I was born in poverty, just before the Great Depression of 1929-32. How poverty can be a good thing will be self-evident as the story of my life unfolds.

My Early Years

At the time of my birth my father worked for the Ford Motor Company in the paint department; the plant was located on the Mississippi River between the Twin Cities of St. Paul and Minneapolis. It was Henry Ford himself who once said that when a person bought a new Ford car he could "choose any color he wanted, just so it was black." My father, as a result of that policy, had only one color to work with, black! Then the Great Depression struck us, as it did countless thousands of others. My father suddenly found himself without work, with no means to put food on the table for his family, to pay the rent, or the many other basic necessities of life. We were thrown onto the mercy of the government.

In 1932 along came Franklin Delano Roosevelt, who was the new president of the United States. Through his efforts, various recovery programs were introduced and my father became a part of that. As a result, my father was able, for a time anyway, to provide some of those necessities of life. My father became a strong supporter of the Democratic Party and was until the day he died. He believed that Roosevelt was truly the savior of the nation and of our family, in particular. I don't believe Dad was very happy about the fact that his three sons were committed Republicans.

Dad had served his country well in the "war to end all wars," as World War I eventually came to be called. Dad was 18 years of age when he went off to fight in France. He was taken into the army as a foot soldier and fought in open trench warfare, right up on the front lines in France. With just weeks of training to prepare him for war, the orders were, "kill or be killed." While many men who were of my father's age were killed and many others suffered the lasting effects of mustard gas the Germans used against the Allied Forces, my father managed to escape the worst of it. He came out of the war without injury by bullets or bayonet; but he did not come home after the war completely unscathed. The intensity of the fighting left my Dad with what was then called 'shell shock,' which affected him through the rest of his life, until he died at the age of 78. I don't remember my father talking much about his part in the war, though one story came down to us at the time. Apparently, one morning, while in a front line trench, he awoke to find himself lying on a dead German soldier, who was probably no older than my father was. Somewhere that young German soldier had a family, who would not find their loved one returning home, as my father did. War is a terrible thing.

Dad spent many of our younger years in the veterans' hospital at Fort Snelling on the far southeast side of Minneapolis. It is there we find the convergence of the Mississippi and Minnesota Rivers. It would be at Fort Snelling where I would go in 1943, during the latter years of World War II, for my physical examination for the purpose of serving my country in the army. I had received a commission in the army with a second lieutenant's rank; this was the result of high marks I received in a special exam I had taken during my last year of high school. And yet, I would not be inducted into the army, for when the examining officer got to my feet, he found that I had flat feet. Even though I pled with the officer that I had a walking job, which took me many miles every day, as well as having been on our high school track team, I was declared physically unfit to serve in the army. Rejected and dejected, I returned home, wondering what God had for me.

I was just a little over three years old when my mother gave birth to my youngest brother, Douglas. By that time she must have given up hope of every having a girl, for there were just we three boys in the family; what a handful we must have been! Some years later, when I was getting ready to enter kindergarten, we moved to a small house on Dupont Avenue North, a few blocks south of Lowry Avenue. The streets of Minneapolis, which run mostly north and south, have names in alphabetical order, starting with Aldrich and ending with Zenith; then they start over again in the alphabet.

I attended kindergarten at Bremer School, which stood on the corner of Fremont Avenue North and Lowry Avenue. I remember very clearly that every afternoon we would have a rest period, which meant that we had to lie very still on the little rugs, which were put down on the floor in our kindergarten room. To me, that was always a fun time. For Mother's Day in 1931 I made a special card for my mother. On the outside of the card I made a row of yellow flowers on green stems. I couldn't write, of course, for I had just turned five years of age the December before; it must have been that the words penned on the inside of the card were done by my kindergarten teacher. Though written down by someone else, they still expressed the feeling I had for my mother. I was so proud to have her as my mother.

> **Mother, my darling;**
> **Mother, my dear;**
> **I love you, I love you**
> **Each day of the year.**

I'm glad my mother kept that card, as she kept so many other family mementos. Looking at that card brings back many happy memories of experiences I had in my boyhood, even though our family lived in poverty. We learned early in life the value of hard work and to be faithful at whatever task we had to do. There were times when I failed to carry out a task assigned to me, but I am thankful that I have a loving God Who forgives us when we fail and recognizing that failure, come to Him in repentance. My father was determined that no matter what it took, no matter how hard a job, whatever job it was, he would put food on the table. Dad was not too proud to do any kind of a job, for that was how he was raised as a boy and that was how he taught us. My parents made sure we would be dressed neatly, even though it might be in clothes that were patched. We boys wore many patched clothes in those early years.

One thing I remember doing in the summer when we lived in that little house on Dupont Avenue North was to chase after the ice wagon in the summer. The wagon was pulled by a horse and as the ice man drove slowly down our street, crying out for people to buy his ice, we boys would run after the wagon, hoping to catch a piece of ice as it fell from off the wagon, so that we could suck the ice. What fun that was. At that time there were only iceboxes to keep food cold. It would get very cold in Minnesota in the winter and the lakes would freeze over as much as a foot thick, or even thicker. Blocks of ice would be cut out of the frozen lakes by special saws and then stacked in a warehouse near the lakes, covered over with a thick layer of sawdust. The ice would remain frozen all summer, or until it was taken out to be sold.

By the time I was in my early grades in school, we had moved eight blocks to the west to a small house on Logan Avenue, just south of Lowry Avenue. We lived in the upstairs of that house and the only way to get up there was by climbing up some rickety stairs on the outside of the house. The house backed onto an alley that ran between Logan and the next street over, Morgan Avenue. What fun we had in the summer playing *Kick the Can* in the alley. Children don't play fun games like that anymore. Hardly anybody in today's generation would even know what kind of a game *Kick the Can* would be. It's a lost 'art.'

I had a friend who lived on Morgan Avenue, down at the other end of the block. In the summer we would set up a game of Monopoly on his glassed in front porch. Those games would sometimes last for days. If it was time to go home for supper, we would leave the game as it was and go back the next day to finish it, or keep playing as long as necessary, until someone won; none of us was willing to give up until we absolutely had to. What fun we had! There were other games we enjoyed playing, as well.

When I was not quite 9 years old I had my first real experience of leaving home to go to camp. I had never been away from home before on my own. It was the summer of 1934. I must have had a great time at camp, for I wrote the following letter home:

> Dear Mother, we arrived here safely about a couple of hours late; therefore, we were forced to take a tent that was old. I have Jerry and Jimmy sleeping with me. We had a fight last night after taps, pulling each other's covers off. They sure do give us good meals up here. We had quite difficulty getting our tent up before it rained. I am trying to get a scalp. I will write my next letter Thursday.
> Your loving son, Kenneth.
>
> P.S. Some other kids and I have to wash dishes for Monday's dinner and supper

Something else I found amongst my mother's things after she died was a poem, entitled
"Vacation." It was published by the Minneapolis Area Council Boy Scouts of America and printed on a 3 x 5 card. I am sure that this must have been an expression of my mother's feelings, as she saw her second son go off to Boy Scout camp, his very first time to be away from home.

> He started off at dawn for summer camp---
> How long he had been waiting for this day!
> Our little lad, whose face still bears the stamp

Of boyhood; who has never been away from
Home at night---who hove a heavy pack to boyish
   Shoulders, sudden, squared with pride;
Departed, laughing, not once looking back;
   I'm glad he did not know his mother cried.
Dear Father-God, take special care of him---
   He's very trusting and he is so young.
Return him sun-browned, sturdy, sound of limb;
   With songs of wind and water on his tongue;
   With friends, adventures, campfire dreams to prize;
   With memories of mountains in his eyes.

During the 4th of July holidays we usually bought packages of tiny firecrackers, called 'lady fingers.' They were all tied together in a long string. We'd light one cracker and watch the whole string of those 'lady fingers' explode, one after the other, as they bounced around on the ground. What a racket! Sometimes we would be very brave, or so we thought. Holding one of the crackers by the tips of two fingers, we would light it and wait until it went off. There was generally no harm done to the fingers, for the 'lady finger' firecrackers had only a very small amount of powder in each one. No one that we knew of ever lost any of their own fingers doing that crazy trick. It was a lot of fun, though I don't think our parents knew that we were doing that, or, I am sure they would have put a stop to our fun. We did something else that probably was not a safe thing to do; we would take a larger firecracker and put it under an empty can turned upside down. With the fuse lying partly outside the can, we would then light the fuse and run away as fast as we could to where we thought it would be safe, holding our ears and waiting for the "big bang." When the firecracker went off, it made a terrible noise and sent the empty can flying high up into the sky. We would see whose can went the highest. Little did we know at that time that nearly 35 years later powerful rockets would send men all the way to the moon.

During those years we lived on Logan Avenue North, my Uncle Walter and Aunt Gertrude Fisher lived across the street from a large park just south of West Broadway. We used to go to their house on the 4th of July to watch all the fireworks being shot off in the park. Aunt Gertrude was Dad's younger sister. My mother didn't much like watching, but I always looked forward to the event with great excitement; what a sight that was! I think it was mainly the loud noises the rockets made as they shot into the air that Mother didn't appreciate and when that time came she would seem to disappear into the house.

When we moved to the house on Logan Avenue, I began attending Cleveland Elementary School, which was located on the corner of Queen Avenue and Lowry. The school doesn't exist today, for the building was later torn down and some kind of commercial building put up in its place. At that time the school system in Minneapolis was set up in such a way that a child could begin school either in September or January. Grades were identified by B and A, B being the 1st semester and A the second semester. When I was in 4th grade I had badly swollen tonsils and had them taken out. I was one sick boy, but I remember that I had to stay in the hospital several days and the only food I could swallow was Jell-O; and from what I can remember, it was red Jell-O. I could eat it by the 'ton.' It was one of my most favorite foods and still is.

Our Move To The Country

When I was promoted to 5A in June 1936, we had to move. Dad didn't have a job and couldn't pay the rent for that very small upstairs duplex. Grandpa Condon, my mother's father, owned two acres of land and a small house on it out in the country north of Minneapolis. The property was on what was then called 'D' Street in Crystal Village. We were two miles from the closest school in the nearby town of Robbinsdale. There was only one way to get to town and that was to walk; there wasn't any bus system then, not even for schools.

The house had one bedroom, where my parents slept with only a curtain over the doorway for privacy. We three boys all slept in one bed near the potbelly wood-burning stove in the living room. The house had no foundation, but sat right on the ground. The outside walls had no insulation in them in those days. We were too poor to buy coal or wood with which to heat the house in the winter. We collected coal from the nearby railway tracks, as well as old wooden rail ties that had been left beside the tracks when new rail ties were put in their place by the railway workers.

There was no running water. An outside pump, as well as one in the kitchen, supplied us with water. Just before the first freeze Dad would pull up the pipe from the outside pump, taking off the small pump and store it for the winter. Our only supply of water in the winter came from that inside pump. In the winter Mother would fill a kettle full of water before going to bed and put it on the kitchen stove. By the next morning the water in the kettle would usually be frozen solid. The temperature in the winter would often go down to a minus 30 or 40 degrees Fahrenheit outside and almost felt that cold in the house. But my mother would turn the stove on and heat the kettle until the ice turned to warm water. She would then pour the warm water down the pump in the kitchen and prime the pump until she got water. Some winters there had been so much snow that when it all melted the following spring we would be flooded out and have to be taken to higher ground by somebody's row boat. Those were the days!

We didn't have inside plumbing, of course; we had an outhouse that sat over a hole. Oh it was brutal to have to go out there in those cold winter days. Whatever we had to do, we did it in a hurry! One summer I was looking forward to going to Boy Scout camp. I was 14 years old at the time and had worked hard, putting my money aside to pay my own way to camp. Well, I was so proud of having my own money for Boy Scout camp; I carried it around in my wallet wherever I went. I can't remember, but I may have even slept with it under my pillow at night. Anyway, one day, with that wallet in my back pocket, I went to the outhouse. Without going into a lot of detail, but just to say, my wallet suddenly fell out of my back pocket and through one of the seat openings, down below into all of that stinky mess! There went all my money I had saved for Boy Scout camp. What was I to do? Had I now lost my only chance to go to Boy Scout camp? No! The little grey cells up in my head began to work furiously. Somehow, if it was the last thing I would do on this earth, I would bring that wallet back up and recover my camp money. With the aid of a long stick, I managed to get hold of the wallet and carefully and slowly recovered it. What a mess! I had no concern for the wallet and any of its other contents, except for my camp money. I recovered the money and managed to wash it and lay each bill carefully out in the sun to dry. Needless to say, the rest of the contents, along with the wallet, found their way quickly into the rubbish to be burned. Camp? What a time I had, but earned at a great price!

I sent a postcard to my mother from camp; it was postmarked August 8, 1940. The camp was located near

Clearwater Lake and the postcard was stamped from the small town of Annandale, Minnesota. The postcard says it all.

> Dear Mother, Camp Wakapoh is open for inspection, Sunday, Aug. 11th. There will be water festivities also. I am passing my mapping now. I received your letter. I am fine, but James' cot ripped along the side and his cot sags.
> Your loving son, Kenneth.

I have always loved to travel. When I was a lad I dreamed of seeing the world. That dream came to pass when Wilma and I began traveling as missionaries to India. I still love to travel and over these many years have traveled to places I had never dreamed of ever seeing. I have never had the experience of being homesick and, unfortunately, I am unable to empathize with those who do go through that experience.

A few miles from where I lived out in the country in Crystal Village, there are two lakes connected together by a small stream; they are known as Twin Lakes and well stocked with fish. Many times in the summer I would walk down the railway tracks to where a trestle crossed over that small stream. There I would sit for hours on the trestle, with my feet dangling over the side, hoping that a train would not come along. With my fishing line tied onto one end of a small bamboo pole and a worm on the hook at the other end of the string, I would patiently wait for a fish to go after the bait. On occasion, I would catch a fish, take it home and have Mother fry it for me to eat. Boy, were they ever good!

One time I decided to go fishing with some of my friends,

who lived near us. I failed to tell my parents where I had gone, which was very unusual for me. I was not a rebellious boy and tried to be obedient and always let them know what I was planning on doing, where I was going and who my companions would be, if any. But this one time I failed to do that. While we were fishing, a heavy storm blew up and we decided we had better head for home. As we walked along the railway tracks on our way back home, I saw someone coming toward us in the distance and knew right away that it was my father. Suddenly, I remembered that I had not let my parents know where I was going. Boy, was I in trouble! When my father came upon us he was as soaked as we were and I could see how angry he was, but at the same time, very relieved to know that I was okay, as were my friends. I managed to escape any kind of punishment, but had learned my lesson well. My father explained to me how worried Mother and he were, wondering where I was in that rain storm, whether I was hurt, or whatever had happened to me; they were quite ready to call the police, for which I was thankful they had not. But never again did I ever disappoint my parents in not consulting with them before I went on any other kind of adventure.

The house in which we lived, sat on two acres of land, one on which we grew our own vegetables and fruit. We had no plow, but only a digging fork and shovel, with which we turned over the soil. We thought we were living like kings. We had raspberry bushes, currents and gooseberries, as well as concord grapes, one crabapple tree and several plum trees.

My father eventually got a job in St. Paul, working as a janitor in one of the state government buildings. Everyday he had to walk the two miles into Robbinsdale, where he could catch a streetcar and from there go all the way through Minneapolis, across the Mississippi River to downtown St. Paul. That trip must have taken him nearly two hours each way, including the walk into town to catch the streetcar. I am sure that my father must have hated that life, especially walking into town in the dead of winter. But I am also sure he was at least happy he had a steady job. On the other hand, I loved every part of that life in the country; that is, except for digging up that soil, one shovel at a time. I also didn't enjoy having to pick those tiny currents. One day my mother said to me, knowing that I hated getting my hands dirty, "Kenneth, when you grow up you'll get a job that requires using your brains and not your hands." Well, if Mother could see me now; I love working in the garden, with flowers and vegetables and I love getting dirt between my fingernails!

I loved the summertime during those years we lived on 'D' Street in Crystal Village. My Grandmother Condon would cook up beets and make pickled beets, one of my favorite foods; it still is. How I loved those pickled beets Grandma made. Then there was something else I always looked forward to in the summer. On the backside of the house that my Grandpa Condon had built many years before, was a single car garage. We didn't own a car and so, we used the garage to store the canned goods that Mother would make from the vegetables we grew, as well as those delicious pickled beets. Dad always made my favorite drink in the summer. He would buy a bottle of concentrated Hires root beer syrup and make bottle after bottle of root beer. The bottles were empty ketchup bottles. Along with the Hires root beer syrup, he bought bottle caps that he put on the bottles with a special machine that pressed down onto the caps and sealed the bottles now filled with root beer. Dad mixed yeast with the root beer syrup, along with water; the yeast gave the root beer its "fizz." What a drink! We could hardly wait until the root beer was ready and the yeast had done its work.

One summer I got a job working on a truck farm. Every morning I was picked up in front of our house, along with a dozen other fellows, by the farmer, who took us out to his farm in the back of his truck. His farm was called a 'truck farm,' because he would haul his produce into town in his truck and sell his produce at special markets. Some days our job was to hoe between rows of radishes, carrots, or onions, or else we pulled weeds; some days we had to pick those radishes, carrots, or onions and wash and tie them into small bunches, with rubber bands. It was hard work for all of 5 cents an hour. One day we decided that we had enough of those "slave" wages. This was my first and only experience of trying to organize a "labor union." I got the others to lay down their tools and we struck for higher wages. We wanted our hourly wages to go from 5 cents to 10 cents an hour, a 100% increase in wages. What union today would be able to make that kind of a demand for their union members? Somehow or other the farmer was persuaded to give us what we demanded and we went back to work. We had won our case, though actually no union was really organized. With the money I earned that summer I bought my first balloon-tired bicycle.

My first bicycle actually had wooden rims and solid rubber tires; the frame was very tall. All I knew at the time was that my feet couldn't touch the ground; but I learned to ride on that first bike. What I wouldn't give to have that bicycle today; it would be worth a lot. But my balloon-tired bicycle was my prize possession. I was very proud of it, for I had paid for it with my very own hard-earned money, working on that truck farm. One thing I remember about the bike was that it was painted blue and had a large basket on the front. I was soon to acquire a newspaper route out in the country near where we lived and that basket on my balloon-tired bicycle held the newspapers I delivered to my customers. I had to ride into town to Robbinsdale to pick up my newspapers at a special galvanized metal shed. After rolling each newspaper into a thick, tight roll and tucking one end into the rest of the newspaper to hold it in place, I'd ride back out into the country, going up and down those country roads, delivering the papers. By having the papers in a tight roll, I could ride past each of my customer's houses and toss their paper, hoping that it would land safely on the porch of the house. Occasionally I missed and the paper would land well away from the house in the grass, or on the gravel driveway. No one had a paved driveway in those days. I don't think that many of my customers appreciated my trying to save a bit of time and energy with that method of delivering their newspapers.

Caught In A Blizzard

I didn't have that paper route very long, but one incident stands out in my mind very clearly, as though it happened yesterday and I have physical evidence to this very day that reminds me of what happened on November 11, 1940. On that date, early in the afternoon, the temperature suddenly dropped from a balmy short-sleeved kind of weather, to freezing winter conditions. It was the beginning of the famous Armistice Day Blizzard of 1940; and I was caught up in the middle of it.

On that day I had to go into town to get my newspapers. The temperature had reached a balmy 60 degrees. It was duck hunting season and there were many hunters sitting in their blinds, waiting for the opportune time to drop a duck or two. Suddenly, the winds picked up until there were gusts as strong as 60 miles per hour and the temperature dropped almost in minutes to below freezing. My mother was concerned and wondered out loud if I should go to town. The snow was beginning to fall and cover the ground. At the time the weather didn't seem to be all that bad; at least I didn't think so. The full fury of the storm was yet to strike. I tried to assure my mother that I would be okay and told her that I had to go and do my job; I had to deliver those papers. She reluctantly let me go. By the time I got into town and reached the newspaper shed to pick up my newspapers for that day's delivery, the snow was coming down so thick I could barely see my hands in front of my face. The snow on the ground was now at least a foot deep and more was falling. In the end there would be nearly 17 inches of snow on the ground. I knew there was no way I could go back out into the country with the newspapers in the basket on my bicycle and cover that route. Besides, the truck that always brought the newspapers out from the newspaper office in Minneapolis had not arrived and there was no way the company had to let me know what the situation was.

At the same time, I knew I could not get back home, for once I left town it was wide open country and the storm was raging fiercely. Later on I read that 49 people had died in the storm, most of them duck hunters. What was I to do? I had to find some place of shelter from the storm; I knew I couldn't stay where I was in that cold, unheated metal shed. I possibly could ask to stay in one of the nearby stores; but then, it was a holiday and the stores were all closed anyway. I decided to try and make it to the house of friends of ours, by the name of Sipe. Mr. Sipe ran the Texaco gas station in town. The gas station was also closed. The Sipes' house was just beyond the high school, or about half a mile from the newspaper shed. I thought I could make it that far. But when I started out, I struggled against the howling wind and blowing snow, which, by this time, was up to my knees; it took me about half an hour to make it to the Sipes' house. When they saw me they took me into the house quickly and said that I must stay there until the storm ended. How good it was to be inside in the warmth of their house, away from the storm. It felt good to get into some warm clothes and get a hot drink down me.

Mother had been frantic, wondering where her second son was in that blizzard, wondering if perhaps I was lying dead in a snowdrift somewhere between home and town. As soon as possible, after making it to the Sipes' house, I was able to call home on the telephone. That was one thing Dad had decided that we must have, if anything, and that was a telephone, whatever the cost might be. In this case, it was a good thing. Fortunately, the telephone lines were not down. When my mother heard my voice, she was greatly relieved and told me to stay where I was until it was safe to come home. I can't remember where my father was at the time; but it is possible he had not yet left for work. Anyway, I was stranded in town for three days before it was possible to go home. I had left my bicycle back at the newspaper shed and later went back to get it and ride back home.

During the storm the days were boring and with being house bound, I was ready for any kind of excitement. Well, it happened the first morning after the storm. One of the Sipe boys and I decided to have a pillow fight and what a fight it was; I cannot remember whose idea it was; but we went at it furiously. Feathers didn't fly, but I think that I did, as the Sipe boy landed a solid blow to my head, causing me to fly right off the bed, landing with my head hitting the edge of a hot water heater by the bed. Blood began to flow freely from the gash on the right side of my head. Somehow, with the help of a cold compress, I was able to stop the bleeding. I have a scar on my head that reminds me of the pillow fight I had with that Sipe boy during the famous Armistice Day Blizzard of November 11, 1940. I don't know if my parents ever found out what happened to me. At least, I never discussed the subject with them; and they didn't say anything to me about it. They must not have known what happened.

Other Adventures Near And Far

A farmer across the road from our house had a small pond on his farm where his cows would come to drink. Some of us boys decided to build a small raft to float on that pond and imagine we were Huck Finn, sailing down the Mississippi River at Hannibal, Missouri. There were six of us who were close friends at school and we did a lot of things together. Well, that farm, with its pond doesn't exist anymore; a number of years ago we had an occasion to visit in the area and noticed that across the road from where our old house on 'D' Street stood is now a cemetery.

One of our group, Keith Rother, lived a couple of minutes away in a large farmhouse. One thing we liked about Keith living in that house was that in the back was a large red barn. The hayloft was always filled with hay and we used to grab hold of a thick rope that hung from a pulley on a track suspended from the inside of the barn roof. Grabbing hold of that rope, we would run as fast as we could and then swing out from a higher part of the barn, out over the stack of hay and letting go, fall down into that hay where we would almost be buried. What fun that was and we would do it again and again, until we tired of it and thought of something else that was just as exciting to do.

Back of the Rothers' house was also a small shed that had been used at one time as a chicken shed; but we turned it into a club house, where we could build our model airplanes. Nearby was a small airport from where small planes would fly. The airport had only a grass runway for the planes to take off from and land. The frames of those small planes were basically made of wood and the cloth covering the frames were made to stretch tight with special enamel painted onto the cloth. We used those same enamels on our model airplanes and would beg a small amount of it from the owners of that little airport. The difference was that our planes flew by rubber band power. We liked flying our model airplanes and would even walk long distances to see model airplane competition. For some reason or other, we never entered our planes in that kind of competition. And yet, we had some great times with our own planes.

As I heard from my mother, she had a brother, whose name was Harold; Uncle Harold flew planes and would fly out of that small airport. It was claimed that my uncle was associated at one time with the famous aviator, Charles Lindbergh. One day Uncle Harold ate a hamburger that must have been bad; as a result, he became sick and died soon after from what must have been ptomaine poison in that hamburger.

One of the fellows in our group was Themeo Ellis, who was of Greek ancestry. Themeo lived in a large log house right across the road from that airport out in Crystal Village. It was actually a restaurant and a saloon together. The Ellises lived up stairs. Themeo went on to become principal of a new junior high school in Robbinsdale; when he retired from the Robbinsdale school system one of my cousins became the new principal of the junior high school.

There was a road that ran down the south end of our property called Corvallis Road. It went for about half a mile until it came to a small hill on which were thick woods. We would sometimes walk down that road to the woods and almost get lost in it, it was so thick. We imagined there had been robbers who had hidden out in the woods after a big robbery and had buried their "loot" in the woods; and so, we would go hunting in the woods for whatever the robbers had supposedly buried there. We never did find anything of great interest buried in the woods. What imaginations we had!

Back of the Rothers' property and on the other side of Corvallis Road was a large field on which the farmer, who owned the land, would plant corn. When the corn was fully grown and nearly ripe enough to pick, we had a lot of fun wandering through that cornfield and, like the woods, would almost get lost. We often didn't know where we were from the road. One summer a cow had gotten loose and wandered into that field of corn; she almost exploded from the feast she had, for she was bloated from all the corn she had eaten.

On the corner, between our house and the Rothers lived another family. We became good friends with the boys in that family and were about the same ages. I had a Red Rider BB gun and sometimes imagined that I was a rough rider out in the Wild West, riding on my trusty steed, hunting outlaws. One day some of us boys decided to have a shootout at the O-K Corral, in the basement of their house. We divided up into two groups and went down to the basement with our BB guns.

Fortunately, those BB guns didn't have much power to them; they were spring loaded and single shot. As a result, when we were hit with a BB it felt more like a bee sting. It was a good thing, as I look back upon that escapade, that no one was hit in the eye; one of those BB's could have caused permanent damage. We later saw the folly of that kind of game and didn't try it again. Neither did we tell our parents what we had done, for, I am sure of this, had they known what we were using our BB guns for, they would have been taken away from us.

Traveling Near And Far

As mentioned earlier, I loved to travel; I wanted to see the world. But when I was a young boy, my world of travel was restricted to short distances. There were those two camping trips, which were only a few miles from home. Another summer, our Boy Scout troop went up to the far north, bordering on Canada. We went by bus and from the end of our bus trip, we went in a large boat with all our camping gear, for what seemed many miles. We camped out on an island and our beds were made of sweet smelling pine boughs. We slept on those pine boughs, lying right on the ground. Back in those days sleeping bags had not yet been invented. What a time we had. At night we could hear the wolves howling in the distance, over on another island, or on the mainland. It almost made the hair on the backs of our necks rise up! We were assured by our scout leader that we were perfectly safe where we were, that there were neither wolves, nor bears on our island. During the day we cooked our meals over an open fire that we had to start by hand, with just a stick and wood shavings; no matches were allowed at our Boy Scout campout.

That was the farthest away from home I had ever been; that is, until the summer of 1942. My Grandmother Condon was going to take a trip to Indianapolis, Indiana to visit some cousins; she wanted to take me with her and would pay my way. I guess that I must have been her favorite grandson; for she did a lot of special things for me like that. We went on that trip by Greyhound bus all the way from Minneapolis to Indianapolis. On the way, we had to transfer buses in Chicago. I was 16 years old at the time and a real greenhorn! The skyscrapers in Chicago were almost overwhelming. I got a sore neck just from staring up at those tall buildings. Some of them were at least thirty or forty stories high. I am sure that people who passed by must have known that I was just a simple boy from the country. In Minneapolis we had one skyscraper, the Foshay Tower, which was all of thirty-one stories tall; it was built in 1929 at the then staggering cost of $25,000,000.

When we arrived in Indianapolis, I wrote a letter to my mother to let her know that we had arrived safely and all was fine with my grandmother and me. One of my relatives must have had a typewriter, for I typed that letter to Mother; I learned to type in high school and got to type quite fast with few mistakes. I was never known to have been a "ladies' man," but I seemed to have had a lot of girl friends, especially those in our church youth group. I had to include that in my memoirs, because of what I wrote to my mother in that letter from Indianapolis. I wrote, in part, "Tell all the girls (that is, those at church) when you see them, that I miss them already. But I don't mind; are there ever a lot of nice ones here in Indianapolis."

My Years At Robbinsdale High School

When we moved out to Crystal Village in the summer of 1936 I had just completed Grade 5B and should have gone into 5A in September. But the Robbinsdale school system did not have that system of grades; there were no A and B classes. As a result, I was promoted up to Grade 6. I think I would have greatly protested had they made me begin at Grade 5 all over again. The grade school building was connected to the high school by a covered walkway. Junior High School included Grades 7-9 and met on the first floor of the high school building. Senior High School included Grades 10-12 and had all their classes on the second floor. This meant that I went through seven grades at Robbinsdale and most of our class that graduated in 1943 was together for that whole time. We were a close knit group of students and very proud of our class and its accomplishments during all those years.

I loved sports of all kinds; but because of my shortness, there were certain sports that I was not able to compete in. Two of them were football and basketball, naturally. My older brother, Warren was about two inches taller than I was and just tall enough in those days to play on the front line of our high school football team. Football was much different when we were young. The team played both offensive and defensive positions. Also, players were much smaller and lighter than they are today. The same seemed to be true with basketball. I remember that if there was a boy who stood six feet tall and played basketball, he was considered to be tall. Our school belonged to what was called the Lake Conference, with seven schools competing in various sports in that conference. One day Robbinsdale played against one of the other schools in our conference. I think it may have been St. Louis Park, which was our chief rival in football and basketball. One of their players was about 6' 4' tall. Boy, was he ever tall! Nobody on our team reached close to that height and it was almost impossible to defend against him.

One sport I really loved and could participate in was track

and field. I ran the 880 (half mile), as well as being on the 4 x 440 relay team. I ran the third leg and handed the baton off to our anchorman, the fastest man on the team. We didn't always win in a meet, but we did a number of times. One time our high school track team competed in a regional meet at the University of Minnesota. We ran on an inside oval track, about a quarter the size of an outside track. We ran on boards specially constructed for that purpose. What a time that was. I loved every minute of it. I remember that while I did not win that race, I did very well, finishing up near the top.

The outdoor tracks were not like we have them today on a special composition surface. Back then they were cinder tracks; i.e., the tracks were dirt and covered with fine coal cinders. Believe me, if a person fell on that kind of a track, he ended up with some pretty badly scraped legs. I know, because it happened to me more than once. Our track shoes were made of leather, very light in weight and had sharp metal spikes to cut into the cinder track for a good grip. Watch out if you were too close to another runner, for you could also end up with painful spike marks, which bled. For the indoor track we wore special rubber track shoes that would grip the hardwood boards. Track is much different and safer today. Our football coach was also the P.E. director. Mr. Sochacki was tough. Everybody called him "Coach," though he was known by many as "Red" Sochacki, because of his red hair. Coach Sochacki was a tough disciplinarian. In those days corporal punishment was given out for certain offenses. Coach had a ping pong paddle with three large holes drilled into it and he used that paddle very effectively, often applying the "board of education to the seat of learning." The purpose for the holes in the paddle was that when Coach came down with that paddle on some boy's backside, the paddle would give a whistling sound. It was a somewhat frightening sound, as the offending boy being "educated" with Coach Sochacki's paddle, waited for the 'whack' to take place. I did my best to avoid Coach's wrath and that paddle. One thing I can say, though, was that Coach was highly respected by staff and students. He was actually a very kind person and respected the rights of every student. Just watch out, though, that you didn't stray from the straight and narrow path!

Miss Loe, our English teacher, was also a disciplinarian, but she used a different approach than what Coach Sochacki used when students got out of line. If any boy crossed swords with Miss Loe, she would grab his hair on the top of his head and march him right down to see Mr. Mielke, our high school principal. Those were the days when the crew cuts were very popular with the boys. Well, if any boy in Miss Lowe's English class, who happened to have a crew cut and had to be hauled off to Mr. Mielke's office, she soon learned to grab the boy with the crew cut at the very front of his hair; it always worked, for there was no escape.

At that time, ice hockey was played outdoors and only during the coldest part of the winter. The hockey rink was enclosed in boards and the ground flooded with water that froze over. Refrigerator systems, as we have them today, were non-existent then. In fact, there were no refrigerators to keep food cold. All we had were iceboxes into which we put a block of ice in the lower part and food up above it. This meant you would have to buy a block of ice nearly every day. Ice hockey was very much a seasonal game and played for only a short time in the winter.

I had no problem making A's in any of my high school

math classes. I enjoyed math, which has always been easy for me. One day I came up with a shortcut to find the solution to the following algebraic equation: $(a + b) \times (c + d)$. It thrilled me to receive my teacher's commendations for my efforts, while also being told at the same time that that method had been known for many years. I did not know that and thought I had come up with something original. At least I came up with the solution on my own and had not read someone else's text on the subject. I was always looking for shortcuts in solving math problems. As a matter of fact, I was always looking for easier ways of doing most any task assigned to me, whether in school, or at home.

My next favorite subject was science, especially chemistry. Our chemistry teacher, Mr. Haagemeister, gave another classmate and me freedom to work in the chemistry lab after school hours and carry out experiments on our own. He must have had confidence in us that we wouldn't blow ourselves up and the school with us, as well. It was not unusual for him to toss us his keys and tell us to lock up when we were ready to go home and drop the keys off in the school office.

My older brother and I were the envy of everybody in school. We had pooled our resources and for just $100 bought a 1930 Ford convertible roadster with a rumble seat in the back and with black leather upholstery. The color of the car was black, of course, just as Henry Ford said it would be. There was no other car at school like it. I got my first driver's license when I was 16 years old and had learned to drive in that roadster with its four-on-the-floor stick shift. A driver's license was very simple in those days. It consisted of just a piece of paper small enough to fit into one's wallet and had on it the barest of information. A driver's license did not expire at a certain time as it does today; my first license was good forever. I wish I had that license today, at least for memory's sake. In the winter we would take our roadster out onto nearby Twin Lakes, which was frozen over solid to at least a foot thick; getting the speed up as much as we dared to, we would then slam on the brakes, making the car do 360's on the ice. Boy, was that fun and how daring we were – maybe a bit too daring.

I Join The Labor Force

One of my most enjoyable jobs I had when I was in high school was working at a local milk pasteurizing plant. Pasteurized milk was filled into glass bottles, both quarts and gallon jugs. The dairy sold its milk to stores, which specialized in milk products, as well as baked goods. Sometimes I would go along in the milk truck to help deliver gallon jugs of milk to those stores. There were five one-gallon jugs to a case. It was not unusual to leave a store with day old bread and even sweet rolls that were given to us free; that was always a help to our family's food budget and my parents really appreciated that. I worked in every department at the dairy sometimes helping the man who operated the automated equipment to be sure that it was working smoothly. I even lugged cases of milk into the huge room-size cooler. The best part of the job was that I could drink as much milk as I wanted to; I liked the fresh chocolate milk especially. But one thing I learned was that after drinking so much milk like that, I soon tired of it and before long, never, or rarely, touch milk at the dairy. Another job I enjoyed was working in the ice cream shop out in front. It was one of the most popular places in town. It didn't take me long to learn how to be a "soda jerk." I learned how to make many different kinds of ice cream dishes, including banana splits, ice cream sodas, malted milks, etc. I could also eat as much ice cream as I wanted; but like the milk, it wasn't long before I had so much of the ice cream that the temptation no longer had an effect on me.

My mother had a cousin who was secretary to the president of Northern States Power Company. She was able to get me a job delivering electric bills. At that time, the bills were not sent through the mail as they are today, but were all hand delivered. I soon learned much of the city delivering those bills every month. In time, I was transferred to reading meters in the homes. Most of the electric meters were located on the inside of the houses. When I got to a house I would ring the doorbell, or knock on the door and then slowly open the door, it if was unlocked, calling out, "meter reader." If no one was at home, I would have to make a note on the page in my book for that house, showing that those people were not at home and I was unable to read their meter; the meter would then have to be read the following month. There were always special notes for different houses, sometimes alerting the next meter reader to a dangerous situation, such as a vicious dog. Some previous meter reader had written a note on the page for one house I came to. The note simply read, "Horse in basement." That was all. Now, when I opened the door to that house and started to open the door to the basement where the meter was located, I suddenly saw a nose poking from under the door; sure enough, that must be the horse in the basement. Well, I didn't have a mind to go down into that basement; not knowing what kind of a horse was there. And so, I turned around and left, adding my note on the bottom of that page; it read, "Sure enough; there's a horse in the basement." Later, much to my chagrin, I learned that the horse was actually a large and very harmless dog. I wonder how long it was before that house had its meter read again.

A Budding Author And Public Speaker

Shortly after my mother's death in 1968, we went through all the things she had saved from each of us three sons. I found a short writing, entitled, "Built On a Rock." It was typed on a half sheet of paper and written on it at the top, in my mother's handwriting, were the words, "By Kenneth." I have no recollection as to my writing this short piece, nor who typed it. But from the style of the writing, it must have been done when I was quite young. I wrote the following:

> From the steeple of the church the tolling bell sends its silvery notes over the sunny mountaintops and the peaceful valleys to call the people to worship. As they wend their way up the mountain path to the church, they hear the organ playing their favorite hymn. Soon the choir joins in the song and the music fills the morning air. A Shepherd hears the music and plays the hymn on his flute. Across the valley another shepherd takes up the melody. From the church the strong voices of the men in the congregation are heard. The shepherds on the hill add an obbligato as the entire congregation sings the closing strains. As the service closes and the people walk slowly down the path, again the bell is heard tolling from the steeple.

At our high school we had a number of clubs, which were considered extra-curricular activities and met outside of school hours, while, at the same time, using school facilities. One of the clubs was the youth branch of the YMCA, called Hi-Y. Today an organization of that kind would not be allowed to have its meetings on school property, even though it wouldn't be during school hours and it couldn't be sponsored by the school either. This is thanks to the U.S. Supreme Court's ruling on separation of church and state. In 1942 the YMCA was seeking to raise funds for its operation in the coming year. I was asked to prepare a speech for its fund-raising campaign and to give that speech at a large public gathering. The title of my speech was, "The 1942 Finance Campaign." This was the early part of the U.S.'s entry into World War II. In my speech I called upon the patriotism of Americans, when I said at the opening of that speech:

> Upon the youth of our nation rests the defense of our great democracy. The youth of today must be strong in body and mind, alert and straight thinking...I am one of the many boys that has shared in and profited by the work of The "Y" organizations. This is only my second year that I have belonged to a "Y" group. But in that time I have met any boys from other groups, have met men from all over the United States that work with the YMCA. It has built a greater character in myself and has helped to open my path toward God...When you invest in the YMCA, you are helping to build any army; the real army, the final line of defense and the young men upon which this great American democracy of ours depends, to keep it the land of the free..."

It must be noted here that I had trusted Christ as my own personal Savior just a few months before and was still a very immature Christian. And yet, God has used various organizations, along with people and situations to bring me to Himself. My participation for three years in the Hi-Y high school branch of the YMCA played a small part in that happening. In those days there was still a strong Christian influence in this worldwide organization. Speaking of the Hi-Y, it was about a year later, on February 24, 1943 that a "Dad's and Lad's Nite" banquet was held at our high school branch of the Hi-Y in Robbinsdale. I was asked to give a short speech in honor of all the fathers there that night. At the conclusion of the main part of the banquet - spaghetti and meatballs were served as the main course - I gave a "Toast to the Dads." Unfortunately, I do not have a copy of the brief speech I gave that evening. I have wondered many time what it was I said that night in my brief speech.

As mentioned earlier, my father was a "dyed in the wool" Democrat, thanks to all that President Franklin Delano Roosevelt did for the country in bringing it out of the Depression. I guess at that time this young lad of not quite 15 years of age must have been an "enthusiastic" Democrat as well. During the presidential campaign of 1940, when Roosevelt was facing Wendell L. Willkie, the Republican candidate from Kansas, I participated in a debate at school and took the Democrats' side.

> Mr. Chairman, fellow students and faculty, the Republicans have said that Roosevelt has ruined business. That's just one great big lie. Facts prove that Roosevelt has actually helped business. In 1933 Commonwealth and Southern, Willkie's company, earned 8 million dollars...If Mr. Roosevelt ruined business, how does the Republican Party account for the fact that business in 1933 was 15% higher than in 1932...

I must have done a lot of research in preparation for my speech, for I gave many statistics that "proved" that

Roosevelt had put 9 million people back to work and brought the country out of the terrible Depression that America suffered, supposedly because of the failure of the 1929-32 administration of Republican president Herbert Hoover. Someone found my speech prior to my giving it and printed at the bottom of the speech, "Take your time on this, Stew." I have no idea who won the debate, but my speech was certainly given with all the enthusiasm of a political campaigner, running for a high office in the country. Just an interesting note here about that presidential campaign, Willkie was actually a Democrat until 1939, when the liberal wing of the Republican party persuaded him to run for office under the Republican banner.

In 1940 I entered an essay contest sponsored by the American Legion for high school students. The title of my essay was, "Our Present National Defense." A brief item in one of our local newspapers announced the following:

ROBBINSDALE PUPIL WINS ESSAY CONTEST

Kenneth Steward, 14, son of Mr. and Mrs. Merl W. Steward of Robbinsdale, has been awarded first prize in the state essay contest sponsored by the American Legion. His essay on "Our Present National Defense" won in competition with essays submitted by students throughout the state. The competition was open to students of junior high schools including the ninth grade. Kenneth's essay will be sent into national competition.

I did not win national recognition for my essay, but winning on the state level over thousands of other entries was more than I could have ever expected. Because of winning on the state level, I was honored by marching with many veterans of the First World War during Memorial Day celebrations that year. I also had the privilege of reading my essay before a large audience and receiving an acclamation from the crowd gathered in the auditorium that day. It was quite an achievement for a poor 14 year-old country boy from Crystal Village, Minnesota.

The following year I entered another essay contest, which was sponsored by the Ladies Auxiliary of the Veterans of Foreign Wars. That time I won second prize, which included a silver medal and $10 cash; that was a lot of money in those days. The title of my second essay was "One Nation Indivisible." This time my picture was printed in a Minneapolis daily newspaper, along with the following article:

ESSAY WINNER

Kenneth Steward, 15, a sophomore in the Robbinsdale High School, was awarded a medal and $10 cash as second place winner in the Minnesota State elimination of the national essay contest sponsored by the Ladies Auxiliary, Veterans of Foreign Wars. Presentation of the award was made by Mrs. Emily D. Olson, state chairman of the auxiliary, at a Robbinsdale High School assembly. High schools over the entire nation wrote essays in the contest on the subject, "One Nation Indivisible."

On the front of the medal are found the words, "Ladies Auxiliary VFW" at the top and on the bottom are the words, "Patriotic Award." On the reverse the following words are engraved, "Presented for Proficiency in Essay Contest on the Cardinal Principles of Americanism by Ladies Auxiliary VFW of the U.S." How proud I was to receive that award as it was presented to me before the whole high school at a special assembly.

I was rather a shy boy under ordinary circumstances; but somehow or other, when I was called upon to speak publicly, I was able to overcome that shyness. On March 12, 1943, not long before my graduation from Robbinsdale High School, I attended the Father's and Son's Banquet, sponsored by the Fourth Baptist Church Brotherhood. Near the middle of the program I was, once again, called upon to give a toast to all the fathers present.

Even though acting was not "in my blood," I loved to perform in plays. In fact, our 6th grade class put on a performance of *Tom Sawyer* and I played the part of Sydney, Tom's "sissy" cousin. What a night that was as we "brought the house down" in what was said to be a successful performance. In high school, I was accepted as a member of the National Thespian Dramatic Honor Society for High Schools and received a certificate in April 1942 "in Recognition of Meritorious Participation in High School Dramatics." Our troupe sponsor was one of our high school teachers, Miss Bess V. Sinnott. While a student at Bob Jones College I played the part of one of King Lear's sons in that famous Shakespearean play, *King Lear.* My performance in Shakespeare would be of great benefit to me later, when we were missionaries in India.

When I graduated from high school, my grandmother Condon bought a watch for me as a graduation present. It was my very first watch and I was so proud of it. In fact, she let me pick out just the watch I wanted. A few days later the watch stopped working. I was suspicious about the whole thing and decided to take the watch to another jeweler to have the watch looked at. I was informed that the watch was, in fact, an old watch put into a new case. I had been duped! But it didn't stop there. Right away, I went to the Better Business Bureau in Minneapolis to tell them what had happened. The store from which the watch had been purchased decided that, to save themselves from being involved in a lawsuit, they had better give me a brand new watch of my choosing. An item printed in the Better Business Bureau Bulletin shortly after this incident about my so-called "new watch" revealed the following:

> "Thank you," says Ken S---, now the proud owner of a fine new watch. Ken's first watch was supposed to be new--but it wasn't. It didn't run right, so he took it to another jeweler for adjustment--- and was greeted with the information that it was a used watch in a new case. Following investigation by the Bureau, the watch was exchanged---for what Ken "thought he bought in the first place."

+ My Beginning Years +

My Father is holding me at
only a few months old.
Standing in front of my
Mother is my brother,
Warren, 2 years old.
The year - 1926

Our old house on 'D' Street in Crystal Village
The year - 1937

Robbinsdale Elementary and High School where I attended from 6th grade through 12th grade.
The years - 1937-1943

My brother, Warren is standing beside me. Notice my pretty dress?
The Year - 1926

Part Two: A Changed Life

January, 1942 - **September,** 1943

A New Creation

"If any man be in Christ, he is a new creature; old things are passed away; behold, all things are become new."
(2 Corinthians 5:17)

I'll Gladly Bear it, Lord, For Thee

I longed to be a child of God,
And do my Savior's will;
And yet the sin that most I feared,
I knew unconquered still.
"Dear Lord," I said, for as I knelt
I saw Him on the tree---
"This heavy burden on my heart,
I'll gladly bear for Thee."

So now, for Him Who died for me,
I'm willing all to bear
Obedient love will never fail,
To bring the answered prayer.

The cold was lifted from my soul,
My burden rolled away;
The light of joy around me shed,
A calm and heavenly ray.
"Dear Lord," I said, "I praise Thy Name
For Thy rich grace to me;
My load is gone and now I rest,
In perfect peace with Thee."

I heard a gentle voice within,
A whisper soft and mild;
"Thy sin was cancelled by His blood,
Who owns thee for His child."
"Dear Lord," I said, "the work is Thine
And Thine the glory be.
My life, my soul, my every pow'r,
I consecrate to Thee."

--- words by Fanny Crosby, 1890

A Changed Life

With all the excitement of my youth, something was missing. While I was enjoying the present life and all it had to offer, I often wondered about the future; what did the future hold for me? By that I meant, what was there after this present life? I was basically a religious person, as was our whole family. Our habit was to be in church on Sunday mornings. It didn't matter what the weather was like, sunshine, rain, or snow; spring, summer, fall, or winter, we were always in church. When we lived in Crystal Village we would have to walk the two miles into town to go to the Congregational church. That was the denomination of my father's people. My mother's family was Methodist. In fact, as I understood it, my mother had a cousin, who was a bishop in the Methodist Church. As mentioned earlier in these writings, my Grandmother Steward's father was a minister in the Congregational church in Edgerton, Minnesota in the middle of the 19th century. By the end of that century higher criticism, which was growing in Europe, began to have its influence in America and changes started taking place in the pulpits across the country. The Congregational denomination was no exception.

As a young teenager, I took catechism classes and was admitted into membership in the church. The minister openly denied the Scriptures as being inspired and without error; he considered many things in the Bible to be just allegorical stories. He claimed that numerous events recorded in the Bible did not happen. I began to question what he said. Did not that Bible I took to church with me every Sunday morning, walking that long distance into town to worship God, have printed on its cover **HOLY BIBLE**? Then, if that was true, the minister must be wrong to claim it was full of errors; how could anything that was holy be full of error? It just did not measure up; I was confused. I wondered about God. Struggles went on within me. Why was God so distant? In my heart I was sure that there was a God; but who was He and where was He? If He really did exist, why didn't He reveal Himself to me? I didn't know at the time that He does reveal Himself to man and that is through the Bible.

Sometimes on a clear night in the summertime, with the stars shining bright, I would look up into that star-filled sky. The stars seemed so brilliant, yet so far away. And that is how I thought about God; if God did exist, He must be far away, probably even farther than the farthest star. Could God, would God listen to me if I called on Him? "God, if you are, if you really do exist, show yourself to me. I want to know you." And so, I cried out in my heart to God, searching for Him. I was always one who searched for new things to learn. I had a very inquisitive mind. But at 16 years of age, I had a deep longing in my soul to go beyond the here and now.

About that time, my older brother had become acquainted with a Baptist church on the north side of Minneapolis. Little did I know at the time, but as a young lad, at the time we were living on Logan Avenue, I had attended a summer Vacation Bible School at that church. God was planting a seed at that early stage in my life that one day would bear fruit. The gospel must have been presented to me, though I could not remember it.

One cold Saturday evening in January 1942, a group of young people from Fourth Baptist Church in Minneapolis was to have a party in the home of one of the church's families, who lived in Robbinsdale. I was invited to the party by a girl in my high school class, Dorothy Groh, who was a member of that church. "Ken, would you like to come to our church young people's party this coming Saturday evening? There is going to be a lot of fun, lots of food and games; and we have some singing and a short message from the Bible?" Why not, I had nothing to do that night and was all ready for fun, food and games. As a matter of fact, I could eat any time! I was a party person. Besides, if there was going to be a message from the Bible, maybe I would hear something about God that would answer many of the questions I had about Him. That night was not only the first night of the rest of my life, more importantly, I was to find the answers to all those questions I had about God. And most important of all, that night was truly the beginning of a new life for me, a life in Christ, for I was "born again."

What fun we had that cold Saturday evening in January 1942, lots of food and fun games. But the songs the rest of the youth sang that night were new to me; they were gospel choruses I had never heard before in my life. God used even those choruses to speak to my searching heart. The whole situation deeply impressed me, for I could see that the rest of them were enthused about what they sang. The youth pastor, Earl Matteson, gave a brief message after the singing. I do not remember what it was that he talked about, but I know that the Holy Spirit brought deep conviction to my heart; I needed what the rest of those youth had. At the close of his message, we were asked to bow our heads and then Earl told us that if there was any one of us who wanted to be saved, to quietly slip out from the group and go upstairs into one of the bedrooms; he would come very soon and explain what it meant to be saved. I did not know at the time what he meant by getting "saved," but I knew right then and there I needed something more than what I then had. I had been struggling with all those questions about God. I knew at that moment that something great was going to happen to me. If getting "saved" meant finding God, I was ready for it. Well, in a few minutes Earl Matteson came upstairs to where I was quietly waiting. He opened the Bible and clearly and simply explained the gospel to me. God brought understanding to my mind and heart and I was deeply moved by all I heard.

I do not remember all the Scripture he read and explained to me that night. Two verses stick out in my mind amongst the many that Earl showed me that night from the Bible and they are the two verses that God used to bring salvation to me when I got saved that cold Saturday evening in January 1942. Those two verses were: 1) Romans 3:23 --- "For all have sinned and come short of the glory of God" and 2) John 3:16 --- For God so loved the world that He gave His only Begotten Son that whosoever believeth in Him should not perish but have everlasting life." I not only realized that I was a sinner, but also I was one of those "whosoevers" and that I was a part of this world; therefore, God must truly love me. That evening in the upstairs bedroom in a house in Robbinsdale, Minnesota, on a cold Saturday in January 1942, I placed my faith in Jesus Christ as my personal Savior; I was truly born again. I went upstairs a lost sinner and came downstairs a found sinner. When I got down on my knees beside the bed in that upstairs bedroom, I put my name into those verses, confessed my sin, admitted that I was a sinner and believed on the Lord Jesus Christ as my own personal Savior. When I did that I was putting my confidence in Christ's finished work on the cross and I became a "new creature in Christ Jesus; old things passed away, all things became new." (2 Corinthians 5:17). Well, almost all things became new. There were still some things in my life that God had to deal with. At the same time, I could sing that chorus with the rest of the young people at Fourth Baptist Church in Minneapolis, Minnesota:

> Something's different now;
> Something happened to me,
> Since I gave my heart to Jesus.

What happened to my older brother and now to me began to affect the rest of the family, my mother, my father and finally, my younger brother, in that order. As a family, we continued going to church, but now it was to a church that preached the gospel, where the pastor preached that the Bible was the very inspired Word of God, without error in any way. We started to soak up the Word of God, like a sponge soaks up water. We couldn't get enough of it. By this time, we had moved back into the city, only four short blocks from the church. We lived on the second floor of a four-plex on 24th Avenue North, between Humboldt and Irving Avenues. We never missed a service at church and that included the midweek Bible study and prayer meeting. But my parents and younger brother were still not saved, though the Lord was certainly working in their hearts as they sat under the ministry of our pastor, Dr. Richard V. Clearwaters. I owe much to him, as to my spiritual growth in the beginning years of my Christian life.

One Sunday morning, in the spring after I was saved, Pastor Clearwaters gave a public invitation, as he did every service. The invitation included those who were not yet saved and knew that they needed to be. In addition, the invitation was also to those who were saved, but not yet baptized. I certainly fitted into the second group. Though I had come to trust Christ as my own personal Savior the previous January, I had not yet been obedient to the Lord in being baptized. God had used the message that Sunday morning to show me that I needed to testify of my faith in Christ through believer's baptism and be obedient to Him in that area of my life. As the invitation was being given, I was one of the first to jump up from my seat to go forward. At our church all the young people usually sat together in the balcony. We were always very attentive during the services and always participated fully in them. My parents always sat downstairs near the back of the auditorium.

As Pastor Clearwaters was giving the invitation I got up from my seat, went downstairs and began walking down the middle aisle to the front, when suddenly I heard a sound behind me. As I turned to see what was happening, who should I see running down that aisle, but my mother; she was coming to get saved and, I guess, couldn't get down there fast enough! Well, praise the Lord for that. It was a great day for our family; at least for my mother and me. In time, my father also trusted Christ as his own personal Savior. My younger brother, Doug, resisted the Lord's calling, which was of great concern to me. In fact, it was not until I was in college that I received a letter from my parents, informing me that my brother had finally gotten saved. Now our family was complete in the Lord.

God Had Other Plans

After I was saved I became involved in the youth program at church. Earl Matteson also played a great part in my young Christian life. He was a musician and played the piano often in church; boy, could he ever play. He would get us young people to sing. In fact, we had an eight-member ensemble that sang, not only in church, but in other churches, as well and going to witness and sing in city rescue missions in downtown Minneapolis. We even had the opportunity of singing over the radio. At that time I sang baritone and my older brother, Warren, sang tenor. In time, I switched from a baritone to tenor. I also got to sing in the church choir.

Fourth Baptist Church had a pipe organ, which was played by Dora Veth, and Earl was choir director, besides playing the piano and being our youth pastor. We were a closely knit youth group. Some of our group went into the service during the Second World War; others went on to Bible college and state universities, while some just went right into the work force and were part of the war effort, making armament and ammunition for our armed forces.

For awhile I became involved with an unsaved girl by the name of Helen. She lived in another town southwest of Minneapolis. It was a long ride from my house to hers by city bus, but that was the only means of transportation I had at the time. I had been introduced to her by another boy in our church youth group, who was dating a friend of Helen. His father owned a corner grocery store and I worked at the store for a time stocking shelves and helping customers with their orders.

Supermarkets didn't exist then and all groceries were on shelves behind the counter. I would have to get down from the shelves the items a customer wanted, put them in a paper bag, as I rang up the price of each item on the cash register. That is something else, for there were no bar codes and machines that automatically registered the prices when the items were passed over the special bar code reader. Everything was done by hand; there weren't even any tapes that the prices were printed on. If the customer wanted a receipt for his purchases, each and every item would have to be written down on a special receipt form. The total amount of the purchase showed on a tab that came up at the top of the cash register and showed through a small window that ran across the full width of the cash register; it would then show 'Total.'

I became deeply involved with Helen, though our involvement went no farther than the "making out" stage. I am so thankful that God kept us from doing anything worse. To that point in my young Christian life, I had not been taught from 1 Corinthians 6:14,17, "Be not unequally yoked together with unbelievers; for what fellowship hath righteousness with unrighteousness? And what communion hath light with darkness...wherefore, come out from among them and be ye separate, saith the Lord and touch not the unclean thing and I will receive you."

One time I asked Helen if she would like to go see a certain movie at the Orpheum Theater in downtown Minneapolis. She had at least heard about my getting saved, though she herself did not understand what that meant. We never discussed spiritual matters, which I have regretted many times. When I asked her about going with me to see the movie, her response nearly shook me out of my shoes! She exclaimed, "But I thought you said that you were a Christian." My reply was simply, "Well, yes I am, but that's okay; we can still go to see the movie." In those days' movies, especially those that showed men and women together were much different than they are today. You would never see a man and woman together in a bed unless it was very clear that they were married and even then, such a scene was rare. There was practically no profanity in a movie. Well, Helen and I went to see the movie in the evening we decided on. I have no remembrance as to what the movie was all about, let alone the title of the movie. God has erased all that from my mind. I remember clearly that we sat in the balcony in the front row and right in the middle. We couldn't have had a better view of the movie; they were two of the best seats in the theater. As the movie progressed I began to get very uncomfortable and soon broke out in a cold sweat. The remark Helen had previously made to me went over and over in my mind, "I thought you were a Christian; I thought you were a Christian; I thought you were a Christian..." On and on it went in my mind and finally, I had enough. I turned to her and whispered, "Come on, let's get out of here." We left in a hurry and I took my date back to her home in St. Louis Park. It was shortly after that our relationship ended and, as far as I remember. I never saw Helen again in my life. I have no idea what happened to her; I have often wondered about it. The one thing I regret that in all the time I had dated her, I never once witnessed to Helen about my faith in Christ, beyond the fact that I was a Christian. I had not explained to her what that meant. But I am sure of this that God used the words of an unsaved girl friend to bring conviction to my soul and deliver me from what later could have been a very unwholesome relationship, which would have changed the course of my life. From that day to this I have never stepped inside a movie theater again.

My older brother, Warren, graduated from high school in 1941 and was working at the time Japan attacked Pearl Harbor in Hawaii. How he was able to keep out of the military draft at that time I do not know; I never asked him about it. In the fall of 1942 he began his college studies at Bob Jones College in Cleveland, Tennessee, along with another young man from our church. From the beginning he began preparing himself for the ministry. One of his interests was in music and in time he became involved in music programs at college. What he had to say about Bob Jones College eventually interested me and played a big part in my going to study there in the fall of 1943.

May 27, 1943 I graduated from Robbinsdale High School in Robbinsdale, Minnesota and received my diploma. No sooner had some of our class received their diplomas than they volunteered for various branches of the military and went off to fight for our country. Out of our group of five, who were close friends throughout our years at Robbinsdale High School, two joined up. Keith Rother joined the army and Glenn Lake joined the air force and became a tail gunner in one of the big bombers. We soon heard that his plane was shot down over the Pacific Ocean and he, along with all the rest of the crew, were not heard from again; all were lost at sea.

My father used to get his hair cut at a barbershop on Emerson Avenue, just north of Broadway in Minneapolis. In time, he became acquainted with our representative in Congress, who got his hair cut at the same shop. I do not know what his name was; but he was able to get for me an appointment to the U.S. Naval Academy in Annapolis, Maryland. I was not interested in becoming a naval officer, partly because of the fact that I didn't know how to swim and I knew that sometime I would have to face the fact of being tossed into the water as an initiation rite. Besides that, I was more interested in joining the army. Earlier in my senior year at high school, I had taken a special exam, along with many others in my class. If I passed that exam with high marks, I would qualify for officers' school somewhere in the States. I passed the exam with high marks and, as a result, received a special commission in the army as a second lieutenant. Shortly after graduation I received orders from the army to report to Fort Snelling for my physical exam, after which I was to go to the University of Iowa for special training. I was so excited I could hardly wait for that to come.

But God had other plans for me. Though I was in top physical condition, one part of me interfered with my plans and almost came between me and God's plan for my life; that part was my feet. You see, I am completely flat footed. When I had my physical all went well until the examining officer got to my feet. I sometimes tell people that my feet are so flat I can rock on them like a rocking chair! Well, those feet did me in; I was rejected, unfit to serve as an officer in the U.S. army. I pled, I argued, but all to no avail. I was sent home, with hardly a wave of the hand. God must have been putting my faith to the test, for I was called up a second time to appear at Fort Snelling for another physical exam. Had there been some mistake? Had they changed their minds? I would soon find out. For a second time, I went down to Fort Snelling and went through the line, stripped to the buff and checked from head to feet. Again, there it ended at those two rocking-chair feet!

God had other plans for me and those plans were for me to attend Bob Jones College in the fall of 1943, ultimately to prepare for the ministry. I decided that as long as I wasn't allowed to go and fight for my country, I might as well go down to Cleveland, Tennessee and enroll in Bob Jones College. I knew little about the college beyond what my brother had told me. But I was willing to give it a try, at least for one year. I could always return home and enter Northwestern Bible College, which met, at the time, in the facilities of First Baptist Church in near downtown Minneapolis. Later, during one summer beak from my studies at Bob Jones College, I took some classes at Northwestern Bible College, which were accepted toward my degree program at Bob Jones College; by doing so, I was able, along with a few correspondence courses, to finish my studies at BJC, as it was commonly referred to, a semester earlier than planned. If I took only one year at BJC, I could even enroll at the University of Minnesota and have very little tuition to pay, while living at home. This was, in fact, what my parents were hoping I would do; but, again, my plans were not God's plans. God's thoughts were not my thoughts and God's ways were not my ways (Isaiah 55:8). In time, it would be, as a student at Bob Jones College, I came to understand more fully God's will and plan for my life. It was there, of course, I would meet my future wife, who became an important part of that will of God for me. It was at Bob Jones College that I would come to understand that God had given me only one life and that He demanded all of that life for Himself; I was to keep nothing of it for myself, nothing of my own interests or plans.

+ A New Creation +

Our family in the back yard at
our house in Crystal Village
The year - 1939

I graduate from
Robbinsdale high school.
May 27, 1943

The church in Robbinsdale
we attended as a family
but never heard the gospel
The years - 1937-1942

Fourth Baptist Church in
Minneapolis where each in
our family heard the gospel,
were saved and became
members
The years - 1941-1974

Part Three: Life At Bob Jones College

September, 1943 – January, 1947

Not **Your Own**

"What? Know ye not that your body is the temple
of the Holy Ghost, which is in you, which ye have
of God and ye are not your own?
For ye are bought with a price: therefore glorify
God in your body and in your spirit, which are God's."

(1 Corinthians 6:19-20)

Life At Bob Jones College

In early September 1943 I packed my suitcase and with the few dollars I had in my pocket, purchased a bus ticket that would take me all the way to Cleveland, Tennessee. I had one change to make in Chicago, Illinois. Thus began a new stage in my life.

How I was admitted as a student at Bob Jones College will probably remain a mystery the rest of my life. I had no guarantee of being able to pay one dime on my tuition and board. Earlier that summer I sent in my application with the application fee. Perhaps I was accepted on the basis of my older brother having been there the year before; I really don't know the reason why, except that the Lord wanted me there and He would take care of the bill. At any rate, just a few weeks after sending in the application form with the fee, I received an answer in the mail, informing me that I had been accepted as a first year student. How excited I was, for now I was officially a college student. As I have already written, I had no money in my pocket, that is, except enough to buy a bus ticket and some change left over. Giving my mother a hug and shaking my father's hand - we were not a kissing family - I boarded the Greyhound bus and headed out for this new adventure in my life.

I was promised a work scholarship, which would meet the very minimal costs of college expenses. The rest was up to the Lord. Many times in the next four years, God would prove the truth of Philippians 4:19, "But my God shall supply all your need according to his riches in glory by Christ Jesus." That first year tuition, board and room cost a total of $550. It might as well have been $550,000. But this poor country boy from Minnesota had absolute, total confidence that God had sent him to Bob Jones College and would honor His promise; He would meet every need. And yet, there were still times when the flesh crept in and doubts arose as to whether I would be able to pay my school bills, as well as take care of all my personal expenses. At the end of one semester I had not paid all my school bills before time for final exams. It was the policy of the college that if our bills were not paid, we could not take our exams. I do not remember exactly how much I still owed, but according to today's standard of living, it was not very much. At that time it seemed to be a small fortune. What was I to do? I had to miss my first two exams; and yet, I knew that somehow God would send in the funds and that, hopefully, I would be able to make up the exams I missed. The morning of the first exams I stood in the lobby at Little Moby's Corner, where the campus post office and snack shop were located. There I waited for the mail to be sorted and put into the boxes. As the mail was being put into the boxes, I waited and looked and waited and looked. Nothing went into my box and I mean, nothing! "God, are you going to fail me now?" I silently cried out. Suddenly, one envelope landed in my box with a light 'thump.' I couldn't get the box open fast enough. Could this be it? It was from the U.S. Internal Revenue Service, an income tax refund check. I ripped open the envelope and out came a check; it had my name on it, Kenneth Norman Steward. Yes, it was mine all right. It was a refund on the amount of tax I had paid the previous year. I took that check over to the college office in the administration building as fast as my legs would take me and paid my bill! God knew the exact amount I would need and held that check back long enough to test my faith, while at the same time, causing me to miss the first two exams, which I was able to take later on. After paying my school bill, I had enough left over to go into town and get a haircut. I needed one badly and the

Lord knew all about that, as well. The length of my hair was getting long enough to begin touching my shirt collar, well, I went to town and celebrated by getting the best haircut I could for those two quarters which were in my pocket. I was able to take the two exams I had earlier missed.

The dress code at Bob Jones College was very strict. Men were required to always wear a dress shirt with tie, whether to meals, classes, chapel, or an artist series program; a suit or sport jacket was a must. I didn't have many clothes, only one suit and possibly only two or three dress shirts, along with two pair of shoes. To save money, I washed out my clothes in my dormitory room sink. In the men's dormitory there were four men assigned to a room in which there were two double-decker metal frame beds, with cotton mattresses. After washing my clothes in the sink I would then hang my clothes around the room to dry. I don't know if my roommates appreciated that, or not. I had the use of an iron to press my shirts. In order to do so, I would put a layer of towels on my desk, dampen a handkerchief and lay it over the shirts. But I would iron only those parts of the shirts that would show when I wore my jacket. I never did iron the back of the shirt, or even the sleeves, except for the cuffs. During that first year at college my shirts began to get a bit thin. Remember that this was the time of World War II and clothes were in short supply; sometimes we would have to stand in long lines, hoping that by the time we reached the front of the line, the particular item of clothes we wanted to buy would still be there, especially in the size we wanted.

My parents were not able to send me much money at college. Dad had a low-paying job with the State of Minnesota. By the time I began college, he had been promoted from janitor to elevator operator. The pay wasn't much better. Mother eventually got her a job with Pako, a photo developing company in Minneapolis.

At the time my shirts were getting thin I wrote a letter of appeal to my mother, asking her to try and find some shirts my size, even colored shirts would do, though white ones were preferable. I wrote a letter home with the following plea, "Dress shirts, oh for some dress shirts. Boy, can I use 'em, even colored ones. I don't know if we have them down here, haven't looked, but will." In a later letter the situation regarding the condition of my clothes seemed to have gotten worse. I must have sounded really desperate, for I wrote again, "...all my clothes are starting to fall apart at once and I mean that literally. I think I will have to dispense with giving the school money for about a week, so that I'll be able to buy myself a pair of pants." I went on to write about the shirt situation, "My shirts are going one by one. I now have only one good shirt left; the others are all mended. Mom, if you can find me any colored shirts at Sears, get me some, will you, brown and blue of any design, about four of them; I need shirts very much. Buy me four as soon as you can and let me know how much they cost, so I can pay for them." In my letter I hadn't given the size of my shirts, though I was sure she knew my shirt size to be 14 ½" in the neck (oh to be that size again) and 32-33" sleeve. I don't know how I was going to repay my mother for the shirts I was hoping she would buy for me, for I didn't have any money to do so. From what I remember, Mother bought those shirts and paid for them herself. That was my mother.

<u>Working On Campus</u>

During my first year at Bob Jones College, I paid off my

work scholarship by working with the cleanup crew. Our job was to clean all the floors in the administration building, the dining hall and hall floors in all the dormitories. The tile floors were made of a rubber composition. We had a special machine with two large circular brushes on them that scrubbed the floors, after which we would apply floor polish and then buff the floors after the polish dried. We did most of the work at night. When we worked in the women's dorms we would have to cry out, "Man on the floor," to be sure that the women were not there, or were properly clothed. Even though our work was at night, after lights were out in the dormitories, I still had to make all my classes the next day. It was a tiring job, but I was glad for any kind of a job that would pay for some of my college expenses. I couldn't afford to be late for classes in the morning, or I would get demerits; 150 demerits meant being "shipped," i.e., having to leave school.

My second year I had a job on the ice cream crew. At Sunday afternoon dinners, the dessert was always ice cream. I enjoyed that job. In fact, one time I wrote home, "I sure do like to serve ice cream. I eat a lot back there in the kitchen and have two or three dishes of ice cream." I got to eat that much ice cream if there was any left over after serving the staff and students in the dining room. In that letter home I wrote that I wondered why I wasn't gaining weight, eating that much ice cream. As a boy and even in college, I seemed to have had a ravenous appetite. Mother always found it hard to keep me filled up.

During those difficult years, when we lived in Crystal Village, Dad used to say that there would always be two things about our family, come what may; first, we would have food on the table, enough to satisfy three growing boys. Then, we would be dressed neatly, even if our clothes had to be patched. My parents never failed in this determination. Both of them worked hard to provide for the family. I appreciated my parents very much and expressed it this way in a letter from college, "Mom and Dad, I'd like to tell you right now how thankful I am that I have you two as my parents. I can't express in words all that you mean to me, but I have it in my heart. You've come through for me in times of trouble and in times of plenty and I'm not going to let you down. Thank you from the bottom of my heart for all that you've done for me. I praise God that I have two Christian parents back home, who are praying for me."

One Sunday, having finished work on the ice cream crew, I was about ready to leave the kitchen for my room in the men's dormitory. The kitchen crew was already getting things ready for the evening meal. Someone had put a large aluminum pot of nearly boiling milk on the floor and had failed to put a lid on the pot. Some of the milk had inadvertently spilled onto the floor near that pot of very hot milk. As I walked past, my feet slipped from under me and as I fell, my hands naturally went out straight, as I tried to keep from falling. As I fell, my left hand went right into that pot of nearly boiling milk, almost up to my elbow, burning my arm and hand very badly. I was taken first of all to the dining room supervisor's office, my hand immersed in very cold water and then I was carried on a stretcher to the school infirmary. Needless to say, I was in great pain. I am thankful that no serious damage happened to my arm and hand. After several days in the infirmary, I was dismissed with burn salve on my burnt hand and a bandage covering the whole arm and hand. I was able to attend my classes again, but it was a trying experience, to say the least. I am thankful for complete healing and that I have not been left with any scars because of the second-degree burns. You can be sure that never again was a pot of hot milk ever put down on the floor again. Who knows why it was done in the first place.

During one of my years at college I had a job waiting tables. By that time, Wilma and I were quite serious about each other. In fact, we were dating no one else; we had been talking about getting married after we graduated from college. It seemed everyone on campus knew it, even the staff and the dean of women, Miss Riley, as well as the dean of men, Dr. Monroe Parker. Ordinarily, if a male student was that serious about a woman student, he would not be allowed to serve her table in the dining room. At Bob Jones College we ate our meals family style, with six persons at each table, including one staff member, who sat at the head of the table. From time to time seating arrangements were changed. At one time I was assigned tables to serve, at which Wilma sat at one of the tables; would you believe it, the staff member at her table was Miss Riley. While I served those particular tables, I made sure that one dish of ice cream on my tray contained a little bit more ice cream than the others. Somehow or other, I managed to hold back that dish and serve it to Wilma. I think Miss Riley must have known what I was doing, but she didn't say anything about it. I am sure, though, that she must have been smiling at the whole affair!

During my last semester at college I was promoted to serving Dr. Bob Jones Sr.'s table, which was always considered to be an honor. The dining hall had two special elevated rooms, which were open to the rest of the dining hall. At one table Dr. and Mrs. Jones Jr. and family sat and at the other Dr. Bob Jones Sr. and Mrs. Jones sat, as well as whoever there were of special guests. One time Scottish evangelist James Stewart was on campus and was the guest of Dr. Bob Sr. At one meal he asked me to bring him a pot of tea. I went back to the kitchen and made this request known to the kitchen staff. One of the staff quickly found a teapot, poured boiling water into it, along with a tea bag. Being satisfied and not really knowing how Scottish people prepare their tea; I put the pot of tea on my tray and took it to Evangelist Stewart. I naturally expected a "Thank you," but almost fell through the floor, when with a roar of a lion, or so it sounded that way to me, Mr. Stewart told me to go back to the kitchen and bring back a <u>real</u> pot of tea. I learned quickly what a "real" pot of tea, Scottish style, was. Returning to the kitchen, I found that the only tea the kitchen had was in tea bags, no loose tea. What was I to do? Well, there was only one thing I could do and so, I did it. I took two tea bags, tore them open and poured the loose tea into a fresh pot of water. Taking the new pot of freshly made tea, along with a tea strainer that someone found for me, I returned to Dr. Bob Sr.'s table and quietly sat the pot down in front of Evangelist James Stewart. This time I received a smile and a gentlemanly "Thank you," from this Scottish evangelist, who was now happy that he finally would be able to drink "real" tea – Scottish style tea. Whew; close call. That was the only difficult situation I was ever faced with in all the time I waited Dr. Bob Sr.'s table my last semester at college.

At the beginning of my Junior-Senior year I inherited a paper route on campus from my older brother. It wasn't long before I had over 200 customers, including students and staff. At first, I delivered both morning and evening editions of the paper; but I found that I was not only having less time to study, but also losing sleep, for I had to get up real early in the morning to deliver the morning edition of the paper. It wasn't long before I had more customers for the evening paper than I had before with both morning and evening editions. All of my customers were on campus. Newspapers at that time cost all of ten cents per copy. I was making enough money that I could pay all my school bills and put the remaining amount into a bank account. I worked out quite a system for both delivering the papers and collecting at the end of each week. I would write the room numbers on each newspaper for those in that room in a particular dormitory who were subscribers; then I would drop the stack of papers inside the entrance of each dorm. At the end of the week I collected from the men and staff, while Wilma collected from the women in their dormitories. If any payments were paid, in part, in pennies, I put them into a large jar. In time, I collected enough pennies to pay for our wedding rings with the pennies I saved from my paper route.

Social Life At Bob Jones College

There were no fraternities or sororities at Bob Jones College; there were what we knew as literary societies. Dr. Bob Sr. placed great emphasis on the principle of preparing students to be ladies and gentlemen. The arts were emphasized. Literary societies had an important part in developing certain cultural skills. Sports played a big part in the activities of each society. At that time there were just four men's societies and four women's societies. The men's societies were Bryan (named in honor of the famous orator and three-time presidential candidate, William Jennings Bryan), Chi Delta Theta, Phi Beta Chi and Pi Gamma Delta. All the women's societies had Sigma in their names, namely, Chi Sigma Phi, Sigma Kappa Rho, Sigma Lambda Delta and Sigma, Sigma, Sigma.

Though my older brother belonged to the William Jennings Bryan Society, I was attracted to Pi Gamma Delta. For one thing, I did not want to follow in the shadow of my older brother, for I felt that I had to follow my own course and make a name for myself. Even then, I came to be known as "Little Stew;" Warren was always referred to as "Stew." It was not until he graduated from BJC that I was able to claim the name of Stew. So it goes for being second in line in the family. Anyway, I was glad I had joined Pi Gamma Delta. I was attracted to it for several reasons. For one thing, the society colors were purple, white and gold, three of my favorite colors. Purple stood for the Kingship of Christ, white represented His Purity and gold symbolized His Deity. The stated purpose of Pi Gamma Delta was quoted in my first year annual, the 1944 *Vintage*. Its purpose was fourfold, "SPIRITUAL --- to make Christ pre-eminent and help spread the Gospel of His Son and our Savior Jesus Christ; CULTURAL --- to instill into the minds of its members an appreciation of the finer things in the realm of art and education; PHYSICAL --- to encourage a well-rounded physical development in each member and a keen sense of sportsmanship and fair play; finally, SOCIAL --- to foster in each member a sense of his responsibility to be courteous on all occasions, to regard every Christian as a brother and to maintain at all times the highest respect for womanhood." The motto of the society was, "His Will --- Our Desire." Whenever we had our regular society meetings, I would faithfully wear my society beanie cap. I've kept that cap to this day as a reminder of all I gained as being a part of Pi Gamma Delta.

During my first year in college I began dating a girl from Gary, Indiana. Grace was actually a student in the high school academy and I became very serious about her. She was very attractive and had beautiful blond hair. I dated her as much as possible to practically every performance on campus. At the end of the school year I gave her my high school graduation ring as a sign of our "going steady." She accepted the ring and I thought it was the beginning of a beautiful relationship, which would one day blossom into something, more serious and permanent. We promised to faithfully write to each other during the summer months until we returned to Bob Jones College in September. But shortly after I arrived home I received a brief letter from Grace, returning my class ring, saying she was breaking off our relationship; no explanation given. I was almost heartbroken, but it was the best thing that could have happened to me. You see, God had someone better for me, who would eventually become the best friend I ever could have, who married me and became my life partner in ministry.

Summer At Home

The breaking up with Grace happened in early summer of 1944. I was living at home at the time and had a job at a small dental laboratory, which made false teeth on special order. I enjoyed the job very much. There were some interesting false teeth orders that came to us from time to time. One man wanted 24-carat gold plates, both upper and lower. At that time gold cost only about $32 an ounce, less than 5% of what it costs today. But then, I am sure the person who wanted gold teeth would have ordered them at any price. We made those upper and lower 24-carat gold plates, with their highly polished ivory teeth. I have often wondered who that man was and how he must have looked in his new teeth, especially when he smiled.

That same summer I took some classes at Northwestern Bible Institute, as it was known at the time; classes met in the facilities of the First Baptist Church in near downtown Minneapolis. Pastor of the church at the time was the well-known Dr. W. B. Riley, who had begun the Bible institute. The school later became Northwestern Bible College and built its own campus.

It wasn't long into summer when I felt pain in my left groin; the pain increased to the point where I needed to see a doctor. A checkup showed that I had a hernia, which needed repair. And so, on June 6, 1944 I checked in at the Northwestern Hospital and was operated on for the hernia. I remember the time clearly, for when I woke up from the anesthesia I heard a nurse say, "The Allies have landed at Normandy, France." It was "D Day" for the Allies, which was the beginning of the end for Nazi, Germany. More than ever, I wished I had been able to go fight for my country. It was quite a summer for me and I was only too glad for the summer to end and get back to my studies at Bob Jones College.

Sports At Bob Jones College

I've always loved sports and participated in those that had no restrictions because of size, or lack thereof. Soccer is one such sport. In soccer a player could be very tall, or quite small. Many men, who have played soccer in world competition, have not been tall men. I had never played soccer before I arrived on campus at Bob Jones College. In fact, it was a sport, which was little known at that time in the States. We certainly didn't know about it in our small town consolidated high school. Well, I learned how to play soccer real fast. When Dr. Bob Jones Sr. began the college in Florida in 1927, the school played intercollegiate football. But by the time the school moved to Cleveland, Tennessee, he saw that intercollegiate sports took too much time of the students from their real purpose of being there and that was to get an education. As a result intercollegiate sports were dropped in favor of inter-society competition. In my third year at BJC we played the other three men's societies twice each and won all six games. We were 6 and 0, while the other teams were each 2 and 4. I played on the front line in what was then called 'right wing' and made my share of goals.

In soccer there are no protective pads worn, just the light shorts and a jersey, with special shoes made for soccer played on a grass field. As a result, when there is body contact, which is bound to happen in a highly competitive sport such as soccer it can be a bit rough and injuries do happen. One day our team was scrimmaging, getting ready for the next Saturday's game; I don't remember which team we were going to play, but I do remember what happened. One of our back field defense men was Fred Afman, who was 6' 4" tall, nearly a foot taller than I am. Fred was playing on the opposite scrimmage team. Our team was going for the ball and heading in Fred's direction, trying to get to the ball before he did. Unfortunately, I was a bit late; Fred got to the ball first and gave it a hard kick to get it out of his part of the field. The ball headed straight for me and there was nothing I could do; it all happened in seconds. The next thing I knew I was laying on the ground, slowly coming to after being knocked out for who knows how long. The ball hit me square in my right eye, which began swelling up immediately. There I was with a swollen black eye, soon to meet Wilma on a date to some special performance in the auditorium. I was more disgusted with myself than anything else, for not having made it to the ball before Fred Afman did. I am glad that we were on the same team and that I didn't have to go against him in a regular game. I don't believe I was able to play in the game that was played a day or two later. It took awhile for the swelling to go down and my eye to return to its normal size and color.

Beginning A Lifetime Relationship

Even though Wilma was in my class at Bob Jones College, we didn't really know each other our first year. It was not until our second year that we became acquainted, when we sat next to each other in Greek glass; we sat right on the front row. Sometime in November, close to Thanksgiving Day, there were to be special activities throughout the whole day, ending with a performance of Romeo and Juliet. My roommate, Bob Waggoner, suggested that we write notes to the LaVoy sisters, asking them for dates for the whole day of activities. Not realizing that Bob intended to write Wilma for a date, I wrote her first and was accepted. When I told Bob what I had done, he was greatly disappointed and graciously sent a note to Wilma's sister, Sylvia. She, in turn, graciously accepted. And so, we "double dated" for the day. As for any continuing relationship between my roommate and Wilma's sister, that did not take place. But as for Wilma and me, it was the first date of many, which have continued these many years.

The activities on Thanksgiving Day, 1944 began with a soccer game between the two best men's societies. One of those societies was Pi Gamma Delta and I was on the team. Thus began our first date, I playing soccer, while Wilma cheered from the sidelines. Our team went on to win, though I cannot remember at this point in time as to whom we played and what the final score was. From then on, Wilma was at every game our team played; she was my most loyal fan! I like to think that it was due, in part, to her faithful support and cheering that every game Pi Gamma Delta played, when I was on the team we won.

Later that day there was a banquet in the dining hall, with all the goodies one could imagine. Remember, it was still wartime and many things were difficult to find, if at all. Mr. R. K. (Lefty) Johnson was responsible for purchasing all the things the school needed, from coal for the furnaces to food for the dining hall. Somehow he was able to get everything needed for a sumptuous Thanksgiving meal. And what a meal it was! That evening was the performance of Romeo and Juliet. Wilma was dressed in her floor length gown and I in my one and only suit. I thought she was the most beautiful woman that God had ever created. I still think that way, even though we are both old and wrinkly. I am sure I must be prejudiced in this one matter. Can anyone blame me?

Wilma was not willing for our relationship to go beyond just a friendship, unless she was sure I was going in the same direction she was, and that was as far as God's will was concerned; i.e., that I was yielded to the Lord's will and had world missions as my goal. She was determined that she would not be deceived by a man and his intentions a second time; as the saying goes, "Once bitten, twice shy." You see, in her first year in college she became very serious about another of our classmates. They were dating quite steadily. At the end of that school year he left college to join the navy. It was not long after that she received a letter from him with the news that he had given up his faith in God. That was the end of their relationship. God was preparing us for each other. Wilma became cautious about any man who would want to date her. From the beginning of our dating relationship, she never revealed any of this to me, as to what happened with her and the other boy the year before.

Dating at Bob Jones College was closely monitored. It

consisted of sitting with a girl in the dating parlor. There was the proverbial "six-inch rule" and women chaperones were always present somewhere in the dating parlor. Dating would involve meeting the young lady in the dating parlor. Her date would then accompany her to a function being held in the Rodeheaver-Mack Auditorium such as a Shakespearian play, an opera, or a recital. Dates were arranged by writing a note to the young lady, who would respond in kind, accepting the date, or - perish the thought - rejecting the invitation.

The tradition of notes going back and forth between the men's and women's dorms was very important in the life of Bob Jones College. Once we became quite serious about each other, there was hardly a night we didn't exchange notes. A time factor was involved and we men had to get our notes written and put into a special box by a certain time, so that the courier could get them over to the women's dorm in time for the women to write a response. I can't remember if Wilma ever initiated the exchange of notes; it may have happened. We have kept many of those notes and closely guard them, for they are private between just the two of us to this day. One day, when we are both gone, they will be available to our children to read. In doing so, they will see how our relationship grew and blossomed into love and, eventually, a lifetime of marriage and serving the Lord together.

Changed Plans

As already mentioned, Wilma was not willing to get serious about a relationship with me until she was sure I was going in the same direction she was going. She had to be sure, first of all, that I was dedicated to the Lord and wanted to serve Him as a missionary, even to the same place where she believed God wanted her to go.

When I enrolled at Bob Jones College I had no thoughts about going there for the full four years in order to prepare myself for some kind of fulltime Christian service. Inasmuch as I could not get into the military and make that my career, I had other thoughts. I was always good in math and had also done well in my high school architectural drawing class. Now that would be a good and well-paying career, as an architectural engineer. I could enroll at the University of Minnesota, live at home and graduate with a degree in engineering in the field of architecture. But God had other plans for me.

That summer at home, after my first year at Bob Jones College, I had some decisions to make; would I go ahead and enroll at the U. of Minnesota, or would I return to Bob Jones College for a second year? I cannot explain the reason for my decision to do the latter, but I did. I went back to Bob Jones College, still with little money in my pocket and depending entirely on the Lord to pay my college bills.

At the beginning of that second year I enrolled in a class taught by a former missionary to China, Dr. Grace Haight. Dr. Haight seemed to live, breath, eat and sleep missions. Her passion for spreading the gospel to the ends of the earth was catching. She was quiet in her ways. Standing less than five feet in height, we thought of her only as a giant for God. It was through her teaching I became burdened for missions. God was beginning to show me direction for my life. In time, I became burdened for India, which, at the time, was still under the rule of Great Britain and had a population of slightly over 400 million. India's population today is nearly that of China, well over 1 billion, with 80% of the population being Hindu by religion.

Two verses in the Bible were drilled into us by Dr. Haight, which, beyond any other part of God's Word, directed my life toward missions and India, in particular. Even though those two verses do not mention India, nor even seem to be "missions" verses, God used them to eventually thrust me out to India to spend nearly 27 years of my life with Wilma in reaching the people of India with the gospel of Christ. Interestingly enough, God used those very same verses to reinforce His will for Wilma's life. Undoubtedly, God spoke to Wilma in a different way than He did to me. The two verses that played such an important part in both of our lives are Proverbs 24:11, 12.

> If thou forbear to deliver *them that are* drawn unto death and *those that are* ready to be slain;
> If thou sayest, behold, we knew it not, doth not he that pondereth the heart consider *it*? And he that keepeth thy soul, doth *not* he know it? And shall *not* he render to *every* man according to his works?

At one morning chapel service, Dr. Bob Jones Sr. told each one of us students to write on a piece of paper what we believed was God's will for our lives. Wilma and I could not sit together in chapel and we did not know what the other had written until later. We had not discussed the subject of missionary service in India, or even about God's plan for our lives, during any of our dates. Until that time; our dating had been only on a casual friendship level. Later in the day we had occasion to ask each other what we had written on the little piece of paper. We came to discover that we had both written one word, INDIA! It was here that I had finally told the Lord, "Lord, I have only one life and I give it all to you; I keep none of it back for myself." We both believed that what happened that morning in chapel was God's sign to us that we were to marry one day and serve together as missionaries in the land of India. There would be many things that had to take place before we reached God's place of appointment for us. From that day in chapel we both had as our goal, the completing of our degree studies at Bob Jones College, get married and go to India as missionaries.

Preaching On The Mountain

For practical experience in preaching one semester, another classmate and I used to preach in a little white church on top of Lookout Mountain, near Chattanooga. We didn't have a car and didn't have enough money to take a bus. The only way we could get to Chattanooga, just thirty miles away was to hitchhike. Hitchhiking was safe in those days and one didn't think of any danger that could happen by accepting a ride from a stranger; that is, except for one ride that we took.

It was, one Saturday morning we got out on old U.S. Highway 11 and stuck out our thumbs, hoping that a car would soon stop to pick us up and take us on into Chattanooga. It was not long before a car stopped and we got in, hoping we would soon reach our destination. We hadn't gone very far when we looked at each other and decided we didn't want to ride in that car any farther. It was plain to see the driver had had one too many drinks; whether it was the home-brewed corn "likker," or store-bought stuff, we didn't know; it didn't matter. We did know we had to get out of that car without delay. We told the man we wanted to get out at the next crossing; fortunately, we had not told him how far we were going when we first got into his car. He did stop at the next crossing and let us out, to our great relief. As we saw him driving on down the road, the car was not keeping very much of a straight path. It wasn't much longer before another car came along and we made it into Chattanooga safely.

As soon as we arrived in Chattanooga on any given Saturday afternoon, we would walk down one side of the city's main thoroughfare, handing out gospel tracts and then return on the other side of the street. I don't know how many tracts we gave out each Saturday, but it must have been in the hundreds. Eventually, we would make our way to the incline railway station at the bottom of Lookout Mountain and take the little car up to the top of the mountain. The "Incline,' as it was commonly called, was quite unique in that all the seats were hinged, so that when the car went up, or down, the mountain, the passengers would still be sitting in a horizontal position. It was like a mountain cable car, only riding on rail tracks that went up the mountain at about a 45-degree angle.

Saturday nights we stayed in the home of a widow lady, whose husband had been a well-known Bible teacher. Mrs. Gregg was a typical Southern hostess and after the morning service she would serve us delicious Southern fried chicken, mashed potatoes and gravy, along with other goodies. I think we enjoyed those Sunday afternoon meals as much as we enjoyed our ministry amongst the people on Lookout Mountain. The congregation was small, but very responsive to the Word of God and accepted these two young Preacher Boys from Bob Jones College. It was a good experience and played a large part in preparing me to serve the Lord on the mission field in India.

Sudden Growth

In the fall of 1945 I returned to Bob Jones College for my third year of studies. The student body had nearly doubled in size. The war had ended in August and our service men and women were now home and moving back into civilian life. War veterans were able to go to college with government aid, called the G.I. Bill of Rights.

The college was bursting out at the seams. Something had to be done and done quickly to alleviate the shortage of housing for students. Dr. Bob Sr. had found out that at the Atomic Energy Commission's facilities in Oak Ridge, Tennessee fifty house trailers were available to the college without cost. All the college had to do was move those trailers down to Cleveland. During the Christmas holiday all fifty trailers had been moved and hooked up to water, sewer and electricity. Temporary board sidewalks were laid down until concrete walks could be built later.
I was assigned to one of those trailers my second semester and also returned to the same trailer for the fall semester of 1946. Eventually grass was planted and permanent walks were poured, but that first spring term the rains had caused one muddy mess and muddy shoes, if you happened to step from off the wooden walks.

Summer Ministry Experiences

During the summer of 1945 Wilma and I both went to New England, along with several other BJC students, to work in vacation Bible schools operated under the auspices of the New England Fellowship. I worked with another male student for several weeks in small churches in Maine. That was an enjoyable experience and the one and only time I have been in the State of Maine. Wilma worked that summer with another female student in the States of New Hampshire and Vermont.

The following summer of 1946 Wilma and I both worked as counselors in her church's camp. The church did not actually own the camp facilities, but rented them for a number of weeks every summer. The camp's name was FA-HO-LO, which stood for Faith-Hope-Love, the name having been suggested by Wilma's sister, Sylvia. That week at FA-HO-LO was a turning point in both of our lives. The special speaker was a youth evangelist and founder/director of Youth Gospel Crusade, Richard W. Neale. Mr. Neale was fondly known as "Uncle Dick." I showed an interest in that type of ministry and during my last semester at Bob Jones College I corresponded with Mr. Neale about the possibility of joining that organization as a youth evangelist after completing my college studies in early January 1947. Wilma was in complete agreement with me that a period of time spent in such a ministry would give us a maturity and experience that could prepare us for an effective life of service in India. As the semester was drawing to a close and I was completing requirements for my bachelor's degree, I applied to the Youth Gospel Crusade governing board as an evangelist. I was accepted and suddenly became known as "Uncle Ken." In time, I would also be known by that name by many M.K.'s (Missionary Kids) in India.

+ Life At Bob Jones College +

We meet in Greek class at Bob
Jones College
The year - 1944

Having a serious
discussion at Bob
Jones College
The year – 1946 (?)

My dormitory the last year
at Bob Jones College
The year - 1946

Graduation Day
Bob Jones College
The year - 1947

Part Four: Uncle Ken and His Gospel Magic

January, 1947 - January, 1949

This **Is The Way**

"And thine ears shall hear a word behind thee Saying, This is the way, walk ye in it, when ye turn to the right hand and when ye turn to the left."

(Isaiah 30:21)

Uncle Ken And His Gospel Magic

In January, 1947, right after I finished my degree studies at Bob Jones College, I moved to Wheaton, Illinois, where the headquarters of Youth Gospel Crusade were located. I lived with the Neales, whose house address was 111 West Union and lay directly across the street from the home of Strat Shufelt, a popular musician and song leader, who worked with a well-known evangelist. Next to the Shufelts' house and at the opposite corner from where I stayed with the Neales, was the home of the president of Wheaton College. My bedroom happened to be the sunroom facing on the south side of the house; it was a pleasant room and I enjoyed my time there. Mrs. Neale was a gracious hostess and made sure I was well fed. I paid no room and board and was treated the whole time I lived there as one of the family.

During those early months with Youth Gospel Crusade, I was Dick Neale's apprentice and quickly "learned the ropes." In March, I was to be in my first meetings with him in a Presbyterian church in Englewood, Colorado, a suburb of Denver. Dick Drove out to Denver with all his equipment, which included a large easel and flannel graph materials for a multitude of stories. The material was called "Scene-O-Felt," for they were scenes painted in oil paints on felt material. Oh, how beautiful they were. Many different backgrounds could be put together with individual pieces, along with figures of people and animals, as well as trees, bushes, rocks, etc, to create different stories, Dick also had projectors, films and lots of illusion equipment; in those days it was called "gospel magic". All of this was to present the gospel to children of school age, all across America.

There wasn't room for me to travel with Dick Neale in his car and so, I went by train. That was the first time I had ever been close to the Rocky Mountains. To me, a boy from Minnesota, those mountains were quite overwhelming. I found it difficult to comprehend the size of the Rockies. Reaching up so high, they seemed to disappear into the clouds above. The mountains of Tennessee, where I went to college are dwarfed by the Rockies. The highest point in Minnesota where I was born and grew up is Eagle Mountain in the northeastern corner of the state; its elevation is only 2,301 feet above sea level. You can imagine that I was awed by the beauty of this part of God's creation. It was quite some years later that Wilma and I would live in the "foothills" of the highest mountains in the world, The Himalayan Mountains in North India.

One day, during a break in our ministry in the Denver area, Dick Neale took me in his car up to Berthoud Pass, at over 11,000 feet above sea level. I thought we would never stop climbing. It was beautiful up there; the ground and mountains were all covered with snow, for it was the early part of March. There is a sign at the pass, showing where the famous Buffalo Bill is buried. I had my picture taken standing beside that sign.

God blessed in those meetings in Colorado, for there were quite a number of boys and girls saved. It didn't take me long to come to love that type of ministry and I was learning quickly as an apprentice youth evangelist. It was not long after we arrived back in Wheaton, Illinois; at Youth Gospel Crusade headquarters that Dick Neale told me that he felt I was ready to launch out on my own with my very own meetings. A week of meetings was set up for me in a small town in the southern part of my home state of Minnesota. God blessed in my very first meetings as a youth evangelist and though I cannot remember all the details of the week of meetings which I had at

First Baptist Church in Albert Lee, Minnesota, I know there were a few boys and girls who came to trust Christ as their own personal Savior. I was thrilled and ready to take on my next meetings.

The following weeks seemed to fly by as I traveled from place to place, holding Youth Gospel Crusade meetings. At the beginning, I had very little money to purchase equipment and supplies, but Dick Neale helped me in that. In time, I was able to purchase my own set of Scene-O-Felt materials, a projector, film stories and special equipment to use for "gospel magic."

Graduation And Delayed Marriage

Almost before I knew it, the time had come for me to travel back to Cleveland, Tennessee for commencement exercises at Bob Jones College, where, along with Wilma, we would receive our Bachelor of Arts degrees, with a major in Christian Education. It was an exciting time for us, for soon we would be married and begin a lifetime of service together, first in youth evangelism in the States and then as missionaries to India. Our hope was to be married on Graduation Day, May 28, 1947; but I had practically no money and no place to take my bride to live. We decided we would wait until August to be married.

Our plans had been to have a double wedding with another couple, right after receiving our diplomas. The other couple did get married at that time, though we were unable to attend for some reason or other. During Graduation, Dr. Bob Sr. made an announcement to all who were there that a "mummy" would come out of the museum to get married and all were invited to attend the wedding. The college's museum was in the basement of one of two adjoining women's dormitories, which were joined together by a beautiful little parlor. We all knew that the mummy was actually Roy Mumme (pronounced as 'mummy'), who had graduated the year before and was marrying a girl in our class.

Wilma's parents had driven down for graduation and after that the three of them drove home by way of the Smoky and Appalachian Mountains of Tennessee, the Carolinas and Virginia. It was hard saying goodbye to my bride-to-be. Being on campus at Bob Jones I couldn't even kiss her goodbye. But we had to part; I making my way back to Wheaton, Illinois and Wilma driving away from campus with her parents, on their way back to Belleville, Michigan.

Expect The Unexpected

We set a date for our wedding, August 22, 1947, and I could hardly wait for that day. I continued living with the Neales in their beautiful home in Wheaton, though I was involved in a number of meetings in Minnesota, Wisconsin and Illinois. While Wilma and I were separated by not many miles, it seemed as though we were half a world away from each other. We kept in close contact by letters and before we knew it, our wedding day was soon upon us. I had just completed a week of meetings and headed for Belleville, Michigan. I stayed in the home of Pastor and Mrs. William R. Rice. Bill and His wife, Lynne, were living in a house owned by the Schulerts, who were members of Berean Baptist Church where Bill was pastor. The church was between the Schulerts' and Wilma's house.

Our wedding day was a time and experience that we will never forget, one in which we should have expected the unexpected. We were to be married in that little white church by Wilma's pastor of her home church, First Baptist Church of Wayne, Michigan, which is less than fifteen miles from Belleville. The evening before, our wedding practice went off without a hitch. Wilma's father was always coming up with something that made a person laugh. The evening of our wedding practice he told Wilma, with a straight face, "Wilma, when it comes time for the pastor to ask, 'Who doth give this woman in marriage?' I'll answer, 'I don't!'" Boy, it would have been just like him to pull off something like that to make our wedding more interesting. Of course, he didn't say that, but, on the contrary, when the question was asked at our wedding, he proudly replied, "I do!"

Well, that wasn't the unexpected we mentioned earlier. As it got closer to the time for our wedding, Wilma received a phone call from her pastor's wife. Pastor Reed had to be rushed to the hospital for an emergency appendectomy! He couldn't perform our wedding. But that wasn't all, for Mrs. Reed was to be the pianist. And to further create a stumbling block in our wedding plans, Wilma received another phone call from the girl who was to sing a special wedding song. She couldn't sing, for she had lost her voice; she had laryngitis. Now what were we to do, no preacher, no pianist and no soloist! Wilma told our soloist to suck on a lemon and come and do her best; on top of that, she would have to also play the piano. But what about the preacher? As we sat in Wilma's dining room, which faced the road in front of the house, discussing what we should do, who should we see going past but Bill Rice? Wilma ran to the door and cried out, "Bill, you have to marry us; Pastor Reed is in the hospital having an emergency appendectomy." His simple reply was for us to be patient and he would be back soon; he was on his way to milk the cow of members of the church, who lived a short distance from there. They had gone away on a short vacation and Bill Rice volunteered to milk their cow while they were away. In the meantime, we discussed our wedding program and finalized as to who was to do what. In the end, no one who attended our wedding seemed to know what had happened. I guess they must have figured that Pastor Rice was to perform the ceremony, in view of the fact that the wedding was being held at Berean Baptist Church where he was the pastor. In the end, everything seemed to go off smoothly. When it was announced that we were now husband and wife, we sighed a big sigh of relief and marched up the aisle with a look of triumph! A picture taken by someone shows me with my mouth wide open, as though I was singing the Hallelujah Chorus!"

Our first night of married life was spent at the Cadillac Hotel in downtown Detroit. We didn't have a car of our own and so, Mr. Schulert drove us into Detroit and dropped us off, bag and baggage at the hotel. We were now on our own. That next morning we received a telegram at the hotel from Maranatha Bible Camp near Muskegon, Michigan. The telegram read, "Reserving Room Three India Nights of 23 and 24. Wire if you wish this held for you. Maranatha" We sent word back right away, "Reserve Room Three India for the Nights of 23 and 24." That morning we caught a train from Detroit to Muskegon and the following week we spent at the Bible camp. Our first two nights at the camp we stayed in a small guest house on the camp grounds, just near the tabernacle where the camp services were being held. The name of the guesthouse was, interestingly enough, India House. After that we were put up at a large dormitory building, which overlooked a bluff on Lake

Michigan. I think we were possibly the only ones staying in that building. At least we didn't see anyone else there. But then, being newly married, we probably wouldn't have seen anyone else there if they walked right past us!

It was a wonderful week, our first week of married life. We did attend a few of the services being held at Maranatha Bible Camp. The week seemed to fly by and we knew that it was time to get back to the realities of life and get ready for a series of meetings to be held in the northern part of Lower Michigan. The first week after our honeymoon Wilma helped me in our first youth meetings together. We were now known as "Uncle Ken and Aunt Wilma." We had a great time and there were a number of young people saved in those meetings.

Our First Year

The following week Wilma had to return to Belleville. Her sister, Sylvia, was to be married on September 12th to Bob Rice, a younger brother to Pastor Bill Rice. Wilma was to be Sylvia's matron of honor. Sylvia and Bob's wedding didn't go without a hitch either. The evening before their wedding Sylvia stepped on a rusty nail. She was allergic to a tetanus shot and as a result, the best thing they could do to stop the possibility of any serious infection, was to burn the spot where the rusty nail pierced her foot. The wedding went on as planned, with Sylvia not walking down the aisle, but hobbling down on the arm of her father. After Sylvia and Bob's wedding, Wilma returned and joined me in the closing days of the meetings I was having in Northern Michigan.

Our first home was a sleeping room in Wheaton, IL. We couldn't even boil water in the room and all of our meals had to be eaten at some local restaurant, including breakfast. It became quite expensive, living that way and we knew that we had to find some other place where we could do our own cooking; but that had to wait until after the first of the following year. On Christmas Day, 1947 we didn't have anything to eat all day, for the restaurants in town were closed for the holiday. What a way to spend our first Christmas together; no food, no Christmas decorations. We were not even able to exchange any gifts with each other, for our "cupboard was bare." By the next morning we were feeling very hungry, to say the least!

Shortly after the first of the year we moved over to the next town, Glen Ellyn, where we moved into an old vacation trailer, set up on cement blocks in the back yard of a house. It had no insulation to it and the only thing we had to keep us warm, besides a small electric heater, was our love for each other. Our bed was the table on which we ate. The trailer measured probably no more than 20 feet in length, if that; but it was a place to stay when we weren't out in meetings. We paid some $30 per month to stay there. One time, during that winter, Wilma didn't go with me to meetings I had, along with another of our Youth Gospel Crusade evangelists. That week of meetings were held in Milwaukee, Wisconsin. The church where we were holding our meetings put us up in a nice hotel and we slept under electric blankets, while Wilma seemed to barely exist in that cold trailer for the whole week I was gone. I felt so badly about the whole matter; but it was beyond my control. I was only too glad to get back to Glen Ellyn and be with my dear Wilma.

<u>Walking By Faith</u>

As youth evangelists, we had no guaranteed salary. We

simply walked by faith and not by sight. God always provided for our needs and we never went hungry, not since that first Christmas Day in 1947. Well, there was one other time and that was the following winter, not that God was testing our faith only in the wintertime. We were scheduled for meetings in the small town of Shell Rock, Iowa, which was about 20 miles northwest of Waterloo. We always traveled by train, wherever we had our meetings, for we had no car of our own. It was a long ride from Wheaton, Illinois to Shell Rock, Iowa. In order to get a train out of Union Station in Chicago, we had to take the suburban train, called the "Aurora and Elgin." Then from Chicago we could get a train to wherever our next meetings were to be held. This time we had just enough money to purchase our two coach tickets and with a Buffalo Head nickel in our pockets left over we headed for Waterloo. Five cents certainly was not enough to buy a meal on the train, not even for one person, let alone for the two of us. And so, the train to Waterloo that day was without anything to eat at all, not a sandwich, not a candy bar! It was late evening when we arrived at our destination and were met by the pastor of the church where our week of meetings was to be held. Nothing was asked by the pastor as to whether we had eaten on the train; he probably assumed that we had eaten and we didn't mention anything about it ourselves. When we arrived at our hostess's house, still nothing was mentioned about food. Our hostess was a widow lady. Her house was a typical Midwest white frame, two-storey house; with no insulation in those days and generally central heating with hot water registers in every room. Somehow the heat did not get up to the corner bedroom where we were to sleep that week. We slept in a double bed, with a thick comforter to keep us warm. We enjoyed our time in Shell Rock, for the people at the church were warm hearted and welcomed this newly married couple with open arms. God put His blessings on us and the meetings, for we saw several youth come to know Christ as their personal Savior that week.

The following months of 1948 took us to many churches in the Midwestern States of Michigan, Indiana, Illinois, Iowa, Wisconsin and Minnesota. We even had meetings in Ohio and New York State. One time we had a week of meetings in Jamestown, North Dakota. That was quite an experience. Our meetings were never in large churches or with large crowds of people. But God always blessed and we always saw young people saved. Only eternity will reveal how many were saved and who they were. One time we even had meetings in the home of a man in Chicago. We were crowded each day into a small room in the front of the house, which was in a run down part of the city.

Another time we had meetings in a small town in Northern Wisconsin in an old bank building, turned into a church. I remember those meetings very well, for on the first night I felt as though there was a dark and heavy spirit present. That evening it was hard for us to complete the meeting and at the end of the meeting, after everyone else had left, the pastor asked us, "Did you feel as though there was some demonic presence in the meeting?" We replied, "Yes we did; why do you ask?" His answer was simply, "She was sitting on the front row." We had prayed much for the power of God and victory over the devil in the remaining meetings. The woman, to whom the pastor had referred, did not come back the rest of the week. God had answered our prayers. The only night of those meetings in which we did not see anyone come forward for salvation was that first night in which the woman in question was there.

Before the first day or night of any meetings we would

usually go to nearby elementary schools and wait for the children to leave for home. At that time we would give to each child a ticket to our meetings, which had our picture on the ticket and the words, "Your Complimentary Ticket to See and Hear - Uncle Ken and Aunt Wilma and their Picture Adventures." The tickets also announced about "Amazing Pictures, Mysteries, Contests, Prizes." Those tickets were quite a drawing card and brought many children to our meetings. Who wouldn't want to win a prize by attending meetings where there was even "magic!"

Lasting Results

We sometimes do not see results of our ministry right away, especially in the matter of people getting saved. In some cases people have made themselves known to us many years later. In the summer of 1948 we spoke at Wood Lake Camp near Grantsberg in Northern Wisconsin. We were not aware of any significant conversions that week, though we knew that some children had made professions of salvation. Many years later, after we had moved to British Columbia to begin a ministry to people from India, who had immigrated to Canada, we had occasion to be in the home of my older brother. Warren had been pastor of several churches in Iowa and Wisconsin and eventually the Lord led him to begin a Christian radio station out of Ladysmith, Wisconsin. Warren and his family lived near Chippewa Falls, which is about fifteen miles north of Eau Claire. As we were getting ready to leave my brother's home to go on to our next destination, we were called back into the house by Warren's second son, Greg. He was on the phone with friends, who were traveling from Minnesota to visit him. They had tuned in on their car radio to my brother's radio station and heard Wilma and me being interviewed by Warren. We were introduced by our given names, Ken and Wilma, which were used more than once during the interview. As the young couple, who were missionaries in another part of the world, listened to the broadcast, the wife became more and more intrigued by the whole situation and remarked to her husband, "I wonder if they are the same Ken and Wilma who were holding meeting at Wood Lake Camp when the pastor's wife at the church we were just at told us how she had been saved at the age of 12 during special meetings being held by an Uncle Ken and Aunt Wilma. Could it be that they are the very same Uncle Ken and Aunt Wilma we have just heard on the radio?" And so, they had stopped along the way someplace to call my brother's home number in order to find out if what they were thinking was true. We rushed back into the house, after being called in by our nephew, to speak to that couple on the phone. Yes, we were the very same Uncle Ken and Aunt Wilma and, yes, we had spoken at Wood Lake Camp back in 1948. We found out the name of the pastor and his wife, who were pastoring a Baptist church just south of Minneapolis, Minnesota.

Some time after this incident took place at my brother's home, I was on my way from Minneapolis to Rochester, Minnesota for meetings in a supporting church. I had that Sunday morning free and decided to stop and attend the morning service at the church where Pastor Bob Gravely and his wife, Edythe, were serving the Lord; it was right on my way to Rochester. What a surprise it was for this couple to see me and what a time of rejoicing, as Edythe related to me how she had been saved so many years before in our Youth Gospel Crusade meetings at Wood Lake Camp in Grantsberg, Wisconsin. After the service that morning, the people of the church were having a picnic at a nearby park and there that pastor's wife had to share with everyone the story of her being led to the Lord by Uncle Ken and Aunt

Wilma and I was that very same Uncle Ken, now many years later.

That same year of 1948 we had meetings in a small country church near Adrian, Michigan. The church was an old clapboard-sided building, which was in much need of a new coat of paint. Once again, there didn't seem to be anything significant that happened that week, though we felt the Lord had been with us and gave us good meetings. We couldn't remember any outstanding conversions amongst the youth who attended the meetings. Just another week of meetings with "Uncle Ken and Aunt Wilma and their Picture Adventures!" Little did we know at the time that God was working in the heart of at least one boy, who came to place his faith in Jesus Christ as his own personal Saviour. Some years later, after we had returned on furlough from India, we heard about that boy, who had gone on to study at a Bible institute and was called of the Lord to work amongst down and out black youth on the near south side of Chicago. We found out where he had his youth center and decided to pay him a visit. He was located in a very much rundown part of the city and we felt a bit of apprehension in going there. But we went, trusting the Lord to take care of us and take care of our car. What a time of rejoicing it was to find this young man, who, as a boy of twelve, had been saved in our meetings in that little country church that needed a new coat of paint. He was now reaching out to a desperate community of poor black youth, who had time on their hands to get into trouble and break the law. As we talked with this young man, we found that he had gained the trust of those black youth. He told us one thing, which we will never forget, and that was that our car would not have been safe parked out at the curb, if he had not been there. Before we would have gotten back out to our car, those black youth would have stripped our car clean, as one would do with fish, leaving only the skeleton.

During our two years of ministry with the Youth Gospel Crusade, there were many unexpected and humorous things that happened. We recall one situation about which we have laughed many times. We were having meetings in a small church in the Peoria, Illinois suburb of Pottstown. The pastor of that church was a student at the time at Moody Bible Institute. It was the fall season and the evenings were beginning to get a bit on the chilly side. One evening, as the meeting was in progress and just at a very important time in the meeting, noise began coming up from the basement. The church was heated by a coal-burning furnace in the basement and the hot air, generated by the coal fire, would come up through a large grate in the floor of the church. It became very hot in that little church and as it got hotter, the noise from the basement got louder and louder. What confusion there was that evening. Well, we got through the meetings, after which we asked the young pastor if he knew what all the commotion was about. He had actually gone downstairs to find out for himself and what did he find, but the church custodian, an old man, who, apparently, was quite drunk, trying to stoke up the furnace with more and more coal. Fortunately, the custodian did not return another night, whether by choice, or by instructions from the pastor; at least we did not have any more noise, or overly stoked hot furnace to contend with.

One time we had meetings at the Great Lakes Naval Training Center, north of Chicago. There was a small congregation that met in one of the dormitory-like buildings on the base. The pastor was also a student at Moody Bible Institute. One day, for some reason that we cannot recall at this time, that young pastor had gone up into the attic, right above the room where we were having our meetings. Fortunately, there was not a meeting going on at the time; but suddenly, there was a loud noise, a shout and the pastor came crashing through the ceiling and landed right at our feet, having fallen a distance of well over eight feet. He was stunned for a moment, then picked himself up from off the floor and stated quietly to us, "I'm alright; I'm alright." We left the base shortly after that, concerned that he might have broken some bones, or gotten a concussion in his head. We thought the latter might have been possible, from the way he spoke, trying to assure us that he was all right.

During those two years we served as youth evangelists, we still had our eyes on the mission field and India, in particular. We believed God had called us to serve Him in that far off country and we had kept that vision before us, waiting for the day when we would begin to take our first steps to reach India. The time did come in the early part of 1949, at which time we resigned from the Youth Gospel Crusade.

+ Our Wedding and First Home +

Mr. and Mrs. Kenneth Steward
August 22, 1947

Cutting the Cake
August 22, 1947

Berean Baptist Church in Belleville, Michigan where we were married on August 22, 1947

Our first home after we were married. Our bed was the "dining room" table.

+ Uncle Ken and His Gospel Magic +

Complimentary ticket used for all
our Youth Gospel Meetings
The years - 1947-1949

Publicity Photo for Youth Gospel Crusade
The years - 1947-1949

We used beautiful scenes with oil paints on felt to portray the gospel in our Youth Gospel Crusade meetings
The years - 1947-1949

Part Five: The **Goal Before Us**

January, 1949 - June, 1965

Idols of wood and brass and of stone

Naught for salvation could ever atone;

Deeply in sin and disease are they

Ignorant of Him, seeking the way;

As God bids us to go, He bids you to stay.

While we are telling, He bids you to PRAY!

"Withal praying also for us that God would open unto us a door of utterance to speak the mystery of Christ…"

(Colossians 4:3)

The Goal Before Us

At the beginning of 1949 we handed in our resignation as youth evangelists with the Youth Gospel Crusade. We had enjoyed our two years of ministry with this outstanding organization, which had as its goal, "Reaching the Youth of America With the Gospel." God used us in some very unusual ways in the lives of many young people of all ages. How many were truly saved in our meetings, we will not know until we get to heaven. But we know that each one who came to Christ, came because they heard the Word of God and God drew them to Himself. We were simply used of the Lord to present the gospel of Christ; we planted the seed. But our goal from the beginning was to go to India as missionaries. Our two years with the Youth Gospel Crusade was a time of training and preparing us for the harder tasks to follow. We were absolutely convinced that God had called us to India and that he would take us there in His time and way and would provide all that we would need to get to India and to keep us there.

Shortly before we moved back to Michigan in preparation for going to India, my mother visited us in Wheaton, Illinois. Mother had a struggle in her heart and mind to recognize God's priority in Wilma's and my life. I don't believe she was actually possessive of me, her middle son, but there was this thought in her mind that we were going to a country where there were poverty, filth, diseases and wild animals. She conveyed this thought to us one evening as the three of us strolled along a street near where we were living at the time. She stated very clearly to me, "Kenneth, you and Wilma will go to India and get sick with some terrible disease and die there, or you will be killed by a wild animal. I am going to pray that God will keep you from going to India." Now, that was a strange thing for her to say, in view of the fact that it was God Who had called us to go to India. My reply to her was simply, "Mother, don't pray a prayer like that, for God will not hear such a prayer." Actually, God does hear prayers like that, but He does not give the desires of such prayers, when it is His will to do otherwise. As for Wilma and me, that 'otherwise' was going to India as missionaries. Little did we know what God would take us through in the next twenty-seven years, or maybe we just wouldn't have gone to India in the first place. That is looking at it from the human perspective. I guess it is a good thing that God does not reveal to us ahead of time things that will take place in our lives.

Upon resigning from the Youth Gospel crusade, we applied to a very well-known interdenominational mission, with its headquarters being at the time in Chicago, Illinois. While we were Baptists by church membership and personal conviction, we knew of only one Baptist mission organization with missionaries serving in India; but for some reason, beyond our understanding at the time, we did not feel comfortable applying to that mission. My own pastor had told us one day that if we would go out under that mission, he could guarantee that my home church would take on the greater portion of my support. We went ahead and applied to the interdenominational mission, knowing that it was a good mission and though it was interdenominational, it was evangelical and held to the same fundamentals of the faith that we held to. It would be some years later that we saw changes taking place in the mission, changes with which we could not agree and it resulted in our parting with the mission.

In February 1949 we were accepted by the mission and attended their candidate school for new appointees going to India. There were a large number of us preparing to go to

India for the first time. It was a thrilling time to be at that candidate school and take this next step in our journey to the land of India, where we would serve the Lord for the next 27 years. We moved back to Belleville, Michigan, where we made our base of operations for deputation ministry. Meetings were set up in a number of churches in Michigan, Indiana and Illinois, in particular. Promises of financial support began to trickle in, but by August we were still a long way off from getting the minimum support needed, as well as funds needed to pay for our tickets on a ship to take us all the way to India, half way around the world. It would cost us $500 apiece for our travel. In August we went to Minneapolis to visit my parents. While there we received an urgent phone call from mission headquarters in Chicago. There was a sailing available on a freighter bound for India, which was scheduled to leave New York on September 30th. Would we accept that sailing? We were almost astounded by the news, but believing that God was in it, we told the mission we would leave on that ship and to go ahead and purchase our tickets for us.

At the time we accepted that sailing, we did not have the funds in hand to pay for the tickets, as well as having all of our needed support for our living expenses in India, along with our ministry to the people. There was so much to do in the few weeks left for us, including getting five or six inoculations in a little over one week before we had to leave and return to Michigan. It was not easy saying goodbye to my parents, knowing Mother was not sympathetic to our going half way around the world to a very backward country with all its poverty, filth, diseases and wild animals.

In the following weeks we took care of last minute

business, packed the few clothes and household goods we possessed, to take with us. We had just three small footlockers containing household effects and a suitcase apiece with our clothes and other personal items. We arrived in New York the day before we were to sail and were met by the travel agent the mission used. There was a telephone message awaiting our arrival, telling us that a church in Dearborn, Michigan had taken on the rest of our support. Funds had also come in to take care of all the remaining expenses for going to India for our first term of service.

We stayed at a guesthouse that night and were met the next morning by the travel agent, who took us to the wharf in Lower Manhattan, from where our freighter was to sail. There we boarded the 9,000-ton Liberty Ship, S.S. Steel King, one of several freighters operated by the United States Steel Company. During World War II, the ship had been used as a troop ship, taking soldiers to Europe to fight in the war.

There was a lot of activity throughout the day as dockworkers feverishly loaded the ship. We were to learn later that the workers, all members of the longshoremen's union, were scheduled to go out on strike at midnight. Little did we know that we would soon be faced with a full-blown hurricane. Because of loading the ship so hastily, it was top heavy, causing the ship to be buffeted about in the ocean, worse than what it would have, had the ship been loaded normally.

Reeling To And Fro

We would soon be reminded of what the psalmist wrote in Psalm 107, "They that go down to the sea in ships, that do business in great waters, these see the works of the Lord and his wonders in the deep. For he commandeth and raiseth the stormy wind, which lifteth up the waves thereof. They mount up to the heaven; they go down again to the depths: their soul is melted because of trouble. They reel to and fro and stagger like a drunken man and are at their wit's end." Psalm 107:23-27.

When the storm struck with all its fury, our little ship was tossed about in the ocean, completely at the mercy of the storm. It seemed that the ship moved in every direction possible. As we looked out from our cabin porthole, we saw only water, for we were actually looking up at the ocean. Because of the storm, we were confined to the inside of the ship. When the crew had to go out on deck, they were tied to a safety line to prevent them from being washed overboard. We thought we would never escape from the storm's clutches. It was not until about the fifth day that the storm abated and we began to get into "calmer" waters. It took us all of nine days to get across the Atlantic Ocean and sail past the Rock of Gibraltar. That was certainly a "sight for sore eyes." We knew that we were about to enter the Mediterranean Sea and, hopefully, calm waters.

While I endured the rough water, Wilma was terribly sick. At the time, we did not realize that she was actually in the first month of a pregnancy with our first child. Lily Ann was, no doubt, conceived in a storm. Wilma could keep nothing down, except for dry soda crackers. But how long can you live on just soda crackers! One morning I went down to the dining room by myself. Wilma couldn't get out of her bunk. We always ate with the officers. That morning our waiter expressed his concern about Wilma's apparent seasickness. When he asked me if I thought she would be able to at least eat a boiled egg, I didn't realize that when I replied it might be possible, he would arrange to send up with me five boiled eggs. After I finished my breakfast, I took the eggs back with me to our cabin. It wasn't funny at the time, but since then we have had a good laugh many times about the whole situation. When Wilma saw the boiled eggs, she fled to the bathroom to bring up what little there was still on her stomach, while I enjoyed those five boiled eggs.

Needless to say, we did survive those five days of the storm, though we wondered at the time if the Lord had taken us out onto the ocean, only to send us to the bottom to a watery grave. Our captain didn't fare so well. During the storm he slipped on some steps and fell, breaking his leg. The first officer was then put in command of our ship while the captain was confined to his cabin, waiting to be taken off the ship when we reached our first port of call, which was Beirut, Lebanon. There he would be able to receive adequate medical attention. The rest of our trip, which took a total of five weeks to reach our destination at Bombay, India, was quite uneventful, as far as any bad weather was concerned.

Life Aboard A Freighter

There was little to do on board ship, though we had a sitting room, along with our two-berth sleeping cabin; in the sitting room we had a small library of books that we could read to occupy part of our time. When we stopped at different ports along the way there were many interesting sights to see. We were eleven passengers on board the S.S. Steel King. Besides ourselves, there were two single ladies, also bound for India as missionaries for their first time. They would be working at the Ramabai Mukti Mission in

Kedgaon, south of Bombay. Their mission cared for homeless girls and widows and was begun by Pandita Ramabai, a convert from Hinduism, herself from the Brahmin caste, which was the highest caste in Hinduism.

Another passenger was a young Indian man by the name of Checkers; at least that was the name by which he wanted to be called. Checkers worked for an export/import company in New York and was on his way back to India on business for his company. There was also a seemingly well-to-do woman on board, decked out in expensively looking jewelry and who stood apart from the rest of us, at least at the beginning of the trip. In time she seemed to warm up to us and was quite friendly. There was a Catholic priest, bound for India, who came from Spain. In taking his vow with the Church, he was not allowed to step foot on his home soil. It was quite a moving experience to see him look longing at the shores of Southern Spain as we sailed on into the Mediterranean Sea. Also, two Catholic nuns tried to keep themselves apart from the priest, not enjoying the smell of his cigars that he continually smoked; the nuns were more friendly to us. We also didn't enjoy the smell of the priest's cigars. We tried to be friendly with him, which was a bit difficult, because of his cigars. Finally, there was another American couple, who kept pretty much to themselves.

On Sundays we had the privilege of having morning services on deck, just outside the radio room. The ship had hymnbooks available and had many hymns with which we were familiar. I was able to bring a gospel message at every service. The priest did not attend, of course, as well as the nuns. Sparks, as the radioman was called, was able to join us for our services, for he was close to his radio equipment, if needed. We came to find out that he was Latvian by nationality, though unable to return to his home country because of it being under the control of the Soviet Union at the time.

Ports Of Call

We stopped at some very interesting ports during our five-week journey to Bombay. The first port of call was Beirut, Lebanon, as already mentioned. We were not able to see much of the city, for our freighter was in port only long enough to discharge its cargo and to make arrangements for our captain to be cared for at the American University, until he could be flown back to the States for proper medical care. Strolling through a nearby park, we came to an open-air meat market. This was our introduction to a typical meat market outside the western world. There would be many more we would see during our years in India.

Our next port of call was Alexandria, Egypt. At that time a king ruled all of Egypt and as we sailed on into the harbor, we passed the king's summer palace with its many rooms. It was rumored that the palace was where the king kept his many wives. As we tried to take pictures of the palace, we were quickly informed by a nearby Egyptian in a small boat sailing past at the time; it was illegal to take pictures of the king's palace. Somehow or other, I was able to get a picture taken of the palace anyway. When we disembarked to go into the city for the day, we had to surrender our American passports. This was probably to assure the authorities that we would return to our ship and not slip off unnoticed into the countryside. Some of the passengers on our freighter refused to part with their passports and had to remain on board. We were able to see only a small part of the city, as we strolled along one of its main avenues. We were greatly surprised to come upon a Christian bookstore.

After returning to our ship, it left Alexandria and sailed along the coast of Egypt until it came to Port Said (Saheed), which is at the northern head of the Suez Canal. We suddenly realized we were now in the heartland of Islam. We're not sure whether we were beginning to get paranoid or not, but an experience that involved a one-eyed man with a fez got us to thinking that we were. It started in Alexandria when we saw such a man standing down on the wharf looking up in our direction. Then, at each succeeding port we seemed to have seen the same man; at least the one we saw looked like the man we first saw in Alexandria port. The last port we touched was at Karachi, Pakistan and there was the one-eyed man with a red fez, standing on the wharf and looking up in our direction as we stood at the ship's railing. Could it be that this man was following us from port to port? If so, what interest did he have in us? We never did solve this apparent mystery.

Each port we stopped at during our five-week journey to India brought something of interest to us. Beirut, Alexandria, Port Said, Port Suez, each one was different than the other. From Port Suez, at the southern end of the Suez Canal, we sailed down the Red Sea to Jeddah, Arabia. There we had to wait five days while pilgrims, who had made their pilgrimage to the holy city of Mecca, were transported back to their ships, which would then return them to their native places. Jeddah, Arabia at that time was just a desert village through which the pilgrims would travel to Mecca. There was no seaport, no wharves, no place for a ship to tie up, no way for freighters to off load their goods. They used large sailboats to unload from the ships, as well as being used to transport pilgrims to and from land. Because of this, we had a five-day wait. The Steel King was carrying steel girders to be used in building the new seaport at Jeddah. In addition, there were wooden crates carrying cars and trucks. As the ship's crew was off loading the large wooden crates, Arabian workers were helping to transfer them from the ship onto the large sailboats. Suddenly, one of the large crates, holding two trucks, broke loose from the rope sling and began plunging into the sea. It seemed that almost in an instant, the Arabian workers had grabbed the rope and diving into the water managed to bring the rope under the crate, as it sank; coming back to the surface, they were able to put that heavy, water-soaked rope back onto the ship's 'hook,' (for use of a better word). As the crate was lifted back up out of the sea, water came pouring out from the crate. We were able to record the whole event, even with the water pouring out of the crate. It was a dramatic event and helped to alleviate the boredom of those five days anchored offshore in the Red Sea. We have sometimes wondered if those trucks had ever gotten rusty from all that salt water which got into the crate as it began sinking into the sea.

While we were anchored offshore for those five scorching days in the Red Sea, the crew of our freighter had time on their hands and life, even for them, began to get a bit boring, to say the least. One day some of the crew decided to do a bit of fishing from off the stern of the freighter. I was able to join them and had a great time as the men began reeling in a fish that seemed to be found only in that part of the world; the fish was round in shape, like the moon and about the size of a dinner plate. As to the name of the fish, I can remember that some of the crew simply referred to it as a 'moon' fish.

After those five days, anchored offshore from the fishing village of Jeddah, Arabia, our freighter sailed on down the rest of the way through the Red Sea to Aden, which is at the very southern tip of the Arabian Peninsula. We stopped at Aden for only part of a day and so, were not able to get off the freighter to do any sightseeing of that seaport. Before we reached Aden, it was exciting to get a view of Mt. Sinai where Moses had received the Ten Commandments from God. This was probably the most exciting part of our whole journey, even more exciting than the storm in the Atlantic Ocean, if such was possible. After Aden it was on to Karachi, Pakistan's seaport on the northern edge of the Arabian Sea. We were in Karachi for only a very brief time before heading on to our final destination, Bombay, India.

Bombay At Last

Our arrival in Bombay was without fanfare; we were just another freighter, ready to unload its cargo and few passengers. The date was November 5, 1949. It seemed to take forever to go through the process of checking our baggage and passports by the Indian officials. We were met at the wharf by a senior missionary, Wayne Saunders. Before saying goodbye to the ship's crew, our waiter presented us with about a dozen bright red apples. We had enjoyed fresh fruit all along the way from New York to Bombay. We didn't know how we were able to get past the customs people with all those apples, but we did; we had not tried to hide them, but somehow the officials seemed to ignore that part of our personal effects. At any rate, as soon as Wayne Saunders met us we offered him an apple and he eagerly accepted all of them! Apples were a rarity in India and when they were available in the markets in Bombay, they were very expensive. Well, we had enjoyed apples all the way from New York and certainly didn't begrudge passing on this apparent luxury to our missionary, who had gone to the personal expense of a trip to Bombay to meet us, which was a day's journey each way.

Our journey "up country" was a very interesting experience, for we traveled the cheapest way possible on the train, Third Class. The coach was crowded with people and most of them were men. There was a special Third Class coach for women, but it was felt safer for Wilma to travel with us in the predominantly men's coach. As the train chugged its way north, everyone tried to find some place to settle in for the night. A few were able to grab hold of a place on the benches above to stretch out. The upper benches were actually meant to place one's baggage. Wilma seemed quite shocked to find some of the men changing into their pajama pants before all the other travelers; but all was done very modestly and without any "to-do." As we arrived at the railway junction town of Jalgaon the next morning, we had to change over to the Tapti Valley Train which followed along close to the south bank of the Tapti River, which is one of India's "holy" rivers. On we went until we arrived at the mission's head station at Amalner.

All the missionaries were meeting in conference and gave us a warm welcome. What an exciting time it was. Our introduction to daytime life in India was really the next morning, when we opened the shutters on the window of the small room in the front of the church where we stayed through the duration of the conference. As we opened the shutters and let the sun stream in through the window, we were confronted with the scene of a farmer across the road, driving a pair of bullocks around, as they trampled out the grain. This resulted in separating the hulls of the grain from the grain itself. That scene has been preserved for us on a 35-mm. slide, as well as in our memory to this day.

Did we have a culture shock upon arriving in India? Not really; except for possibly Wilma's experience of seeing

Indian men changing into their pajama pants on that train traveling from Bombay up country to Jalgaon. We were greeted by the typical "yells, bells and smells" which made India so unique. Coal-fired engines, belching out their black smoke to cover everyone alike on the train, the strange language, which would soon be our language of communication with the people to whom God had sent us with the Gospel of Christ. We experienced many new things during those first days in India, but culture shock was not a part of them.

Life In India Begins

Right after the end of the missionaries' conference and all the missionaries, who were not stationed at Amalner, left for their own mission stations, we were able to move into the mission bungalow. The missionaries built their bungalows much after the fashion of the British, who had ruled much of India for nearly three centuries. There were four large bedrooms at the four corners of the bungalow. Attached to each bedroom was a dressing room along with a bathroom. In the middle of the bungalow, separating the bedrooms on each side, were the living and dining rooms. At the very back of the bungalow was a large screened-in porch and attached to that, but separate from the bungalow, was the cookhouse. Surrounding the bungalow on three sides was a wide-open verandah. Large columns supported the roof over the verandah. Because of the usually hot climate in that part of India, the ceilings were about fifteen feet high. Buildings in India were generally built of stone and brick, with cement plaster on the walls and whitewashed with a lime solution. Because there was no running water, the toilet facilities were very primitive. It was not long before we made a vow that as soon as we were situated in our own mission station and found such primitive conditions, we would do our best to install more modern plumbing with a septic tank.

While India had gained its independence from Great Britain two years before our arrival, there was almost a servile attitude on the part of many people, especially the lower caste people. Ultimately, a seemingly superior attitude toward the lower caste people was transferred from the white man to the high caste Indians, who took over power from the British. We found, much to our dismay, that there was a similar attitude of lordship over the Indian lower caste people shown by some of the older generation missionaries. One situation which prevailed, for which there did not seem to be a solution at the time, was the dependence of the Indian Christian on the white missionaries. This was, no doubt, caused by an open rejection of the convert by those of the high caste Hindus. In effect, the new convert to Christianity was considered to be of a still lower caste, almost bordering on a level with, or even below the outcaste. At the time of her independence in 1947 India was declared to be a secular state and adopted a constitution, which guaranteed the equality of all religions and all peoples. It must be remembered, though, that Hindus constituted nearly 80% of the population. As a result, many laws and rights guaranteed by the constitution were simply ignored.

Our first responsibility, as soon as we moved into the mission bungalow, was to buy a bed for ourselves. Until such time as we were able to go down to Bombay to buy a bed, we were loaned one by the senior missionary with whom we lived. As soon as possible, we took a train to Bombay and found just the bed we needed at a department store run by an English company called Whiteway and Laidlaw. The bed was a double bed, with coil springs and a thick cotton mattress. Arranging to have it shipped up to Amalner, we returned to begin our language study with a private tutor.

Our tutor was the unmarried daughter of the local national pastor, David Chopda. Tarabai knew English very well and had been studying at a university. We enjoyed our beginning studies in Marathi, the language we would use almost exclusively in our future ministry. The program of study was so set up that we were to learn only one tense at a time. At the beginning we could speak only in the present tense. Thus, it was impossible to talk about anything that happened yesterday, or possibly might take place tomorrow. We were living only in the present.

Green Eggs And Ham

During our first months in India, we not only had to struggle through our studies in Marathi, trying to converse with the local people, but both of us had struggles with health problems. Wilma was dealing with early months of her first full pregnancy. Nothing seemed to taste very good to her.

We arrived in India a little over four years after the end of World War II and many things were still in short supply and rationing was in effect. We were allowed only one liter bottle of kerosene per month, which was to take care of our kerosene lights and pressure stove used for cooking. One or two pounds of sugar could be purchased per month and then the quality of sugar was quite poor, being almost as course as rock salt. Flour for making bread was in short supply and petrol (gasoline) for vehicles was hard to come by, that even being carefully rationed.

It was not long after our arrival in India that I became sick with dysentery and lost a lot of weight; at least, that is what we thought the problem was. My sickness would continue over the next 2 - 3 years and culminate in major surgery. I lost a great deal of weight and went down to about 125 pounds in all. I never wrote home about my illness to my parents, for, you will remember, my mother had told us we would get sick and die there in India, possibly from cholera, or some other terrible disease. At the time of our first child's birth, I made the mistake of sending a picture to my parents of me holding the baby just in front of the house we were living in at the time. Less than two weeks after I had sent that picture to my parents, we received a letter from my mother, asking me, "Kenneth, have you been sick?" I can't remember now what I wrote in answer to her question. Not wanting her to worry; I must have written something that alleviated her concerns about my health, for she wrote nothing further about the matter. I felt at the time that my illness was probably just due to getting used to the food and water in India.

It didn't take long for us to acquire a taste for the foods of India. Rice and curry is quite a staple diet for many of the people, though the type of curry varies from one part of India to another. In Bombay State (now called Maharashtra) not many people had rice as part of their daily diet, possibly because they could not afford the rice. At any rate, they ate *dal,* which is a type of lentil, with orange dal being the most popular kind. There is a black lentil that is also popular with the people, especially the poorer villagers. It is called *moong dal.* We never did eat it for it had quite a different taste and didn't appeal to us. We came to love the *chapatti*, flat bread made without yeast. It is made with special whole-wheat flour. We still love to eat the *chapatti* or *roti*, as it is commonly known in much of the country. Usually, when the word *roti* is used, it actually refers to the whole meal, whatever that might include in addition to the *chapatti,* or *roti*, itself.

While we lived with the Mebergs in Amalner, we ate a lot of powdered eggs. They weren't powdered when we ate them, of course, for they were usually scrambled. Powdered eggs were a surplus food left over from World War II and came in very large tins that could be bought in Bombay at a provision store in the local *bazaar* (market). The powdered eggs were probably safe to eat. At least none of us ever got sick from eating them, to the best of my knowledge. But one thing about those eggs that didn't exactly make them appealing to us was that when cooked, they were green in color. From what I can recollect, Wilma did her best to keep from eating green eggs. Fortunately, ham was not a commodity found in India, at least fresh ham, in view of the fact that the village pigs were totally scavenger animals, eating anything they could get hold of; and that is not a pleasant thought, to say the least!

Language School In Mahableshwar

By the following February, we were beginning to get a grasp of Marathi and even graduated to verb tenses other than the present tense. February is the beginning of the hot season and time to get away to the hills. "Getting away to the hills," meant going up to a mountain resort where the British would go when it got too hot on the plains. During our first two hot seasons we attended language school in Mahableshwar, south of Bombay and at an altitude of about 5,000 feet above sea level. It was cool and pleasant there. We stayed in Mahableshwar for three months, during which time we spent several hours every weekday in a classroom situation and then later, had an hour of special study with a *pundit* (language teacher). There was also a lot of free time in which we could enjoy the sights, take hikes and even, for those of us brave enough to do so, scale some of the nearby mountains.

During our first two years of language study there was a large contingent of new missionaries, which arrived in India, not only with the mission we were serving with at the time, but with many other mission agencies working in that part of India. The same must have been true in other language areas of India. Our Marathi language school was very large and held in the local Anglican church, which sat on one of the high points in Mahableshwar. During our first hot season we were a total of fourteen new missionaries, all living in a large house that had been rented by the mission for the season. Zaida England, one of our senior missionaries, was put in charge of our household. I must have been the envy of the local Indian men, especially the merchants who came to the house to sell us milk, eggs and other food items. One man in a house of thirteen women; what a harem I must have had! We have laughed often about that. We went out of our way to let people know that I had only one wife and was faithful to her. Yet, we are sure some of the people must have thought otherwise.

Not far from Mahableshwar was another mountain, commonly known as "Saddleback," for it resembled from a distance a saddle on the back of a horse. One day, some of us male language students decided we would try to scale that mountain, returning back to Mahableshwar, all in one day. No one had ever succeeded in doing that before, as far as we knew. Early one morning, packing a supply of food and water, we set out for our goal. The trail up Saddleback was steep and sometimes a bit precarious; but we made it to the top and still had several hours to get back. I, for one, was not prepared for such an attempt and had not built up my lung power or strength in my legs. The last hour going back was quite a struggle and I wondered if I would ever make it back. But I did and when I returned to the house where we were staying that hot season with the other language school students, I was ready to just flop on our bed and not move for a week!

Wilma gave me a good back rub and massaged my legs. Some time after arriving back in Mahableshwar after our hike to Saddleback Mountain, I found out that another couple in the mission, who were living in a house some distance away, was making homemade ice cream and had invited us to join them. We had no idea where they got the ice from to make ice cream in an ice cream churner, or where they even found an ice cream churner, but the idea sounded appealing to me. Under ordinary circumstances I would have declined such an invitation; but who was I to pass up homemade ice cream. It took me several days to get back to where I was able to walk up and down the hills without crying out in pain; but, in time, I finally got my mountain legs and lungs.

Language On The Plains

Just before the beginning of our first monsoon season, we returned to the plains and to what would be our home for the next two years. Nasik City was about 114 miles due north of Bombay and right on India's national highway that ran from Bombay to New Delhi, capital city of India. The mission had rented two old houses that sat on a large lot directly across from the city post office. The name of our property was "Rasul Bagh". One of our other new missionary couples, along with two single ladies, lived in one house and we, along with three single men, lived in the smaller of the two houses.

Later on the two single ladies moved over to the compound of a women's mission society, which was a short distance from our two houses. At that time another couple, who had recently arrived in India, moved into the larger of the two houses. These two houses were at least one hundred years old at the time and the walls, which were made of sun-dried bricks, were 20 inches thick. Every window and every door in the house in which we lived were of a different size. The door leading into our very crude bathroom was so short that even Wilma had to duck to get into the bathroom. The ceilings were of whitewashed burlap sacking. Sometimes at night we would hear noises up above the ceiling and knew that it had to be mice or rats running around playing tag! The floors were all of concrete, except one, which was a dirt floor plastered over with dried cow dung. Shortly after we moved in we arranged for that floor to be poured with concrete, for when a cow dung plastered floor became wet, it gave off quite an offensive smell.

Language study consisted of one hour a day with a private pundit. Practical study consisted of shopping in the local bazaar, while we practiced our newly learned Marathi on the merchants. We are sure that many times we must have caused the locals to smile behind our backs; but they seemed to tolerate our crude attempts to speak their language. In time, especially as we completed our language study with private tutors on the plains and hot season language school up in Mahableshwar, we gained a certain amount of proficiency which enabled us to present the gospel clearly. We felt that we had attained that proficiency when we not only thought in the Marathi language, but even dreamed in it. Even though we had both passed our final language exam, including both written and oral exams, we really did not feel at ease in the language until we had lived amongst the people in a village situation. In time, I was able to preach in Marathi, using a minimum amount of notes.

Our First Child Is Born

As Wilma got closer to the end of her first pregnancy, we became more concerned as to whether we would make it to the hospital, less than a mile away, in time for the baby to be born. We were still language students in Nasik at the time. Howard Johnson, who lived with his wife and two small children in the larger house, said that when it came time for our baby to come, he would take Wilma out to Canada Hospital in his jeep. Now, there was one small problem. As already mentioned, at that time there was still petrol rationing and it was in short supply. Howard usually ran his jeep on a highly refined form of kerosene, called *powereen*. He always kept a supply of petrol in a can so that when he started the engine he would first pour a small amount of petrol into the carburetor and that would get the engine started. From time to time, he would have to remove the head of the engine in order to scrape away the carbon collected on the inside of the engine head. Then he would carefully bolt it back onto the engine, hoping that in the process he would not have ruined the head gasket. As it got closer and closer to the time for our baby to be born, Wilma would ask Howard, "Howard, are you sure you will be able to get the jeep started when it is time for me to go out to Canada Hospital?" Even though he tried to assure her that, yes, he would be able to get the jeep started and would be able to get her out to the hospital in plenty of time, she still had lingering doubts. Wilma thought that if worse came to worst, she could always ride out there in a horse *tonga* (a cart used as a local taxi). The *tonga* had no springs, making for a very uncomfortable ride, especially for a woman about to deliver a baby. A ride to the hospital in a *tonga* just might have brought on the baby even before reaching the hospital.

On July 2, 1950 Wilma's labor pains began to intensify and, yes, we did make it to the hospital in time in Howard's jeep. Even after Wilma got to Canada Hospital, she had to wait until the doctor, Dr. Pleasance Carr, got home from the nearby Anglican church that evening, for Dr. Carr was the church organist. The baby waited until the doctor got back to the hospital and was born Sunday evening at 9:30 p.m. We had a daughter and she weighed in at 6 ½ lbs. The delivery room at Canada Hospital, so named because it was built with funds that came from Canada, was all open at the top between the walls and the roof. Because of that, birds were able to fly in and out at will. After our baby was born, cleaned up and put into typical newborn baby clothes, mother and daughter were wheeled into their recovery room and I was able to go in and see for the first time my new baby daughter. Wilma asked me what we should name the baby. When I saw our infant daughter for the first time she reminded me so much of the purity and whiteness of the Lily of the Valley flower, so small and delicate. Without any hesitation, I replied, "Her name is Lily Ann." And so she was named and registered with both the Indian and American governments.

Several months after Lily Ann was born, one of the young men living with us in our little house in Rasul Bagh looked at our baby daughter with her nearly bald head and said, "All she needs is a cigar in her mouth and she would look like Winston Churchill." Winston Churchill was prime minister of Great Britain at the time and was always seen with a cigar in his mouth; he was nearly bald and had a round face. It wasn't long before Lily Ann had a full head of beautiful curly blond hair.

The following hot season we were back in Mahableshwar for our second year of language school. At that time we stayed in a bungalow by ourselves. By this time, Lily was nine months old and had yet to have even one tooth show through her gums. She cried a lot and we knew it was due to the pain of her teeth trying to break through, for she was ordinarily a very contented baby and slept through most of the night. One day we decided to take things into our own hands for we tried rubbing her gums with the edge of a spoon. It must have hurt her terribly and we almost felt like crying with her. But one day we awoke to find her first tooth had come through; we were ready to celebrate and liked to think our efforts with the spoon hurried up the process.

Our First Encounter With Leprosy

We had previously hired a young woman as our *ayah* (nurse maid) to take care of Lily while we were in language class, as well as helping us with other household duties. Shakantala had been taken in at the Ramabai Mukti Mission when very young and had grown up to be a very pretty woman. Unfortunately, unknown to us at the time we hired her, she had been married by her father to a man who was a leper and was being treated at a nearby leprosy colony in Nasik City. Shakantala left her husband when it was made known to her that her husband had leprosy. When we came to find out about it, we were informed that she could be a carrier of leprosy and could pass it on to someone else through close contact, without herself contracting the disease. We were also told that if, by some chance, she was a carrier and passed on the leprosy to someone else, that person might not know if he/she had leprosy until up to twelve years later. How true all this was, we could not tell at the time, but, needless to say, we were devastated by the news. There was only one thing to do and that was to let Shakantala go. It was a difficult decision to make, for she had become almost a part of our family and Lily took to her very well. In the end, we were very thankful that Lily did not contract this terrible disease, which has left so many people in India disfigured and cast out of their family, as being "outcastes." Today there are wonder drugs, which help to cure a person without leaving that person disfigured, provided the infected person is treated in the early stages of the disease.

Our First Encounter With Indian Police

At the end of our second year in language school, we returned to Nasik to complete language studies with our private tutor. When we arrived back at our little home in Rasul Bagh, we were shocked by the scene that met us inside the house. Someone had broken into the house for there were cigarette butts lying all over the floor of the dining room. Our ayah's house, right beside ours, had also been broken into. Not only that, the young man we had hired the previous year to be our cook was missing. We soon found out what had happened. A neighbor came to inform us that the local police had used our house as a stake out. They supposedly had news that some *dacoits* (highway robbers) were in the area and they waited in our dining room smoking their cigarettes while they waited. Also, they had arrested our young cook on suspicion that he had been hiding the *dacoits* in our *ayah's* house. This was our first experience, not yet two years in the country, of dealing with Indian police about critical issues.

When hearing of what happened, I immediately went to the police station to inquire about our cook. Meeting with the superintendent of police, I found him to be very adamant about the fact that our cook was in on the whole thing, guilty of hiding the *dacoits* in our ayah's house. My heart ached for our cook, when the police official told me, "He will talk when we give him the third degree." I found out a few days later that they did give him the third degree, being beaten mercilessly by the police. When I returned to see the police to lodge a complaint, I was told by the superintendent of police, "Well, Mr. Steward, we have decided that your cook is innocent after all, but we advise you to tell him that he had better leave town as quickly as he can!" There was little else we could do, but, for his own safety's sake, let him go and advise him to return to his village. That was not the only encounter we had with the police, for less than two years later I would have a very traumatic experience with Indian police, which left me quite shaken.

Our First Assignment

By the fall of 1951 we had passed our final language exam and were now ready to be assigned at our mission's annual field conference to our first ministry. We had become acquainted with most of the mission's stations and there were some, which did not appeal to us as a place to serve in village evangelism. We had thought in our minds that if there was one station we did not want to be assigned to it would be Yaval. This was a small village located across the Tapti River, which would cut us off from the rest of civilization (so we thought) during the monsoon (rainy) season. The only way to cross the river at that time of the year was in a barge-like ferry that was propelled across the river with a long pole. It was not unusual for the ferry to end up on the other side of the river a mile or more downstream from where it was intended to land. Also, it was not unusual to see the ferry loaded with many more people than what it was built to hold. Well, it was to Yaval that we were sent. As we look back on the whole situation, we are convinced that God put us in that place, for there were many lessons God wanted to teach us. There were testings God wanted to put us through that could not have happened anywhere else.

Immediately after the conference finished in Amalner, we were taken by missionary Ray Rhutan to Yaval. Ray and his wife had been serving in Yaval and were soon to return to the States on furlough. The Rhutan did not return to India after that. All we had with us the day we went to Yaval were a couple of suitcases of clothes and other personal items, along with our bedding roll. To reach Yaval from Amalner, we had to take the train that ran along the Tapti River, as far as Bhusaval, about a two-hour journey. From there we went by bus, another hour's journey, though the distance was only twelve miles. It was the beginning of the cold season and water in the Tapti River was down, allowing the bus to cross over on the low causeway to the other side of the river. The mission bungalow in Yaval sat on a high hill across a small river from the village. This time, when we arrived in Yaval and got our two suitcases down from the top of the bus, we had to wade across the river to get to the bungalow on the other side of the river. We hired a coolie (village porter) to carry our suitcases for us. We had arrived at our first place of ministry in India

The mission bungalow was empty, except for a few dishes and cooking pans in a small cupboard in the kitchen/dining room. Ray Rhutan introduced us to the mission workers, which included John Vasavi, our national village evangelist, along with his wife and three small children; then there was Mr. Salvi, our English-speaking evangelist, in addition to the mali (gardener) we had inherited from the Rhutans. As soon as introductions were made, Ray stated that he needed to catch the next bus back to Bhusaval; and so, he left. That was our introduction to Yaval and our first mission assignment in India. We were still new to the country, having had just completed two years of language study.

Our working knowledge of Marathi was quite limited and we knew there was still much to learn. There was no furniture in the house; just the four bare walls. Besides that, we had with us very little food to cook. Bu we were excited to be there and could hardly wait to begin our ministry. We managed to survive and were able to get a few fresh vegetables and fruits from the local bazaar.

In the meantime, we had to do something about getting all our furniture and other personal belongings shipped up from Nasik. Everything was still there at Rasul Bagh, locked up in our 100-year-old house. Until then, we had no vehicle of our own. We did have a pair of unevenly matched horses and a tonga, which we soon got rid of. Those horses were more trouble than they were worth and it cost to feed them, even when they weren't pulling the tonga. Something had to be done about buying a vehicle we could use in our village ministry. But first, leaving Wilma and Lily at the mission bungalow in Yaval, I took the bus back to Bhusaval and caught a train for Nasik. As soon as I could, after arriving back in Nasik, I made sure our things were all okay. I sought out a local trucking company, which would be willing, for the right price, to haul our things up country to Yaval. That was quite an undertaking. It took me several days to get everything prepared. I knew Wilma would be concerned as to where I was and what was happening, for there was no way to communicate with her, except by telegraph. Even then I was not sure she would even receive the telegram if I were to send one. But I went ahead anyway and sent her a telegram, letting her know I had found a truck and would return home as soon as possible. After loading things onto the truck, I entrusted all our possessions to the driver, returning to Yaval by train and bus. Wilma was greatly relieved to have me back home in Yaval, as I also was. We were surprised to find the truck arriving shortly after I did and that all our things were safe; nothing had been stolen and nothing was broken. We had to but give thanks to the Lord for His watch care over all our possessions and over us.

A Self-Made Mechanic

It was not long after our move to Yaval that we found a jeep for sale in Bombay and within our means to pay for it. It was a World War II jeep built by the Ford Motor Company under license to the Willys Jeep Company. It had a Ford 4-cylinder engine under the hood and even had a distinct Ford sound to it. Though it was in good condition, considering the fact that it had been through the war, it still needed a lot of work done on it. I had never repaired a vehicle in my life; but thanks to the help of Wilma's father, he was able to obtain a mechanic's manual for repairing jeeps. He also shipped out to us all the parts we needed for a major overhaul, sending the parts by air parcel post. The parts all arrived in good condition. None of the parcels had been opened by Indian customs and no custom charges levied. Wilma's father had paid for all the parts we ordered and paid for the expense of shipping them out to us. Every part had been removed from their original boxes, carefully wrapped in Kleenex and put into other boxes. Kleenex was an unheard of thing in India at the time and so; it was an enjoyable luxury for us.

What a time I had repairing that jeep. Wilma even helped me in some of the repair. The engine block was a straight four in top condition, needing no reboring. That, in itself, was a miracle, for all we needed was to put in slightly oversized rings. The valves were held in place by two half-round pieces that had to be dropped down into the seat of the valves. Wilma helped in this by using some tweezers and while I was able to hold each valve up against the springs, she dropped each half-round piece into its own spot. We were a team, both rookies at the job of doing a major overhaul of the jeep. But we were a fantastic team, if I do say so myself! When we completed the job, the jeep was in perfectly new-like condition. We were even able to set the timing right, without having the use of a timing light; as a matter of fact, we didn't even have a timing light, let alone know how to use it. That was probably the greatest accomplishment of my life in all the things I have had to repair over these many years. There have been many construction jobs and many home repairs. I think I have every right to stick out my chest in pride for a job well done.

Laborers Together

Our first term of service was full of many experiences, which tried our faith. Aside from one trying experience in particular, we loved those years we had in Yaval. We enjoyed going out into the villages with our World War II jeep, which had apparently been used by the American army somewhere up close to the Burma/China border. We also had an old army trailer in which we hauled all our gear when we went out to the villages. We enjoyed going out to the villages with the jeep and trailer loaded with equipment, as we went preaching the gospel where it had not gone before.

There is a stand-up calendar in our living room, with a Scripture verse for each day, with some comments on that verse. For October 14th, the verse is 1 Corinthians 2:9, "We are laborers together with God." The comment below the verse is the following:

> We are in partnership with God, not God in partnership with us. Sometimes we come to Him, saying, "Dear Lord, I am going to work here today; I want to serve you here; come and help me." But He has the right to tell us where He wants us to serve. We should say, "Lord, where do you want to use me today?" Place me there and use me." Only in this way will our labor bring Glory to God.

We were yet to learn the reality of that. God would take us through some deep-water experiences before we learned the lesson well.

Life In An Indian Village

Our life in Yaval was very simple. While the village had a post office and even a bank, there were no paved streets and no electricity. There were not the conveniences that life in America had to offer us. But then, we were not there to enjoy the conveniences of life in America. God called us to serve Him in India and placed us in that small village in Western India, with no paved streets and no electricity. Our house was a simple two-room stone and brick house along with a very small dining room and a bathroom without any facilities, as we know them to be in any bathroom in the

States. Bathroom facilities were quite crude at their best.

We often said we had running water; we had to run to the well, draw our water out of the well with a small metal bucket on the end of a long, thick rope and then run back to the house with the water. On the front of the house was a very small room that we used as an office and in addition, there was a screened in porch, or verandah. Rural houses in India usually do not have kitchens as part of the house itself, but are separate rooms close by the house; such was the case for our little house in Yaval. We cooked on a small *shaygardee* (round charcoal burner), as well as a raised fireplace where we cooked on an open wood burning fire. No electric, or gas cooker, no microwave oven, not even an electric toaster to toast our bread. We made toast by putting slices of bread on a piece of tin held over the hot *shaygardee*.

Our house had a roof of simple half-round baked tiles laid over some bamboo slats. It had a ceiling of cement-asbestos sheets, which helped to keep the rats and other small creatures from getting into the house. The floors were of roughly hewn stone. All the windows had bars on them, which gave us a certain amount of security, and the screening over the windows helped to keep out some of the bugs, especially mosquitoes. And yet, we made sure that every night, as we climbed into our simple wooden-framed bed, with its woven cotton tapes, upon which we laid our thin cotton-filled mattresses, the mosquito net would be tucked in firmly under the mattresses. It was quite a procedure, just to get into bed. We had door sills that were about three inches high and this came in handy in the hot season. At that time of the year the temperature could rise as high as 110-115 degrees. Fahrenheit. During the day we would often lay towels across the window of our bedroom, which was on the west side of the house and then soak the towels with water. The hot winds, blowing against the towels, evaporated the water, which helped to cool down the bedroom somewhat. Also, when we did sleep in our bedroom during the worst part of the hot season, before settling in for the night, we would literally flood the stone floor in the bedroom with water, right up to the top of the door sills. By morning the floor would be absolutely dry!

Whenever it got too hot to sleep in the bedroom, we took two army cots outside and slept on the cots. We had a double size mosquito net, which we put up over the cots. But there was one problem we had to deal with and that was a full moon. There were two small trees in front of our bungalow that protected the bungalow somewhat from the hot sun during the day. But on any full moon night we would start out the night well protected from the glare of the full moon. Eventually, as the moon advanced in the sky, it would begin to shine down on us. I could sleep through such a situation, but not Wilma. It wouldn't be long before she would awaken me and say that the moon was shining on us. We would then have to move the cot and the mosquito net, which had been draped over a crudely made frame. I couldn't be sure at that time whether she took literally, as did Miss Swanson, one of our elderly lady missionaries, what is recorded in (Psalm 121:6), "The sun shall not strike thee by day, nor the moon by night." Thankfully, we didn't sleep outside very often. When it got too hot for us to carry on any ministry in Yaval, we headed for a hill station, where it was much cooler and stay there for about six weeks during the worst of the heat on the plains.

Missionaries, who had served at Yaval before us, whether it was the Rhutans or someone before them, had erected a steel drum outside the bathroom, laying it on its side on a high wooden platform. A half-inch pipe was attached to the drum, which went into the bathroom with a faucet connected to the end of the pipe. On the side of the barrel was an opening through which water, brought up from the well, could be poured into the barrel. In that way we could have running water in the bathroom. It was alright to take a quick shower, but it had to be done during the hot time of the day, else one would end up with a cold shower, for the water from the well was always cold.

Rat In The Water

We always made sure we boiled our drinking water, for even though the well was deep and there didn't seem to be any nearby pollution which could seep into the well, we were not willing to take any chances by drinking water straight from the well. We stored our drinking water in *murdkas* (black earthen pots), which sat on a special metal stand. As the water slowly seeped through the wall of the *murdkas*, it would cool down the water inside the *murdkas*. How cool and refreshing that water was, especially during those very hot days in the hot season. Though we made sure that we even used drinking water to brush our teeth, one day I must have been in a hurry and didn't take the time to get a glass of water from the *murdka*; instead, I drew water from the faucet in the bathroom and used that to brush my teeth. As I began to brush my teeth, a foul smell came from the glass of water I had drawn from the water tank outside the bathroom. What was that awful smell? What a terrible taste to the water! I decided to go outside, climb up and look at the water in the drum. What I discovered was that the mali had failed to put the large cap back onto the hole in the side of the drum, after filling the drum with water. What should I see floating in the water, but a dead rat! I quickly ran back into the house and cleaned out my mouth with, yes, you guessed right, boiled drinking water. I told our mali what had happened and reminded him that he was always to make sure the cap was placed back over the hole in the side of the drum, - and the cap made tight. Thankfully, the Lord kept me from becoming sick from putting that polluted water into my mouth. We poured out all the water from that drum and cleaned the inside of the drum as thoroughly as we could. You can be sure that after that I always brushed my teeth with boiled drinking water!

Village Bazaar Day

Every village in India had its weekly *bazaar day* when the farmers brought their vegetables and fruit, along with other goodies, to sell in the bazaar. It was usually located in the *chowk* (village square). While we were able to buy a few necessities during other days of the week, *bazaar day* was the time when we bought most of our fresh food. During certain times of the year the selection was not very good. But we generally were able to get tomatoes, potatoes, onions and hot chilies, along with such fruits as bananas, mangoes, papayas and guavas most of the year. During bazaar day we also bought such necessities as rice, sugar, and *gur* (unrefined brown sugar). White sugar was very coarse in those days and looked almost like rock salt. *Gur* was sold in large bales, or blocks, which were formed when the hot brown sugar syrup was poured into metal pails, lined with burlap. When the gur cooled down and became solid, the burlap was sewn around the block of gur. While we did not require a whole block of *gur*, we would tell the sugar merchant about how much we wanted and he would break off that much and weigh it on his balance scales.

Whenever we bought things by weight, we made sure the merchant would not have his finger on one side of the scales when weighing out rice, wheat, or some other product. The weights used to balance the scales had imprinted on them the special government markings to indicate weights as being accurate. Even then, there were times when we questioned whether those weights had been tampered with. We were sure there were times when we must have been cheated.

We had no way of keeping food cold, for we had no refrigerator. What cooked foods were left over after a meal, along with such things as butter, bread, etc., were kept for a short time in a small screened in cabinet called a *pinzara*, or food safe, as the British called the cabinet. Food would keep only a day, at the most, with such arrangements. We used to have problems with ants. In order to keep them from getting into the *pinzara*, we put its four legs into small tins filled with water. That helped only as long as there was water in the tins. If we had milk left over at the end of the day, we had to boil it again, or else, by the next morning it would be spoiled.

Co-Co Our Water Buffalo

One day a letter came in the mail from a children's Sunday school class at Covenant Community Church Dearborn, Michigan, the church that had taken on the remaining support we needed when we set sail from New York in 1949 for that first term of missionary service. The children had sent us a sizeable check, which was enough for us to buy our own water buffalo, so that we could have our own milk supply. When we bought milk from a local milkman, it was always a battle to see that he did not add water to the milk before selling it to us. Years later, when we served at the boarding school for MK's in Chikalda, we tried to get the milkman to bring his buffalo to the school yard and milk it right in front of us. We had a special tester, by which we could test the specific gravity of the milk and tell whether any water had been added to the milk. One time the milkman admitted that, yes, he did add water to the milk, "But, memsahib, at least it is clean water!" We used to tell the milkman that we wanted to buy milk from him and were not interested in buying his water; if we wanted water in the milk, we would put our own water into it. Well, back to that check from the children at Covenant Community Church in Dearborn, Michigan. When the check arrived, as mentioned, we made a decision to buy the best water buffalo possible, one that was already giving milk. We found such an animal and brought it to our mission compound in Yaval. We kept the buffalo in the old horse shed, but when it was time to milk, we brought the buffalo up by the back of the house every morning. That buffalo was very temperamental and I couldn't get near it, or it would shake its horns at me. Of course, I had never milked a cow in my life and I wasn't about to try milking that water buffalo. The only one who could get near the water buffalo to milk it was our *mali*, or general handyman. Oh, how delicious that milk was. We fed it cottonseed, which helped to make the milk richer and produce more cream. From what we were told, a water buffalo's milk had a butter fat content of 7%; now that is rich milk! We had all the milk we needed and were able to provide milk to our national co-workers who lived on the mission compound with us. We turned some of the cream into butter, having so much that we heated the extra butter until the solids coagulated and separated from the liquid, giving us *ghee* (pure butter oil).

We decided to have a contest to give the water buffalo a

name. We wrote to the children at our supporting church in Dearborn, Michigan, asking them to give the water buffalo a name. Several names were suggested to us and the one that we finally chose was Co-Co, standing for Covenant Community Church. It seemed to be a very appropriate name for a water buffalo, which we had during the three years we were stationed at Yaval.

Our Family Increases

On December 5, 1952 God gave us our little Irish daughter, Kathleen Dawn, who was also born at Canada Hospital in Nasik City. This time we had to go down to Nasik about a month before the baby was due, to be sure we were near medical help at the time of delivery. Though there was a woman doctor at the small clinic in Yaval, she didn't have the facilities for safe delivery of babies. Most Indian women had their babies delivered at home with the aid of an uneducated *dayabai* (midwife) and under somewhat unsanitary conditions. Girls are not thought of very highly in India. Sons are considered more important and are doted upon by their parents. When we had our first daughter I was very happy; in fact, I had told people that I actually wanted a daughter. The local people must have thought this white man from America must have been mentally unstable to want a daughter and not a son, especially as his first child. When our second daughter was born I was just as happy as with our first daughter. But, again, the people must have thought I must have been even more unstable in my brain. Two daughters and still no son? How strange that I had not left my wife to take another wife who would give me the son I needed. Little did most village Indians know at that time that the father, not the mother, determines the sex of the child. Well, God not only blessed us with our Irish daughter, but in time He gave us two more daughters, four in all; and still no sons!

Madam Sahib, Did Sahib Leave You And The Children?

One time we decided to visit some of our other mission stations. By this time we had two children and it would have been rather crowded in the jeep with all four of us and what we needed for the time we would be away from Yaval. We left Yaval with the trailer being pulled behind and quite full of our belongings. Eleven miles from Yaval we came to the Tapti River. As we approached the river, going down a gradual slope to the river, we suddenly heard a loud noise and then felt the trailer going "bump, bump." We had been going at only about 25 miles an hour and it did not take long before we came to a complete stop. Looking off to the right, we saw a wheel from the trailer rolling off into the field beside the road. When I took a look at the axle to which the wheel had been attached only moments before, but now with the wheel lying some distance away in the field, I saw the source of the problem. The wheel bearing, still sitting on the axle, had been chewed to pieces. Now what were we to do? I remembered that there was an auto supply store in the town of Jalgaon, about an hour's drive across the Tapti River from where the wheel had come off the trailer and rolled off into the field. Perhaps that auto supply store just might have a wheel bearing that would fit our jeep trailer; it was worth a try to drive over there and find out. I managed to bring the wheel back up to the trailer, which I had disconnected from the jeep. Leaving Wilma and the girls behind to guard our trailer and our belongings, I headed for Jalgaon. Just as I was driving off in the jeep, a few village women came upon the scene. One of the women asked Wilma, "Memsahib, did the sahib leave you and the girls to go find another wife?" Seeing that we had only girls, they assumed that I must have had a fight with my wife and had gone off to find another wife, who would give me sons and not daughters. I was hardly gone two hours when I returned with a new wheel bearing in hand. It was not much longer before I had the wheel back onto the trailer and we were safely on our way to visit our other mission stations. What a relief; I hadn't left my wife after all!

<u>The Famous Famine of '53</u>

The previous year I had planted a number of young trees along both sides of a long driveway, leading up to the front of our bungalow from the main gate of the mission property. Before we left on our hot season vacation in 1953 I instructed our *mali* to allow anyone who wanted to draw water from our well for themselves to do so. Wells had been drying up all over our district and water in many places was costing more than milk. I gave a long rope to the *mali* to which I had tied rags along every foot of that rope. I then told him to drop the rope down into the well every day. He could tell how much water was in the well by how many of those rags came back up wet. If the level of the water went down even one foot, he was to stop watering those young trees. When we arrived back after our vacation we found that people had come to get water from our well. During the nearly two months we had been gone the level of water had not gone down even one foot! Our *mali* had faithfully watered the trees every day and they were flourishing. How we wished we could have said the same things about the people. Not only was water scarce for the people, but so was food. There was little in the bazaar for the people to buy, even if they would have had the money to buy the food. Jobs were scarce, as scarce as the water and food. People began eating whatever they could find even weeds, that is, when they could find them.

One day villagers came to our bungalow to ask if they could dig up the weeds in the yard; we had plenty of them. We had heard that in another district people were peeling bark from off the trees, soaking the bark in water to extract the tannic acid and then chew on the bark to get what nourishment they could get out of it. We were able to get free powdered milk and gave milk to the people who came to our bungalow. We never gave them just the powder, for they would inevitably take the powder into town, sell it to someone else and use the money to buy *birdis* ('beer-dees' - Indian style cigarettes).

A Frightening Experience

While our well was deep and the water cool, it was an open well, with no protection to keep people from falling into the well. We always had a concern that one day a child would go too close to the well, slip and fall in. It was easy for people to simply drop a pail down into the open well, with a long rope tied to it, and draw cool, refreshing water from the well. Little did we realize the real danger until one day our mali came running up to the bungalow to let us know that Lily was down at the well, leaning over and looking down into it. When we asked him if he had picked up Lily and taken her away from the well, he replied that he didn't think of it; he was so excited about seeing our little girl, now about two years old, looking down into the well, all he could think of was to come running to let us know what she was doing. Needless to say, our hearts went into our throats. Instead of rushing down to the well ourselves to rescue our little girl, or even yelling at her to get away from the well, Wilma quietly called to Lily and told her to come back to the bungalow; Lily looked back at us standing in front of the bungalow and, not questioning at all what Mommy wanted her to do, she turned and simply came back to the bungalow. Even now, we shudder to think of what might have happened. The Lord was gracious and did not allow anything to happen to Lily; God's angel surely was watching over her at that time.

Needless to say, right after that incident, I had a local carpenter, who did odd jobs for us; put a covering over the well, with a hinged door on it. Instructions were given to all our people to make sure the well was to be kept closed at all times when they were not drawing water from the well. A warning was given that if ever we found the well left open, a lock would be put on the well and they would have to come and get the key from us. We are glad to say that they kept the door on the well closed, as we had instructed them to do; we had never found the well left open after that.

The Trial Of Your Faith...

"the trial of your faith, being much more precious than of gold that perisheth, though it be tried with fire, might be found unto praise and honour and glory at the appearing of Jesus Christ." --- (*1* Peter 1:7)

One Sunday afternoon, as we met with our national Christians for the usual Sunday afternoon service in the little church that stood at the front entrance to our mission property, a crisis took place, which would affect each of us in the church that afternoon. After the service was over, we went back to our bungalow, only to discover that the office had been broken into and a drawer in my desk forced open. It was the end of the month and all the money that was due to be paid to our national workers was stolen out of the drawer that had been broken into; not an anna (less than one cent in American currency at the time) was left. Our mali, who had been working for us at that time, was not a Christian and did not attend the service that afternoon. We found him gone and the room on our mission property, where we let him stay, was locked; he was nowhere to be found. As we began to think more about the situation, we recalled that there were times while I was working in the office, he would pass by one of the windows, trying to see what I was doing. It was possible that at some time or other, when he was passing by, I might have been putting money into that drawer. There was only one conclusion that we could make of the whole affair. Circumstantial evidence pointed to our mali as the thief. I had to take responsibility for what happened, for I should have been more careful in where I kept the workers' money, for that money was not ours.

When I revealed to our workers what had happened, that it was their money that had been stolen, I told them that now they had to go from trusting the missionaries to trusting the Lord. We ourselves did not have even one anna to our name, for it was also the end of a yearly quarter and we were waiting on funds to arrive, which would take care of us for the next three months. How could our workers feed themselves and their families? We looked in all our cupboards and, like Old Mother Hubbard, found them to be bare, that is, except for one shelf. There on that shelf we found some old tins of army surplus vegetable soup, along with a bag of dried beans we had received at some time in the past from friends back in the States. We decided to distribute evenly among the people whatever we had in the way of food.

A few days later I was in our village and stopped at a local teashop. Word had gotten around the village about the theft and when I greeted the shopkeeper, he told me that if we had a financial need, he would be very glad to loan us whatever money we needed. I politely thanked him for his offer, but told him that we had a great God, the Living God, Who would meet every need we had and the needs of all our people. We would soon see that God would do what was humanly impossible.

There were yet two serious matters with which I had to deal. First, I had been responsible to see to the security of our workers' money and also, see that the money was somehow replaced and that the workers were yet to be paid. The other matter was of a more serious nature. Word had come to us via a person in the village that if our thief, the mali, caught any of the workers' children in the village, or even our own, he would slit their throats. We considered this to be a real danger, though we were not yet ready to report the whole matter to the police. While we were willing to trust the Lord to not only meet the need of replacing the money that had been stolen, but also the safety of the children, we decided to take some matters into our own hands. I went to the servants' quarters and with a hammer, broke the lock from off our mali's door and proceeded to put all his belongings that I found in the room on the outside of the barbed wire fence that surrounded our property. Sometime in the night, realizing that his "goose was cooked" and that we had possibly gone to the authorities, he must have come and taken all his things away; we never heard from him again. As we looked back upon what happened, we realized that it was rather a foolish thing to do. From the beginning, we should have gone to the police and reported the theft, as well as the threat that had been made against all the children on our mission property.

But what were we to do about replacing the money that had

been stolen out of the desk in my office? It was some 300 rupees (equivalent to about 45 dollars) and might as well have been 300 dollars! Not long after the theft had taken place and we had heard about the threat to any and all of the children, including our own, we fell on our faces on the stone floor in the living room of our bungalow, crying out to the Lord for His help. We told the Lord that if He did not meet that need, we would pack up all of our belongings, get on the next bus out of town and go back to America. We didn't have enough money to buy a bus ticket to take us to Bhusaval, twelve miles away, let alone buying tickets to sail half way around the world and return to our home country. What a foolish thing to demand of God! It almost sounded like Elijah, after he fled from wicked Jezebel, who cried out to the Lord, asking the Lord to take away his life (1 Kings 19:1-4). Instead of taking away Elijah's life, the Lord sent an angel while Elijah was sleeping under a juniper tree and told him to eat the cake that was baked on the coals and to drink the water that was in the bottle (verses 5, 6). Besides, had I not told that shopkeeper that our Living God would take care of us? Well, God did for us what He had done for Elijah, only in a different way. He sent the cake and the water to satisfy our souls and meet our need. What follows tells the whole story of God doing what was humanly impossible.

While we were youth evangelists with the Youth Gospel Crusade, we held meetings in a small Baptist church in Bartonville, Illinois, a suburb of Peoria. Little did we know at the time, but one teenage girl was deeply moved by our ministry and, already being a Christian, she had given her life to the Lord to serve Him one day as a missionary on some foreign soil. The story unfolded a few days after the theft of the 300 rupees, when a letter arrived in the mail from the mother of that teenage girl. Along with the letter was a check in U.S. dollars that, when changed into Indian currency, came to exactly the amount that had been stolen! The mother wrote in her letter about her daughter, who was no longer a teenager, had married a wonderful young man, expecting to serve the Lord together. She had become pregnant with their first child and at the time of delivery, the young mother-to-be suddenly died; the baby survived. At the funeral, the mother requested that in lieu of flowers, money should be given for missions. The mother went on to write in her letter that she knew her daughter would have wanted that money to go to us. God has promised to supply all our needs "according to His riches in glory by Christ Jesus" (Philippians 4:19).

By the way, that mother had mailed her letter to us from Bartonville, Illinois about a week before the theft had taken place in Yaval, India.

Medical Experiences

Even though there was a small *davakhana* (medical clinic) in our village, with an Indian woman doctor in charge, the closest good hospital was our mission hospital in Chinchpada, nearly a day's journey by train, with one change of trains on the way. One day Wilma suddenly became sick and it was not long before her skin turned yellowish and the whites of her eyes turned the same color. We knew it was infectious hepatitis, commonly known as jaundice. There was not much in the bazaar that Wilma was able to keep down, but she did like stewed tomatoes. We had called the woman doctor in our village and asked her to have a look at Wilma to confirm that it was hepatitis; but the doctor had never before seen a white person with hepatitis and didn't recognize it as such. When the Indian people contract the disease, the color of their skin and eyes turn a strange shade of gray. She confessed there was not much she could do about the situation.

Wilma was too sick for me to transport her at the time to our mission hospital. All I could do was to be sure that she had plenty of bed rest, drink lots of fluids and eat stewed tomatoes. Praise the Lord that there was an abundance of tomatoes in the bazaar at that time of the year. Eventually Wilma gained enough strength so that I felt I could take her in the jeep to the mission hospital. I made up a small bed in the back of our jeep and with our two daughters, Lily and Kathy; we headed for Chinchpada, taking five days to get there. We stopped at two of our mission stations on the way to give her as much rest as possible. At the Chinchpada mission hospital Wilma was able to get the medical attention she needed and, in time, recovered from her case of infectious hepatitis. Fortunately, she suffered no damage to her liver, from having traveled such a long distance over bumpy, dusty village roads. When Wilma was strong enough to travel again, we made preparations to leave for a hill station in South India to spend nearly two months away from the heat of the plains. During that time Wilma was able to recover fully.

About a year after we arrived in Yaval I decided to clean up the old horse barn. There was a piece of rolled up expanded metal (heavy type of metal screening) lying on the ground. I decided to toss it up onto a shelf instead of wisely getting a ladder and placing it carefully there. As a result of my foolish action, when I tossed that roll of heavy metal screening onto the shelf, it suddenly came back down and hit my right arm. This resulted in a deep gash, with blood beginning to flow from the arm. I am usually not one given to showing much excitement in an emergency and so, quietly putting the flesh back in place, while holding my arm tightly to try and stop the bleeding, I walked back to the bungalow and announced to Wilma that I had cut my arm. She suggested we go to the village clinic and have the woman doctor stitch up the arm; but I was not for that. Instead, Wilma made a butterfly bandage with a piece of adhesive tape and taped a sterile bandage over the gash. I figured that the arm had bled sufficiently to protect me against any possibility of tetanus, though medically speaking, that may not have been true. Fortunately, I did not get tetanus. To this day I have a wishbone-shaped scar on my right arm.

One day I was doing some other work in the old horse barn and picked up some bricks, which lay on the ground. There was always one rule of thumb; when picking up an object from off the ground, first make sure there is not a scorpion underneath. Ignoring that rule, I reached for a brick to pick it up and suddenly was stung on my right thumb – I think it was that 'rule of thumb' - by a small brown scorpion, which was underneath the brick. The sudden pain of the scorpion sting was intense and caused my thumb to throb, until I thought it would shake from off my hand. Again, I quietly walked back to the bungalow, holding my thumb tightly. Wilma quickly made a poultice of dry mustard and applied it to the spot where the scorpion had stung me. Interestingly enough, the pain did not go any higher than the base of my thumb. I don't know if it was the mustard poultice, or if I was immune to scorpion stings, which confined the pain to the thumb; I was not willing to test out the possibility of immunity to scorpion stings by picking up another brick without first looking. At any rate, I had learned my lesson and was never stung by another scorpion during the rest of the time we lived in India.

God's Grace is Sufficient

We lived in India at a time when the incidence of cholera was very high, especially during the monsoon season. Smallpox was prevalent throughout India during those years. There was always the possibility of other diseases and yet, through all of this the Lord protected us. God's Grace was always sufficient in times of great need.

There was one illness that I struggled with from shortly after our arrival in India until the hot season of 1953. Even here, as we look back upon all the circumstances at the time, the Lord was with us to protect us, even from physical danger that was to follow eventual surgery at a mission hospital south of Bombay.

My illness seemed to have intensified during our hot season vacation spent in Mahableshwar in 1953. We stayed at a very nice hotel operated by a Parsee family. Parsees had originally lived in the old Persia (now Iran), but when the country was conquered by the Muslims in the 7th century, many of the people, who were followers of the Zoroastrian religion, fled to India. Most Parsees in India live in the city of Mumbai (formerly Bombay). A doctor with the Nazarene mission was staying with his family in a nearby cottage. We had all been in language school together and so knew each other quite well. Late one night I awoke with terrible pain and decided that I should awaken our Nazarene doctor friend to get his opinion as to what the problem might be. His conclusion was that it must be my gall bladder, for that was where the pain was concentrated. It was drawing close to the time when we would have to leave Mahableshwar and return to Yaval. The monsoon was but a few weeks away and when the rains began there was the possibility of the Tapti River being in spate (flood state), preventing us from getting across the river and to our home in Yaval some ten miles distant. The small river between our village of Yaval and our bungalow, could flood at any time after a heavy rain and keep us from getting across to our bungalow. After talking with another doctor, who had been born of Presbyterian missionaries in Korea, it was decided that we should go to Miraj, to the Wanless Memorial Hospital where he served as head doctor. He would do an exploratory surgery to see exactly what the problem was and then correct it. So, that is what we did. Instead of heading home to Yaval, we drove right down to Miraj, south of Bombay nearly a day's journey. Our daughter, Lily Ann, who was not yet three years old, had been having serious problems with her tonsils. It was decided that she should have her tonsils removed while we were at Miraj for my surgery. The end result was that Lily had her tonsils out and I had my appendix out, for that was what my real problem was. There were some adhesions that had built up around the gall bladder, which masked the pain in my appendix.

The problem with my appendix had been building up for the past three years and when the doctor opened me up he found my appendix ready to burst. There could have been tragic results had we not have gone to Miraj and, instead, gone home to Yaval, where the monsoon season would begin and cut us off from good medical care. We were convinced that this was all of the Lord's timing and provision, even concerning what was soon to follow. Truly, God's grace is sufficient in time of need.

Because the monsoon season was soon to begin we felt that we should head for home as quickly as possible. Our main concern was crossing the Tapti River on the low causeway that served as the only bridge across the river. Once the rains set in, the river would rise and we would not be able to drive the jeep across the causeway. The doctor cautioned me about driving home in our jeep so soon after my surgery; but we assured him we would take several days to get home and would rest along the way. We were not sure as to where we would be able to stay. But trusting the Lord, we loaded up the jeep with all our belongings and headed north toward Yaval and home. By now the rains had already begun, but we were prepared with side curtains for our jeep and when they were all in place we were kept very dry. The windshield wipers seemed to be working overtime, clearing the rain away, so that I could see where to drive, especially where the edge of the road was and to be sure that we were on our side of the road.

We were making good progress, when suddenly we saw a government bus headed in our direction on our side of the road. The driver certainly could not see us, for the wipers on the bus were not working and there was a driving rain. In a few seconds it seemed that there would be a head on impact, unless I did something drastic. As the bus got closer I suddenly turned the jeep toward the ditch on our side of the road. At that moment, the impact took place, as the bus struck our jeep on the right side behind where Wilma was sitting and holding Kathy in her lap. Kathy was hardly six months old at the time; Lily was sitting in the back seat of the jeep, surrounded by baggage. The impact by the bus tore the canvas top from off the jeep and broke to smithereens a clay water pot sitting on the side seat, just back of Wilma. How thankful we were that none of us was injured and the jeep stayed upright as it plunged down into the ditch.

A few moments after the accident took place, a small car stopped to find out what had happened. Who should it be, but the young Indian family who had been in the cottage next to us at Wanless Memorial Hospital in Miraj. Their son had been operated on for a serious kidney problem. They graciously offered to take Wilma and the girls about seventy miles up the road to the next town where there was an American Marathi Mission doctor and family. We had become acquainted with the doctor while we had been language students in Mahableshwar. And so, the young Indian family took Wilma and the girls in their small car, along with some of our baggage, to that American mission station; there they awaited my arrival several hours later. I assured Wilma that I would be okay and would see her and the girls soon. I had to stay with the jeep until the police arrived, for there were a lot of legal matters to take care of with the police. The end result was that I was charged with driving recklessly and on the wrong side of the road. How was this possible, I do not know, for our jeep was sitting in the ditch on our side of the road. That didn't matter to the police; I was to blame and that was that.

In the end, we were thankful for the Lord's protection in this very dangerous situation. I was eventually able to make my way back to the jeep, after having been interrogated by the police for at least an hour at the police station. While I was away from the jeep a local village man assured me that he would watch it and make sure that nothing would be taken from the jeep. He was true to his word, for when I got back, everything was just as I had left it. I am glad that I was able to get the jeep out of the ditch and drive it to where Wilma and the girls were waiting for me. The canvas top of the jeep was torn and one of the bars supporting the canvas top was broken, but the jeep itself was just fine, hardly a dent in it where the bus struck us. The American missionary doctor and his family were so gracious to us and put us up for the night. The next morning I found a welding shop in town. It was not long before the canvas top was back in place and we were on our way home. We made it across the Tapti River before it rose to cover the causeway. Once again, we experienced God's grace and protection.

Lasting Impressions

During our early years of village evangelism in Yaval, we had gone to our nearest mission station about thirty miles away to visit the missionaries who lived there. That day we went out to a nearby village with our fellow missionary, along with our national co-workers. We had gone to hand out gospel tracts as well as to gather the villagers together in the village *chowk* (center of the village) to hear a gospel message. The men and boys gathered around the jeep, listening intently to the gospel recordings, along with a message by one of our national co-workers. We had given out many gospel portions to the people that day, though we never gave them free of charge, for they would have had little value in the eyes of the villagers. We always charged an anna, or two. At that time there were sixteen annas to a rupee and approximately nine rupees to an American dollar. An anna would be worth less than a penny. One of those gospels must have been purchased by a young lad, for as we left the village that day, we saw the lad sitting on a rock at the edge of the village, reading the booklet very intently. Several questions have remained in my mind since that day so many years ago, such as, "which Gospel was he reading?" and also, "What did he do after reading that Gospel? " Where is that lad today? Did he ever understand what he read and believed on the Lord Jesus Christ as his own personal Savior? Will we ever see that lad in heaven? We will not know the answers to these questions, of course, until we ourselves meet our Savior in heaven.

During our first term of service in India we had a number of occasions to go to Bombay for special shopping, or for some legal matter at the American Consulate. On one occasion we were walking down Hornby Road, the main road in downtown Bombay. As we walked along the road, we noticed a beggar sitting on the sidewalk. He had beside him a small metal cup into which a few coins had been tossed by others as they passed by. It was apparent that those who had passed by before us were quite indifferent to his condition. What was startling to us was not that he was a beggar, waiting for people to fill his cup with coins, which would give him enough money to provide something to eat for another day. It was his physical appearance that drew our attention to him. He had apparently been in a terrible fire at some time, for his face was badly scarred. He was blind and where there should have been outer ears, there was nothing but more scars. He could neither see nor hear, though he could talk. The first thought that came to us, as we saw that man was, "How could we ever possibly convey the gospel of Christ to him? It would be an impossible task. Our hearts cried out to him, as well as to God to have mercy on this pitiful creature, who could neither see, nor hear. We could only trust in a merciful and compassionate God on his behalf. At the same time, we realized that there were many other beggars in India, who needed the gospel, who could see and hear and we were determined to do our best to give the gospel to them whenever and wherever we met them.

As I drove across the causeway over the Tapti River one day in my jeep, I headed up the hill on the other side, just outside the railway town of Bhusaval. The scene which I saw at the river side will never leave my mind, for it conveyed to me a picture of the hopelessness of life for a person in India, a hopelessness for anyone else in the world, besides those living in India, who was without Christ. It is not an uncommon sight to see a body being cremated at the edge of one of India's holy rivers. As the flames leaped high into the sky, I could not help but believe that the soul that once resided in that body now being consumed by those flames, was now suffering a worse torment in hell, where "the fire is not quenched" (Mark 9:44, 46). Oh God, that person had only one life, as I have, and now he has perished, probably without ever having heard of Christ. Help me to take the Gospel to these people, who walk in darkness, having no spiritual light at all.

Evangelism Opposition

We arrived in India a little over two years after the country had gained independence from Great Britain. In those early years of independence there was much opposition to anything that could be identified with the British. Names of streets in large cities were changed, as were the names of towns and cities, names reverted back to their ancient Indian spellings and pronunciations. Statues of English royalty were town down. The government even tried to wipe out the use of English in schools and government departments. There was a growing opposition to foreign missionaries and in many places the cry went up, "Missionary, go home!"

Opposition to foreign missionaries and their white man's message of Christianity was no more evident than when we had invited an Indian national evangelist from Hyderabad in South India to come for special meetings to be held in our village. Because we had no electricity in Yaval, our loudspeaker system had to be run from off the jeep battery. As the Indian evangelist began preaching, with the portable microphone in his hands, someone in the crowd cut the wires that led from the jeep battery to the loudspeaker system. When it was discovered and the wires put back together again, the wires were cut a second time. By this time the crowd sitting on the ground in front of us became more and more rowdy. It wasn't long before someone in the crowd began throwing rotten vegetables at us, along with other objects, some of them quite hard. When we saw the anger of the crowd was getting worse and worse, louder and louder, it was time for us to make a move to a safer place. And so, we all backed up against a storefront. As the noise of the crowd got still worse, it must have reached the local police station, or else someone had gone running to let the police know what was happening. It wasn't long before a band of police came around a building, with *latis* (long bamboo sticks) in their hands and shouting to the people to sit back down and listen to the message of the Christians. It was a frightening experience, but we praise the Lord for His protection that night. God must have sent His guardian angels to watch over us.

In the early part of 1954 I received an invitation from a missionary friend serving with another mission in the Central Indian city of Secunderabad. They were planning on holding several weeks of gospel meetings in the adjoining city of Hyderabad. The whole area had a strong Hindu element and at that time, Hindu leaders were seeking to oust all foreigners from the country especially Christian missionaries. There was one group of orthodox Hindus called 'Arya Samaj, which went to no end to attack national Christians and foreign missionaries. I was invited to be one of the main speakers at the meetings. A large tent top was set up in the open courtyard of a large church, right across the road from Hyderabad's train and bus stations. It was an ideal spot for such meetings. A group of local Christians volunteered to hand out printed notices of the meetings to people at the stations. Every night the tent top, referred to as a *shamiana,* was filled with people sitting on the ground. It seemed that we had wall-to-wall people.

The Arya Samaj heard about our meetings and was able to also get a permit to use a loudspeaker. They set up their loudspeaker right across the road from where we were holding our meetings. As our meetings progressed, they would play loud Hindu music. When we turned our loudspeaker up for the people to hear our message, the Arya Samaj turned their speaker up still louder to try and drown us out. This went on for several days until one evening, one of the Arya Samaj men came across the road to our tent and while I was speaking, yanked the microphone out of my hand and began shouting at the people sitting on the ground before us. Needless to say, I was able to get the mike back and somehow the meeting went on, after that person suddenly left to return to his microphone across the road, once again, trying to drown us out with his loud music. The missionary who had organized the meetings felt our safety and that of the people coming every night for our meetings, was in jeopardy. The next day he consulted with the local police superintendent, who ordered several police, with their *latis,* to be present at the rest of the meetings. The job of the police was to see that there was total peace and that we were able to continue with our meetings without harassment from the Arya Samaj. I need to add that we had no further problems from the Arya Samaj during the rest of the week of meetings and, to my knowledge, they gave up trying to drown out our messages with their loud Hindu music.

Another Daughter

Gloria was born at Canada Hospital in Nasik City on

December 30, 1954. She was supposed to have been our Christmas baby, but delayed her entry into the world by five days. We had already decided that if God gave us another girl, her name would be Gloria; we also gave her Wilma's middle name, Ruth. She was delivered by a young English doctor, Dr. Pam Dodson. As soon as I was permitted to see Wilma and Gloria, I went into the room where they were lying in bed. As I stood looking at my third baby daughter, the first words that came out of my mouth were, "She has a pointed head!" Well, it wasn't long after she was born that everything was okay; her head didn't continue to be "pointed." I couldn't help but see that she was a beautiful baby. When Gloria was in her early teens she had a picture taken and someone remarked that she looked like a princess. Well, she truly was our special princess.

Those Strange Americans

The year was 1955 and in February we returned to America for our first furlough. We had been away from our homeland for nearly 5½ years. This was to be the first time we traveled on a passenger ship. It was a long process clearing through Indian regulations, just to be able to leave the country. During our time in India, we not only needed an entry permit, or visa, to get into India, but we needed a permit to even leave the country. Every year, while living in India, we had to apply for renewal of our residential permit. Sometimes it would be granted just before it was time for the permit to expire; we would then have to go through the process all over again in applying for the following year's permit. Red tape usually unwound very slowly in India. When it came time to board the ship for the first leg of our journey back to America, red tape was no exception. Men and women were processed separately and children were required to go with their mothers. The official who processed Wilma's papers declared that Wilma would not be allowed to board the ship, inasmuch as our Gloria, now only about six weeks old, did not have any kind of vaccination certificate. Even though Wilma informed the official that Gloria was well protected against diseases, in view of the fact that she was nursing the baby; that didn't seem to impress the official very much. Everyone else had boarded the ship except Wilma and our three daughters. I was already aboard the ship and beginning to get quite concerned, wondering where they were, when suddenly Wilma and the girls showed up. When I inquired, with great relief, as to what happened, Wilma replied simply that when the captain of that large passenger ship, became quite agitated that the ship was being held up, he had gotten off the ship, went to the Indian official and declared that it was perfectly alright that this mother and her three daughters, including baby Gloria, be allowed to board the ship. That was that!

It took our ship just three weeks to reach London. What an exciting time we had. We felt as though we were traveling in luxury, though we were crowded into a small cabin, which was in one of the lower decks. We were awed by everything. One problem we had to deal with was the feeding of our girls. We were traveling on a P. & O. Steamship Line ship, a British company. At that time it was the custom of the English for children to eat earlier in the afternoon, separate from adults. With our girls being so young, we felt it best that one of us be with them when they ate. And so, Wilma chose to sit with Lily and Kathy, four and two years old, respectively, to see that they were fed, while I remained behind in our cabin caring for Gloria. Later, when it was time for adults to eat, I had my turn, while Wilma stayed in our cabin with the girls. On ships sailing across the Atlantic, the situation was different. Because there were so many Americans traveling on English ships from New York to England and back, children and adults ate together. There was plenty to do on board those ships, with games, parties and a lot of deck space in which to walk for exercise. There was shuffleboard on deck to keep us occupied. We knew we had to get as much exercise as possible, for we were being fed as though we were royalty; at least, that is how we felt.

The day after we arrived in London, we were to sail out of Southampton for New York on the new English passenger liner, QEII (named after Queen Elizabeth II, who had come to the throne only two years before); but plans were suddenly changed, for the ship was taken out of service to be retrofitted with stabilizers. Instead, our booking was changed and we were now scheduled to sail from Liverpool on another P & O ship. During our time in London, we stayed at the Ivanhoe Hotel, not far from the British Museum. We checked into the hotel shortly before time for the evening dinner. When we arrived downstairs at the dining room, the headwaiter recognized us as being Americans. Having our three girls with us, which, as already mentioned, was not an English custom at dinner time, he decided to seat us at the very back of the dining room, well away from the other customers. Children in England were generally fed by about five in the evening and then shortly after that, put to bed. It was probably a good thing we were put so far away from the other diners, for that evening the menu included roasted chicken. While we knew that the English never ate chicken with their fingers, we preferred to eat our chicken the good old American way, with our fingers! We only hoped the head waiter would not be too embarrassed by having those strange Americans eating chicken with their fingers in his dining room.

Our trip across the Atlantic was calm, in comparison to our trip out to India on the S. S. Steel King in 1949. We crossed the North Atlantic fairly close to icebergs floating down from Greenland. That was the first time we had ever seen an iceberg, except in pictures; it was an awesome sight. Our ship stopped briefly at Halifax, Nova Scotia before sailing on to New York and the end of our journey from India. What a thrilling time it was to sail into New York harbor. As we stood on deck and viewed the Statue of Liberty, we heard a sound behind us. Standing at the ship's railing was a middle-aged couple from England. As they stood there, looking in the direction of the Statue of Liberty, they began to weep unashamedly. They remarked to us that they had looked forward to this sight for many years, for they were immigrating to America to begin a new life in the "land of the free and the home of the brave." We shared their sentiment and felt like weeping with them. We were home at last, after being away from our homeland for 5½ years. For us, though, there was still a long way to go before we would really be home.

Wilma's parents had arranged for us to fly from New York to Detroit. This was the first time we had ever been on an airplane. Our flight was on one of the famous DC-3's, a two-engine propeller plane. The day after we arrived in New York we went to the air office in downtown New York and awaited the call to board a bus that would take us out to LaGuardia Airport for our flight to Detroit. In all the noise and confusion at the air office, we had not heard the call to board the bus and it was not until we decided to check with one of the officials that we discovered we were left stranded. There was only one solution and that was to take a taxi, at our own expense, out to the airport. The taxi driver assured us that he would get us there in time, that is, if he could take a shorter route over a toll bridge and if we paid the toll; we readily agreed to the taxi driver's request. We seemed to be flying in that taxi, but we made it on time and got into the plane just as one of the crew was beginning to shut the door of the plane. We were finally on our way on the last leg of our journey from Bombay, India to Detroit, Michigan. When the plane touched down at the old Willow Run Airport, which served at the time as Detroit's only airport, Wilma's parents were there anxiously awaiting our arrival. We were tired and a bit confused, but glad to be back in familiar territory once again; but was it so familiar? The following account will answer that question.

Catching Up To The Twentieth Century

Many changes had taken place during the 5½ years we had been away from our homeland. When we left India on September 30, 1949, we had seen only one television set, which was on display in a department store in Detroit; the television set was in a wooden case with an oval screen. There had been no supermarkets; only the typical corner grocery store. Computerized cash registers were not known at the time as were bar codes now found on every thing sold today. We had never seen an escalator and when we got on one for the first time, we did it with great trepidation. Credit cards had not yet been invented. There were no divided highways before we left for India. It was frightening to us to drive on these new highways, for in India we drove on narrow roads with animals and people vying for the right to walk where vehicles were meant to go; the top speed we could make on such roads in India with our jeep was hardly more than 25 miles an hour! But in America, on these new divided highways, cars were speeding along at 55 mph! It was truly a frightening experience.

One day I went to a Kresge Five and Dime store in Wayne, Michigan, near where we were staying on furlough. I bought an item that cost no more than a dollar, or so. I didn't know where to pay for what I had bought. I didn't see any cash register, or a clerk who would take my money. But I did see some people going up toward the front of the store and so, I decided to follow them; maybe they would show me where to go to pay. As I followed them I saw that they were lining up behind others, who were giving whatever they were purchasing to a woman standing behind a cash register. As I soon found myself standing before that woman, who, when she took that one item I was buying, asked me if it would be cash, or charge. I didn't know what she meant by that question. And so, I asked her, "What do you mean, will that be cash, or charge?" Her simple reply was, "Do you want to put this on your credit card?" My natural response was a simple, "What do you mean, credit card?" I had no idea at the time what a credit card was; I had never heard before of that system of paying for something; at least we didn't have that before we went to India in 1949. That clerk must have thought I was from outer space! Everyone knew what 'charge' meant; well, everyone, except for us, for we had a lot of catching up to do to catch up to the twentieth century.

The year we were home on furlough was mostly an enjoyable time for all. We stayed in an upstairs apartment in the Schulerts' house. The church where we had been married was between Wilma's parents' house and the Schulerts' house. When we were not traveling to visit supporting churches, or to visit my parents in Minneapolis, the girls were at their Grandpa and Grandma LaVoy's house. You can be sure their grandparents enjoyed that very much. In fact, they had the opportunity of watching Gloria, who was only about two months old when we arrived back in the States, to being nearly a year and a half by the time we returned to India for our second term of service in the spring of 1956. We were told by Wilma's mother that after we left for India, her dad found a little sock of Gloria's that we had left behind; he had put that sock under his pillow to sleep on it at night. I wish, for memory's sake we had that little sock today; but we don't, unfortunately.

Crises Situations

We had arrived back in the States on Saturday and the next day, being Sunday, we knew we were expected to be in church. Our home church was already aware that we had arrived back from India with our three daughters and the people were eagerly waiting to see our three little "Indian" girls and us. We were warmly welcomed by everybody. But right after the morning service, Lily got separated from us and soon we heard a sound from another part of the church auditorium, "Mommy, Daddy, where are you?" Lily had become very frightened in being separated from us. She was not used to seeing so many white-skinned people, all speaking English. In India, her playmates were brown-skinned Indian children, all speaking Marathi, which she spoke as well as did the Indian children. Had we realized what would happen, we would have arranged to arrive back in the States on a Monday, not Saturday. That would have given us nearly a week to get our girls somewhat used to being amongst Americans speaking English. We had learned our lesson well, but a bit too late for that situation. To quote a cliché', "Hindsight is better than foresight." As a result of this first crises situation, Lily developed a serious case of hives, which took nearly six months for her to get over this problem.

We were not always aware of how our children watch and mimic us. Sometimes the result is not very pleasant. For awhile, we wondered whether our second daughter, Kathy, was accident-prone. She was just two years old at the time, when I had to be away for meetings, while Wilma stayed home with the girls. One day Wilma was using her mother's sewing machine, while Kathy sat on a high stool near the machine. As Kathy began bouncing around on the stool, she suddenly fell off and hit her head on the edge of the sewing machine, resulting in a gash, which began to bleed very profusely. Fortunately, Wilma's father was there and they rushed Kathy to the emergency at a nearby hospital; she came back home with a souvenir of several stitches in her head. Her remark was simply, 'Mommy, I yumped!" Our second daughter always walked on her toes and was the "bounciest" little girl we had ever seen.

A few weeks after Kathy had injured herself on the sewing machine Wilma and the girls were with me in Chicago for a missions conference. We had been unpacking our suitcases and suddenly noticing Kathy holding a double-edge razor blade in her hand and blood rushing down the side of her head. Knowing one of our mission doctors was nearby in the same building, I ran to tell him what had happened to our daughter. He immediately dropped what he was doing and came to give first aid to Kathy. He as able to put pressure on the spot on the side of her head where she had cut herself with the razor blade and temporarily stop the bleeding. I quickly rushed her to the emergency at a nearby hospital. It took a staff of four people, plus myself, to hold Kathy down while the doctor probed around to find the location of the cut and then stitch it up. It was a heart-wrenching scene at the time, for the bleeding began again and as the blood was running down into her eyes, she cried out, "Daddy, Daddy, where are you?" The reason why all this happened was that at sometime or other, Kathy had watched her mommy trim her own hair by using one of my razor blades. It must have been that Kathy wanted to do the same thing with her hair when she saw a razor blade lying in my opened suitcase that day. As soon as I could, I got rid of my razor with the double-edge razor blades and bought an electric razor. This was another lesson we had to learn under difficult circumstances.

Gloria And Green Paint

Gloria always made life so very interesting for us. It was getting closer to the time for us to return to India for our second term of service. Wilma's father had made some little seats to take back to India for the girls; they were made in such a way that they could be stacked up on one another and used to store their toys, as well as being used to sit on. I was in the process of painting the little seat boxes one day, when I saw Gloria get up from one that I had just painted with bright green color paint a few minutes before; the paint was still very fresh. Oh no! Gloria had soaked her diapers and they had fallen down to her ankles. There she was, standing up on her wobbly legs, with a big bright green circle of wet paint on her bare bottom. The day before, I had told her to try out one of the other seats that also had been painted bright green, but was perfectly dry. She had apparently thought this second seat was the same one she had sat on the day before. Gloria, hardly a year old when this happened, put up a brave front without even a whimper, as I cleaned off the green paint with turpentine. From then on I made sure that she was not around while I finished my project of painting all those seats. We had learned another lesson at the expense of our daughters.

When Gloria experienced her first Christmas in the States she heard the Christmas carol, "Angels We Have Heard On High," in which the chorus begins with the following: "Gloria in Excelsis Deo." When Gloria heard those words being sung, she would cry out, "Mommy, Daddy, they're singing my name!" Our Gloria was quite the girl!

Left Stranded High And Dry

One question our daughters didn't tire of asking during that first furlough was, "When are we going back home?" Home to them meant India. We assured them that it would be soon and that time finally did arrive. It was the month of May, 1956 and time to go "back home to India." This time we were booked to sail on the S. S. United States, the fastest ship afloat. In fact, it was so fast that we arrived in LeHavre, France nearly a day ahead of schedule. From LeHavre we sailed across the English Channel to finally dock at Southampton, England.

Before catching our train to London, I placed a call to the P & O Steamship Company head office in London to verify the sailing time of our ship out of London the next day. I was informed that, yes, everything was in order and the ship would be sailing as scheduled. Upon arriving in London, we took a taxi to Ivanhoe Hotel, where we had stayed the year before, on our way through to the States from India. The next morning, after having had breakfast in the hotel dining room – this time the headwaiter didn't put us way in the back of the dining room as had been done before – and packing up all our things, we checked out of the hotel. From there we took a taxi to the train station in order to get the "boat train" down to Tilbury Docks on the River Thames, from where our ship was to sail. When we arrived at the station and asked a man standing at the gate where we were to board the boat train, he inquired as to which ship we wanted. When we told him the names of the ship we were informed, "Oh! That ship left last night." What a shock! There we were with no place to go because we had checked out of our hotel. Now what were we to do? We were left stranded, high and dry.

Returning to the Ivanhoe Hotel, I asked the desk clerk if Wilma and the girls could stay in the lobby while I went to the P & O office. When I explained to the gentleman what had happened, he was quite happy to grant such permission. As soon as I arrived at the P & O office, I was ushered into the office of one of the shipping company's officials. When I related to him what had happened, I was told to return at noon and by then the company would have a solution worked out for us. At noon I was back at the P & O office to meet the same official. He told me that they had two offers for us and whichever one I chose would be acceptable to them. At no time did the man ever admit that the mistake was theirs. At any rate, one of the offers was to wait in London until the next ship sailed, which had room for us. The company would put us up in a hotel at their expense, as long as was necessary for us to find accommodation on the next ship available. The next ship was a month away and we had no desire to stay in London for at least that length of time; it could have been longer. The second offer was for us to wait in London an additional four days and we could fly from London to Athens, Greece, from where we would travel on an air conditioned bus with Greek immigrants to Australia and meet the very ship we had missed at a small fishing village in the southwest part of Greece. All of this would be at the P & O Shipping Company's expense. We chose the latter plan, which sounded like an exciting adventure. We were put up at a very nice hotel near Hyde Park in the heart of London for the next four days, awaiting our flight to Athens, Greece.

A Greek Adventure

We flew to Athens, as planned, and stayed at the Hotel Athenee in downtown Athens. The next morning, as we sat in the hotel dining room having our breakfast, we began to hear explosions, which sounded nearby. Wondering if perhaps there might be a coup in the making, we asked our waiter what was happening. He explained that it was the Greek Orthodox Church Easter Sunday and ships in the harbor were shooting off their big guns with blanks, in celebration of Easter. This seemed to be one of the many interesting customs of modern Greece. Later that morning we boarded one of two buses that would take us on a two-day trip across the Pelloponnesus Peninsula to the small village of Pylos on Navarino Bay. There we would await the arrival of our ship that left London without us. Not long after we left Athens, the two air-conditioned Mercedes buses in which we were traveling, along with all the Greek men and women emigrating to Australia, crossed over the deep canal that separates the Peloponnesus Peninsula from the rest of Greece. We stopped for lunch on the first day of our trip across Greece in the town of Korinthos, better known as Corinth, where the Apostle Paul had preached the gospel and a church was established, to whom he had written 1 and 2 Corinthians. We did not see any signs of a church, but if there were, they had to be Greek Orthodox churches. We ate at a lovely little outdoor café and soon found out that the water was so bad to drink the people drank only beer. We were offered some by the waiter, but thanking him for his gracious offer, we decided to take a chance with the water. Fortunately, we did not get sick from the water, or any of the food we ate on that trip. From Korinthos it was on to another small town for mid-afternoon refreshments. Only one on our bus spoke English besides ourselves. An official of Greek origin from the P & O Steamship Company served as our interpreter the whole journey across Greece. Our daughter, Kathy, who was three years old at the time, seemed to have become a favorite of the Greek passengers. As we traveled along, she began singing, "Jesus loves me this I know." It wasn't long before she was sitting on the lap of one of the Greek men sitting near us.

When we stopped at a small village for a mid-afternoon snack we sat around some tables that were underneath an arbor, sheltered from the heat of the sun. We were asked by a waiter if we would like to have a lemon soda. We thanked the waiter, thinking that he would bring us a cold bottle of lemon soda. Instead, he brought each of us a glass of cold water, along with a tin of lemon powder (left over from World War II) and a box of baking soda. The action of the lemon powder, mixed with the baking soda, gave it a "fizz" when mixed into the glass of water; voila', we had lemon soda! After our snack in that quaint little Greek village we continued on in our two-day journey across Greece until we came to another village. There we stayed for the night at a small hotel; it certainly was not the Holiday Inn, but it was a place to sleep for the night and that was all we needed.

The next day we arrived at our destination at the village of Pylos, facing on Navarino Bay, to await the arrival of our ship. It was not long before we found a cute little open-air restaurant. No one there spoke English and we didn't know the Greek they spoke. I had taken four years of Greek at Bob Jones College. But the Koine Greek of the New Testament is not the spoken language of Greece today. Our Greek interpreter was nowhere to be found and we were hungry. There was only one thing to do and that was to go right back into the kitchen to see what I could find. As I lifted up the lids on all the pots set in the warming tray, I noticed one filled with what looked like spaghetti and meatballs. Finding it swimming in olive oil, it didn't appeal too much to my appetite, as hungry as I was. I did not know at that time how healthy food is cooked in olive oil and that is practically all we use today to cook our food. Well, I thought that maybe the waiter might know what the word 'omelet' meant. When I said, "omelet," his eyes lit up and he repeated, "omelet." And so, that is what he brought. I had told him, though, "no onion," but that was one English word the waiter didn't understand, for he proudly presented to us an omelet loaded with onions and swimming in olive oil.

Navarino Bay and its little village had no wharf for a huge passenger ship to tie up to. When our ship finally arrived in the bay, we all had to go out to it in a large motorboat. We climbed up the gangway which was let down over the side of the ship. As we walked up that steep gangway, it had a tendency to sway, which was not very good for a person who got seasick, especially for Wilma. I could remember her experience on the S. S. Steel King in 1949 as we crossed the Atlantic in hurricane waters. Well, we all finally made it up to the ship, we five, along with 75 Greeks, who were on their way to Australia, the ultimate destination of the ship. Apparently the word had gotten around that there was an American family, which had missed the ship in London and would be meeting it there in Navarino Bay, along with the Greek emigrants. There was no doubt in the minds of all the passengers, gathered along the ship's railings, as to who were the Americans.

Back Home Again

The rest of our journey back to India was quite uneventful. We were just glad to be back in the place of God's appointment for us and the girls were glad to finally be "back home again" in the land of their birth. After clearing our baggage through customs, we caught the first train we could to go up country to the mission station at Raver. Raver was only about 30 miles away from Yaval by road, where two single ladies were now stationed. They had been assigned to village evangelism, rather a strange arrangement for two single lady missionaries. It was necessary for us to get our household goods hauled over to Raver; but, in the meantime, we had to also await the arrival of our jeep station wagon that had been shipped from New York to Bombay by freighter. We had purchased the station wagon during our first furlough and used it in our deputation ministry. It was bright red and easily seen by anyone else on the road. As soon as word reached us that the station wagon had arrived in Bombay, I took the train down there to clear the vehicle through customs.

Post Office Red

At the time I filled out all the papers to clear the vehicle, I was told by a customs official that I couldn't bring it into the country. The only vehicles in India that were allowed to be red were post office vehicles. The customs official claimed that the color of our jeep station wagon was "post office red." What was I to do? I took a quick glance at the documents I signed when we bought the jeep station wagon from a dealer in Michigan. There it was, printed very clearly on the documents; the color was not "post office red," but "president red." I informed the official, "Sir, my jeep station wagon is not post office red; it is president red!

Here, look what is printed on this document." The official had nothing further to say; as he studied the documents and he quietly marked our vehicle as cleared through customs. Now I could drive it away and head for our new home at Raver; but could I?

Twice Bought

Little did I know at the time I was dealing with this problem of what color our jeep station wagon was, whether post office red, or president red, that another problem had already taken place. As soon as the vehicle was cleared through customs I got into the driver's seat, put the key into the ignition to start the engine. The engine turned over all right, but wouldn't start. What was the problem? The battery was okay; I had left the station wagon in New York at the wharf with a full tank of gas; there must be an electrical problem somewhere. When I looked under the hood it was obvious that someone had stolen the carburetor somewhere between New York and Bombay. Could it have been right there at the customs shed in Bombay? I had no doubt that that was what happened and it was already somewhere in Bombay's *tsar bazaar* (thieves' black market).

I was able to hire a pair of bullocks to pull the station wagon through the streets of downtown Bombay about two miles away to Bombay Baptist Church, where a missionary friend from Canada was pastor. Leaving the jeep station wagon in the church compound, I took a taxi to Malabar Hill, which was close to the ocean and where there was an auto parts store. When I inquired of the salesman as to whether they had a carburetor for a 1956 Continental engine, the man told me, "just a minute, I'll go back into the stock room and see what I can find." A few minutes later he returned, holding a carburetor in his hands; it was not in any kind of a box that would identify it. "Sir, we just happened to have one in stock!" No questions asked. I paid the price for what I was convinced was the actual one that had been stolen from off our jeep station wagon. The continental engine was built by the Continental Engine Company especially for that model of the 6-cylinder jeep station wagon. It was highly doubtful that there was another vehicle in all of India of that make and model and that there would be a call for such a carburetor to be in stock by a small auto parts store on Malabar Hill in Bombay. This much I knew, I was desperate for a carburetor and without it, that 1956 jeep station wagon was going nowhere! We settled on the price; I paid it and took the carburetor back to Bombay Baptist Church to install it in our vehicle. It was twice bought.

I was only sorry that before we shipped the station wagon from New York we had not fitted it with a locking system, which could not be opened by anyone else without a special key. This certainly was a hard and expensive lesson to learn. As soon as I fitted on that carburetor, the engine started up; what a beautiful sound that was. I quickly packed my things into the station wagon, said my thanks to our missionary friends and headed out of Bombay to drive some 250 miles up country to Raver. Fortunately, it was the hot season and there were no flooded rivers to cross along the way. As I drove our bright red jeep station wagon, I was confident that our president red (not post office red!) vehicle could be seen by the people walking along the dusty roads, or riding in their bullock carts; I wasn't so sure about the many animals walking along the roads. Colors of vehicles didn't seem to matter to them one way or the other; they walked on whichever side of the road that pleased them at the moment. There were always two parts to a vehicle that were important in India and those were a horn and brakes.

Off To Boarding School

Lily Ann had her 6th birthday on July 2, not long after we arrived back in India for our second term of missionary service. It was not a very happy birthday for her, for she had to leave for her first year of boarding school. The interdenominational mission we were working with had cooperated with several other missions to operate a boarding school for missionaries' children (commonly referred to as MK's, which term we will use throughout the rest of these memoirs). The school was known as Sunrise School, which was also the name of a bungalow owned by the Christian and Missionary Alliance mission, on whose compound most of the school was located. Sunrise School was in the mountains of Central India at the edge of the village of Chikalda. Chikalda was about 30 miles up a winding road from the Conservative Baptist Foreign Mission's head station at Amravati, where they had their hospital. Chikalda was at nearly 4,000 feet altitude and served somewhat in the early British days as a semi-hill station. The unique thing about where the school was located was that it was right on the edge of a very large government reserved forest.

Wilma went with Lily to Chikalda to get her settled into her boarding school home and enrolled in school. They rode with another missionary and his children, who were also students at Sunrise School. We regretted how Wilma had to leave Lily at Sunrise School, for she had gone off to school expecting to see Wilma at the end of that first day of school. Wilma had told her that she would see her later in the day when she got back to her boarding home. But the missionary with whom they had ridden up to Chikalda was anxious to leave and get back to his mission station. As a result, Wilma had to write Lily a note and explain what happened. Again, hindsight is better than foresight. Looking back now, after so many years, we were sorry that we had not all gone as a family to Chikalda in our almost new jeep station wagon and spent a few days in Chikalda to be sure that our daughter was settled into her temporary "home-away-from-home" at Sunrise School. This could have been somewhat of a family outing. The one uncertainty was that this was during the time of India's monsoon season, making travel a bit harder, with the possibility of rivers suddenly being flooded. I am happy to say that Lily did settle in well into boarding school life and we helped, somewhat, by being sure she received letters from home every week.

Cobras In The Roof

Cobras were in the roof? How is that possible? The roof on the mission bungalow at Raver began to leak so badly that we actually had to take an umbrella with us into the bathroom. After the rainy season was finished I hired some men who were skilled in the trade of laying roofing tiles. We found that all the tiles had to be removed from the roof before laying down all good tiles. The roof had four layers of tiles, one layer face up, the second layer with tiles face down, overlapping the first layer; then the next two layers repeated. The workmen were beginning to remove all the tiles when I heard one of them yell, "Come Sahib, there is a nest of cobras in the roof!" There sat a nest of very small cobras apparently just-hatched. A baby cobra is just as dangerous as an adult cobra. Like fully-grown cobras being disturbed they had their hoods spread and hissed at us. Needless to say, we removed those baby cobras and destroyed them. In the meantime, the question arose as to where was the mother cobra was. Well, maybe she figured later on in one of two other confrontations we had with cobras at our mission station at Raver.

Who Was Scared The Most?

One day I heard a commotion outside our bungalow at Raver. As a loud cry from Wilma seemed to pierce the air, I rushed out to find her trying to get away from a cobra. She had been on her way into the bungalow when suddenly she saw a cobra on a ledge by the door. As she ran in one direction to get away from the cobra, it slithered along the edge of the bungalow's foundation in the same direction Wilma was fleeing. When she changed directions, so did the cobra. In the end, we were able to kill the snake, but the question remains, "Who was scared the most? Who was trying to get away from whom? We have laughed about this incident with the cobra many times since.

Cobra In The Wood Shed

One day our cook rushed into the bungalow shouting that there was a cobra in the woodshed. He had gone to get some wood for the kitchen stove when he saw the cobra trying to escape through a small window. Needless to say, our cook forgot all about getting firewood and fled, thinking to save his life from the cobra. I went out to the woodshed to confirm what the cook had said was true, sure enough, there was the cobra, trying to climb up the wall, trying to reach a window; but kept falling back down to the floor. I made a quick decision to remove the wood from the woodshed so that we could more easily kill the cobra. Just then, the cobra disappeared. Where had he gone? We needed to find the cobra and kill it before it struck someone with its poisonous fangs. The snake had to be somewhere in that large stack of firewood. As I picked up one piece of firewood at a time and handed it back to the cook, who was standing right behind me, I kept watch for the cobra. He could have been anywhere, under any one of those pieces of wood I picked up. After some time I had removed every piece of wood from the shed, only to find that the cobra was not there; he had disappeared. Where had he gone? He certainly did not climb up that wall and escape out through the window; nor had he slipped between my legs and fled through the door of the shed. He had to be in that room somewhere; but the room was absolutely bare. Ah, there was only one place he could be. At one time the room had served as a place for an *ayah* to stay, who had worked for a previous missionary family. In one corner of the room was a bathing place right beside the door. A small pipe of about one inch in diameter stuck a few inches outside so that at bath rime, the water could drain out onto the ground through that small pipe. We usually stuck the neck of a bottle loosely into the opening of the pipe, which would allow the water to flow out, but not allow snakes and mice to get into the house. At some time I had placed a brick against the opening of the pipe on the outside of the shed; nothing could get into, or out of that ayah's bedroom-cum-bath, now turned into our woodshed. That cobra had crawled into the pipe, which was too small for him to turn around and crawl back out. I sent the cook to bring a kettle of boiling water, which he always kept ready on the stove in the kitchen to make a cup of tea for us. The boiling water would now serve a better purpose. When I poured it all down into that pipe it cooked the cobra!

As we think of these incidents with the cobras (there were others, as well), we remind ourselves of God's hand of protection upon us while living in a land of cobras, wild animals and life-threatening diseases. Truly, God's grace is sufficient in time of need. (2 Corinthians 12:9).

Scorpions And Tigers

There were two creatures we were always on the lookout for: cobras, or other poisonous snakes, and scorpions. In India there are both the small brown scorpions and the much larger black ones. Black scorpions are the most deadly of all scorpions. I already had my experience with a scorpion sting, but Wilma was to have a more terrifying experience with a scorpion. One winter season, while we were stationed in Yaval during our first term of service, we packed up all our camping gear, including a large three-room tent, along with our cooking utensils, food supplies and gospel literature, as well as our hand-wound gospel record player. We had a supply of records provided by Gospel Recordings in the States. The gospel records were all in Marathi, the language of the area in which we were involved in village evangelism. Whenever we went out to the villages to preach, we would always go to the village *chowk* (much like a village square in America). There we would play the gospel records and wait for the people, almost entirely men and boys, to gather around to listen to the music being played on the records and see what these white people had to say.

After loading up all our gear into the jeep and trailer that day, we drove to a village at the foot of the Satpura Mountains, which was the boundary between our district of East Khandesh and the next district to the north of us. By the time we had set up our tent, got our sleeping cots unfolded and set up and our cooking gear laid out in the cook room at one end of the tent, it was late in the day and too late to go into the nearby village. At the opposite end of the tent the other small room was used as our bathroom where we had a portable toilet. The large middle room served both as dining room and bedroom. After darkness had set in that evening, Wilma stepped outside the tent for a moment, when suddenly she let out a loud yell of pain and ran back into the tent where I was with our girls. She had been stung by a scorpion on the bottom of her foot. She was wearing a sari and had a pair of *chappals* (leather sandals) on her feet. As she sat on her cot, the pain began to creep up toward her heart. We quickly made a poultice of mustard and applied it to the spot where she had been stung. I applied heat to the spot by putting our kerosene pressure light as close to that spot as possible. Neither of us slept much that night. Fortunately, the pain went up only as high as her waist. By the middle of the night the pain began to ease. It was a frightening experience, knowing that a scorpion sting could kill a person, especially a very young child, or older adult.

Another encounter with a "wild" creature took place during that same campout. One very dark evening the tent began to shake quite violently. Right away, Wilma thought it could be a tiger! The name of the village near where we had set up our tent in a farmer's field was "Waghjira" (village of the tiger). We knew there were tigers in the area. Armed only with a flashlight, I bravely went out to see if it was a tiger trying to get into the tent. What I found was a village water buffalo scratching himself against the tent pole. So much for the tiger! We had quite a laugh over that affair.

A Curious Crowd

Most people are curious about something they have heard about, or never seen before. Some people will go to any length to satisfy that curiosity. The people of India, especially villagers, are curious. One hot season we drove with one of our other missionaries to South India to a well-known hill station. We needed to get away from the heat of the plains, which could get as high as 110 to 120 degrees Fahrenheit. At noontime during our second or third day of travel, we decided to stop for a picnic lunch beside a quiet flowing stream, with a grassy spot nearby. It was just the place for a picnic lunch. There didn't seem to be a soul in sight; we didn't even see a village anywhere near there. After laying down a tablecloth on the ground, we got out all our picnic things and then had prayer to thank the Lord for our food and a safe journey to that spot. As we opened our eyes and looked up, what did we see but a crowd of people, all gathered around, wondering what these strange white people were doing.

At another time, we were returning to Raver, during our second term of missionary service. We had been to our mission hospital in Chinchpada, nearly a day's journey by jeep, having gone for some medical attention. In fact, I had a very large mole removed from the middle of my back by the mission doctor. The doctor had told me very clearly that I was to be careful and not do any heavy lifting, or anything else that would put a strain on my back and cause the stitches to come out before the back had healed up enough to take the stitches out. As we got into the town of Bhusaval, on the south edge of the Tapti River and only about forty miles from home, the rear left tire of the bright president red jeep station wagon went flat! In order to get to the spare tire, I had to unload all our baggage from behind the back seat, which was packed right up against the spare tire. The jack was also attached to the back of the spare. When I tried to jack up the station wagon with that scissors style jack, I had little success. Wilma and the girls had gotten down from the station wagon and were standing around watching our baggage, for a large crowd of villagers had come to see what the sahib and his family were doing. As I was struggling with trying to get the station wagon jacked up enough to remove the flat tire and put on the spare tire, I looked up toward a nearby house. At the back of the house a truck was parked. It was one of the large trucks used to haul goods from town to town. When I went over to ask the owner if I could use his large jack, he gladly let me take it. As I was preparing to put the jack under the jeep station wagon, one man in the crowd spoke up, "Sahib, do it this way" and he began gesturing, indicating the way I should do it. That was enough for me; standing up, I extended the jack handle in his direction and replied, "If you know so much about how to work a truck jack, then you can do it; here." Backing off, the man replied, "No, no, Sahib, that's alright; you are doing it okay." My answer was simply, "Then keep quiet and let me do it, okay?" I soon had the station wagon up high enough to change tires; it wasn't long after we had everything loaded back up into the station wagon. I returned the truck jack to its owner with a word of appreciation and we were soon on our way the rest of the way back home to Raver. Later that day we discovered that in all my effort to change the flat tire, I had burst open the stitches in my back; just what Dr. Holt had warned me against doing. As a result, when my back finally healed up, it left a large scar, another one added to my long list of body scars.

Gloria And A Tin Of Tar

I used to keep a small tin of liquid tar in the woodshed for painting the base of tree trunks; this was to prevent white ants (termites) from climbing up the trees. Unfortunately, the woodshed door had been left open by someone. Gloria, who was about two years old at the time, found the door ajar and she decided to go inside to investigate. She found that small tin of liquid tar with a large brush set in the tar. The next thing we knew was that she had gotten into the tar, resulting in one sticky little girl! What a time we had cleaning the tar from off her. Again, kerosene came to the rescue. I made sure after that tar incident that the door to the woodshed was always closed. Besides keeping Gloria from the temptation of another paint job, was the possibility of other cobras getting into the woodpile stored in the shed.

Life At A Jungle Boarding School

After a year of village evangelism in Raver, we were transferred to Chikalda to serve at Sunrise School. Gloria was just 2 ½ years old at the time and some of our missionaries wondered whether it would be possible for us to give our full attention to the boarding school ministry with such a small child. We had been at Sunrise School for no more than a year, when we proved to the doubters that, yes, it was not only possible, but we were doing a good job of it, and our Gloria proved to be an asset to the ministry. We served as house parents at Sunrise Cottage and I was asked to teach the 5th -7th grade classes. All three classes met together in what had once been a garage, but with some remodeling the former garage had become a very nice classroom. Teaching those three grades was challenging and though I had never taught a grade school class before, I soon learned and enjoyed that part of my ministry very much.

Near the gate to the school compound was a large elephant shed, where a female elephant was kept. The government forest department used the elephant for clearing the jungle of scrub trees in preparation for planting young teakwood trees. The children at Sunrise Cottage had fun from time to time riding on the back of the elephant when the *mahoot* (elephant driver) brought it up to the bungalow. A seat was strapped onto the back of the elephant, which looked like an upside down bed. The children would ride a short distance, with the *mahoot* prodding the elephant with his special stick. Oh, that was a lot of fun.

One day we were all seated for our lunch, when we heard a loud noise coming from somewhere near the bungalow. Suddenly, a village man came bursting in to announce that a woman had jumped into an abandoned well near the elephant shed and was screaming for someone to come and rescue her. I told our cook and his helper to bring the coil of rope we kept in our storage room. When we reached the well, sure enough, there was the village woman down at the bottom of the well. Fortunately there was no water in the well, but a black, slimy mess had covered the stones that lined the well from top to bottom. The distance to the bottom of the well where the woman, now covered in the black slime, was standing and shouting, was about 20 feet. We came to find out that the woman had jumped into the well to commit suicide, possibly because her husband had abused her. She had survived her fall into the well and apparently decided that she didn't want to commit suicide after all. That black slime was too much for her and she would rather have suffered the wrath of her husband than to remain in that mess any longer. In a few minutes we had her out of the well and on her way back to her hut to have a bath, put on a clean sari and whatever fate awaited her at the hand of her husband. We have no idea what happened to her when she got home and her husband found out what she had done. We were only thankful that we had helped to rescue the village woman from a smelly well.

Attacked By A Horde Of Bees

Occasionally we took the school children for a hike, or picnic on a nice day and when schoolwork was not so pressing. One day we packed up a picnic lunch and with all the students, we hiked to a place where we loved to go from time to time. The *Panch* (pronounced as 'ponch', meaning 'five') *Bowl*, where five streams flowed out and down into a large ravine below, was a beautiful place for a picnic. We hiked down to one of the streams and gave the students some time to relax and wade in the water, while we staff prepared to lay out the picnic lunch. One of my students always seemed to get into some kind of mischief or other. Seeing a large hole in the side of the cliff that rose above the stream on one side, the mischievous student in question picked up a stone and threw it into the hole on the side of the cliff. Without warning, a horde of angry bees came swarming out of that hole. They came by the thousands and began attacking us. Wilma managed to quickly gather together all the small ones and move them away from that area and back toward higher ground. For myself, I knew there was only one way to escape and that was to dive into a small pool of water near where I was standing. I had pulled my short sleeve shirt up and over my head to protect my head as much as possible, even though both arms were exposed. While I was under the water the bees could not sting me, but I could stay under only so long and had to come up for air. But every time I came up for air, the bees were there seeming to wait for me. I hadn't thrown that rock into the hole to disturb them; why were they attacking me? It was not that they were just attacking me, but also other staff and students, who were still in that area.

I had no idea what had subsequently happened, where the

students and other staff were, or how badly others might have been stung. For me, the next thing I knew I was lying on the floor in a room with others and my head was in the lap of a Catholic nun. There was a Catholic convent school not far from Sunrise School and someone from the Catholic convent school had found me lying unconscious on a hill close by and brought me to the Catholic school. The nun was carefully pulling every stinger out of my head. How many stingers were in my head, I do not know, only that there were many. Another nun came into the room, carrying a cup of warm milk and told me to drink it. It was not long after I had drunk that warm milk when I began vomiting the milk back up, along with the poison from the bee stings. I was fortunate in that most of the stingers were in the top of my head, despite the fact that I had covered my head with my shirt. Others of staff and students were not so fortunate, for they were stung in their faces, arms and other parts of their upper body. Some of the others had badly swollen faces. It wasn't long before the Conservative Baptist missionary doctor came up to the school from their hospital in Achalpur, thirty miles away, bringing with him serum that would counteract the poison from the bee stings and help to bring down the swelling. Those of us who had felt the wrath of those angry bees were one sorry bunch of people.

As a result of the attack by those bees, I became allergic to any kind of a sting, including stings from certain kinds of flies and ants. On more than one occasion I experienced such stings when we were back in the States. I used to keep special medicine on hand in case of any kind of sting. One time I was stung by a large fly and had to be rushed to a nearby hospital for emergency treatment.

It was not unusual to find beehives hanging in the trees

near our school compound in Chikalda. For the rest of the time the school was located in Chikalda the smell of honey seemed to make me feel sick and I lost all desire to eat honey, wild, or otherwise. In time, that feeling disappeared, as the incident with the bees became more and more remote in my mind. Today I love to eat honey of any kind.

A Wild Boar That Didn't Get Away

Sunrise School campus was on the very edge of a government-reserved forest; in fact, the whole area was thick forest with tall teakwood trees, along with many different kinds of scrub trees. In addition, there was a pretty, but very thorny bush called *lantena*. Though the thorns were very small and hardly noticeable from a casual glance, they could do damage to bare skin. There were many wild animals in the jungle, including tigers and leopards, as well as several varieties of deer, or elk. There was one type of wild ox, called *gaur*, which stood at least six feet tall and almost as broad, so it seemed. Its horns were much like that of bullocks and the animals were dark brown in color, with white stockings on each leg. The *gaur* were protected from being hunted. At that time there were a few pea fowl in the jungle, but being the national bird of India, were also protected. One large animal found in the jungle was the *nilgai* (neel – guy), or blue bull, very tasty to the palate. There was even the occasional wild boar, along with the porcupine, both of which met their fate at the hands of this huntsman.

I owned a semi-automatic seven-shot 12-bore shotgun, along with a cute little 30-caliber carbine that packed a lot of punch for its size. All firearms in India had to be registered with the government and whenever we left the country to return to the States on furlough, we had to leave our weapons with the local police.

During the hot season, while Sunrise School was on summer break, some of our fellow missionaries would come to Chikalda for a brief time of R & R. That was a great time to get a month's license to hunt in one of the reserved blocks. No one else was allowed to hunt in that block for that particular month, except for those whose names were listed on the license. One hot season several of us, or even just two of us, would go out every day to hunt. We had so planned the day that we took with us bedding and cooking gear, along with a day's supply of food, so that if necessary, we could stay over for the night in a small government dak bungalow (rest house generally meant for the use of government workers, but available to us, as well). We never had to stay out, for each and every day that we were out hunting that particular hot season; we brought back some kind of game. Early one morning, one of our missionary friends, Mel Slack, from Calgary, Alberta, and I went out in his jeep. The sun was just beginning to come up and there was a bit of light, as we entered our hunting block, barely enough to see our way along the trail. I happened to be sitting out on the jeep, in order to see better, as Mel slowly drove along the trail. Suddenly, there appeared from our left, a wild boar, which ran across the road in front of us; he was heading toward the thick *lantena* bushes to our right. It all happened in a few seconds, as I raised my carbine and got off a quick shot. As I did so, there was a loud piercing sound from the boar. I knew that he had been hit, but how badly, I couldn't tell, for he suddenly disappeared into those *lantena* bushes. Not wanting to lose him, I slid off from the jeep and ran after the wounded boar, right into that thorny *lantena*. In a few moments I had caught up to the boar, which, by this time, was lying in a small gully below me. As he lay there with one eye seeming to look in my direction, I got off another shot to finish him off. Just then, Mel appeared above where I was standing; he had driven the jeep through a small opening in the bushes, coming as close to this scene as he possibly could. The next thing I heard, Mel was laughing in his typical Mel Slack "guffaw." My response was, "Well, what are you laughing at?" To which Mel replied, "Ken, you should see yourself in a mirror." I was more interested in getting that boar up and out of the gully and into the back of Mel's jeep than I was in trying to find out the reason for Mel's laughter.

Fortunately, Mel had thought of bringing along a long roll of heavy rope, which we used to tie around the boar and then to the bumper of his jeep. With little effort, we brought the boar up so that the two of us could lift it up and toss it into the back of the jeep. We decided that boar was enough for us to handle for the day; and so we decided to head back to Sunrise School with my prize wild boar. Besides having Mel and his wife, Enid, and their boys staying with us, we also had the Buhler's, Les and Verna and their children also staying at Sunrise Bungalow. Les learned how to cut meat while he was a student at Prairie Bible Institute in Three Hills, Alberta. Les was our "official" meat cutter that summer, whenever we brought any wild game home from the jungle. And so, Les had the job of cutting up that boar, which was a young one and very tasty.

After returning to the States on our next furlough, I gave the four tusks from the boar to Wilma's father. Dad LaVoy was a great hunter in his day and I knew that he would be thrilled to get those tusks. I was only too happy to present them to him as a remembrance of my hunting in India, especially as he had given me both that 30-caliber carbine, and the 12-bore semi-automatic shotgun, along with a large supply of cartridges for both guns. The next time I saw those tusks they were mounted on a wooden shield and hanging in my in-laws' living room. I later inherited those mounted tusks after Dad LaVoy died in December 1997; they are now hanging in my office at home. Below the tusks is a sign that reads, "Tusks from a wild boar I shot in the jungle near the village of Chikalda, Amravati District, India in the hot season of 1958." By the way, I finally did get to look in the rearview mirror of Mel's jeep, after we had managed to get that boar up into the back of the jeep, and saw that blood was pouring down my face from where I had been scratched by the tiny thorns of the *lantena* bushes through which I had run, while pursuing the wounded boar. It didn't matter how I looked, for I had succeeded in recovering the boar and I have his tusks hanging on the wall in my office to prove it. That was one boar that didn't get away!

A Tiger And My Bright Idea!

One hot season, two missionaries with the Free Methodist Mission and I went out for a hunt in another block about five miles down the mountain from Chikalda village. We came upon a group of village men gathered around an open fire, having their breakfast; it was still early in the morning. The men were working in the jungle, clearing some of it for planting young teakwood trees. As soon as they saw us, they became excited and one of them cried out that they had been troubled by a marauding tiger, which was killing some of their cows and goats; would we help them kill that tiger? Two of the men volunteered to lead us up the nearby dried up river bed, to where there was a small pool of water where the tiger was known to come for his early morning drink.

As one of the village men led the way, we three missionaries followed, with the second villager bringing up the rear. I happened to be third in line, with one of my Free Methodist missionary friends in front of me carrying his 30-06 rifle. Just before we came to a bend in the river, the villager in front of us turned and pointed up the river to indicate that the tiger was nearby. We continued walking on silently and slowly; as we came to the bend in the river, the tiger came into view. He had smelled us before we saw him, for we happened to be upwind from him. At that moment he bounded ahead of us and leaped up onto a high bank about a hundred feet in front of us. My missionary friend in front of me got off a quick shot, as the tiger leaped up onto that high bank. As he landed onto the top of the bank he let out a loud roar; we knew that he must have been hit. But then, all was silent and not another sound came from where the tiger had landed onto the top of the bank before us. Was he lying there dead, killed with that one quick shot; or was he wounded and breathing out his last? We couldn't tell from where we were standing. There was no way we could go after that tiger at that time, not knowing what his condition was. We had always been told that when sitting up in a tree, waiting for a marauding tiger to come for a *kill* (a goat, or some other small animal) tied at the base of the tree as bait, we should be at least 10 feet up the tree. Well, when we got to the base of the cliff where we had seen that tiger leap, we estimated the vertical distance from the river bed up to the top of the bank; which we believed it to be about 15 feet! So much for the 10-foot suggestion. One of the village men suggested that we ought to climb up onto the bank on the opposite side of that dried up river bed and see if we could see the tiger, hopefully lying dead on the other side, or at least lying mortally wounded. We saw nothing; not even a blade of grass seemed to stir. Just to make sure, we shot several times across to the opposite bank, but still nothing moved. Figuring that he must have crawled into the thick growth of the jungle, or could have even been lying dead nearby, we finally went over to that side of the river, cautiously, with our rifles ready to fire, in case he was still alive and able to attack us. We found only a small pool of blood and a trail of blood leading off into that thick jungle growth, where there was a small opening, just large enough for a tiger to crawl through.

As we stood there debating in our minds as to what we ought to do, I came up with a plan. "Let's all crawl through that small opening in the jungle growth on our hands and knees and follow the trail of blood," I suggested. One of my companions replied, "Okay, Ken, seeing as how it was your suggestion, you go first and we'll follow." It was no use protesting that maybe that wasn't such a good idea after all; I soon found my self down on my knees, beginning to crawl through that small opening as I dragged my 30-caliber rifle after me! I hoped that my two missionary friends were right behind me; catching a quick glance of them crawling after me, I proceeded, following the trail of blood. We were on the alert, expecting to see that wounded tiger at any time. But as we went further into the jungle, the trail of blood became less and less, until finally, as we came to a large opening, the trail of blood stopped completely; no blood and no tiger. What had happened to him?

It was Saturday afternoon and the next day we had our church service back in Chikalda. At the same time, we realized that it was our responsibility to follow up on the tiger and keep searching until we found him, dead or still alive. What were we to do? We prayed about it and all three of us were of the same mind that it would be more honoring to the Lord if we were in church on Sunday and not out in the jungle. We committed the whole situation to the Lord and prayed that He would protect the villagers nearby and not let the tiger harm either the villagers, or their animals. We told the villagers what we were going to do and assured them that our God would protect them and their animals from the tiger, while we went back to worship Him on His special day, Sunday. We promised them that we would be back early Monday to once again search for the tiger until we found him, dead or alive. And this we did.

Early Monday morning we searched the jungle, but found no sign of the tiger. While we were resting in a nearby *dak* bungalow, there was a sudden noise of a voice shouting, "Sahibs, sahibs, I have found the tiger!" The voice belonged to a village boy, on his way back to his village, when he spotted a hawk circling overhead. Thinking that possibly there might be some animal lying in the jungle, having been killed by the tiger we had been looking for, he decided to go to where the hawk was circling overhead. If there was such a dead animal, he could take it home for food for his family. As he carefully worked his way along a narrow jungle trail, he suddenly came upon the tiger, lying dead in the path. By the time the boy had reached the tiger, the hawk had disappeared. Had God sent that hawk to lead the village boy to where the tiger was lying dead in the path? Perhaps. Needless to say, we were excited and told the boy to show us the way, as we drove into the jungle in my Free Methodist missionary friend's Land Rover. Sure enough, there was the tiger, as dead as dead could be; and there was not even one fly buzzing around, not even a hawk, or a vulture. The tiger had been dead only a short time before the village boy had come upon him, for all his fur was intact and not even one single fly was buzzing around. With the help of some of the village men, we were able to get the dead tiger into the all-steel trailer my missionary friend had thought of bringing along with us when we left on our hunt that Saturday before. Back up the mountain we raced, returning to Chikalda and a spot near the other missionaries' bungalow, where we could skin the dead tiger.

By the time we got back to Chikalda, word had spread throughout the village that the sahibs (white men) had brought a dead tiger back to the village and were about to skin it. We soon had quite a crowd of village men gathered around. It was of utmost importance that we make sure no one would try to pull out any of the whiskers, or claws of the tiger, which they would put into their amulets to be worn around their necks. By doing this, the villagers believed they would be protected from all future danger in the jungle. The men were allowed, though, to take the tiger meat. The tiger skin, of course, belonged to my Free Methodist missionary friend who had gotten off that quick snap shot. It was an exciting time and we were all only very thankful that the tiger had been found and would not give any more trouble to the villagers, or kill any of their animals. There were other hunting adventures I had while we lived in the jungles of Chikalda; but, in time, I sold my weapons and began hunting in the jungle with a camera, which was almost as much fun.

The Last Laugh

Remember the incident about my killing the wild boar, only to be met by our missionary friend from Calgary, Alberta, as he stood there in the jungle by his jeep, laughing for all he was worth? He was laughing at the sight of me with blood pouring down my face and arms, having been scratched in many places by the lantena bushes, as I pursued the wild boar I shot. Well, later on I had the "last laugh." You see, that hot season, my missionary friend and some of the other men had gone out hunting, while I stayed home. They were told about a pair of marauding leopards giving trouble to the villagers and had been killing their animals. That evening my friend from Calgary, Alberta returned, all excited about the experience they had of finding and killing one of the leopards. The men had seen both leopards frolicking in the road ahead of them. The leopards soon ran off into the tall grass beside the road, but by that time it was getting darker, the sun having gone down some time before, and it was getting difficult to see clearly. The men began to fire in the direction where they thought was the outline of one of the leopards, with his red eyes shining in the light of the jeep pointed in that direction. One of the men was finally able to kill the leopard, much to the relief of all. What happened to the other leopard, they could not tell.

The next day Mel was too tired to go out with us on another hunt. The other men, who had been out the day before and shot the leopard, told me that they would show me where the whole incident of the leopard had taken place. When we got to that spot, what did we find, but the other leopard, lying dead in the tall grass. The men had shot, not one leopard, but both of them. By the time we arrived on the scene, it was getting quite hot in the sun and when we pulled at the fur of the dead leopard, the hair came right out; it was too late to keep his hide; but then, even if the fur was alright and the skin of the leopard in good condition, one of us could not have kept the leopard, for we had only one leopard on our block license. At any rate, we had to report the matter to the local forest officer. But, what about that "last laugh?" This is the rest of the story. I cut off the two front paws of the leopard and brought them back with me to the house. It was late when we got back, but I had already formulated a plan in my head. I slipped into my missionary friend's bedroom, knowing that he was fast asleep. I proceeded to shake him awake and whispered in his ear, not wanting to disturb his wife lying beside him also fast asleep. "Wake up, my good friend," I whispered, "You haven't heard the rest of the leopard story yet; here!" And I thrust those two leopard paws in front of him. Boy, was he ever startled out of his sleep; I don't know how long it took him to get back to sleep that night, after I told him the rest of the story about how they had actually shot both leopards the night before. I do know this; I had the "last laugh!"

A Major Move

There were a number of factors that caused us to make the decision to move Sunrise School. We needed to locate the school where we were able to get good medical help in case of sickness, or an accident. Difficulty in getting fresh food was also another deciding factor. For all the years the school was located in Chikalda, practically all our food had to be brought up from Achalpur in metal boxes on top of buses, which plied between Achalpur and Chikalda. That included all our fresh fruit and vegetables, as well as fresh meat, when we could get it. We had engaged the services of one of the hospital workers at the Baptist hospital in Achalpur, to do all the purchasing for us and ship the food up to Chikalda on top of a bus. It was not an ideal situation, for we did not know, first of all, if we were being cheated by the worker and also, how fresh everything would be by time it got to us in Chikalda, especially during the hotter time of the year. Also, our water supply at Sunrise Cottage was limited. There was a large concrete tank attached to the side of the bungalow. Gutters all around the bungalow would catch the rain water as it ran off the roof and direct it into that large tank, from where it would be pumped back up into the bungalow. But eventually, the water supply in the tank would become exhausted and then we had to buy water. We bought our water from a villager, who hauled it up to the bungalow in steel drums on his bullock cart; the closest stream from which he got the water was some miles away and thus, the water became quite costly to us. The other two bungalows, where our students stayed, did not have the convenience of a storage tank as we had at Sunrise Cottage. All of their water had to be brought up from the stream.

When it came time to decide on a place where we should relocate the school, what better place to move the school than to Nasik City, where there were all the modern facilities one could expect in a large city in India at the time. As for medical facilities there was none finer than what we could find at Canada Hospital, which was operated by what was then called the Zenana Bible and Medical Mission. The hospital was named Canada Hospital because much of the funds came from Christians in Canada. *Zenana* is a word used in the east to mean that part of the house where women were usually kept in seclusion. The mission's ministry was to the women of India and their missionaries were entirely women, with the mission coming under the direction of the Anglican Church.

Besides the excellent medical care we would receive, Nasik had the advantage of electricity and a city-supplied running water system. Of course, there was much to be desired as to the quality of the water, which we would have to boil for drinking. Also, Nasik City was a good source for food of all kinds. Then too, we had easy access to Bombay, only a few hours by train, or car. The decision was made to move the school at the end of the school year in 1959. For those of us on the staff at Sunrise School, there was no time to have a hot season vacation that year. There was much work to be done to get everything ready to move some three hundred miles away. Trucks were hired to haul everything to the new location; all the staff worked almost through the night loading up all the school furniture, as well as our own belongings, onto the trucks we had hired.

At the Nasik City there was also much work to do to get the buildings ready for the new school year to begin in just two months. But we were able to do it, even to the point of putting up a new building, which would be used for our dining room, including a kitchen and laundry room.

Two long stone buildings, with six rooms in each building, side by side, were to be used for the boys' and girls' dormitories. Wilma and I were appointed as dorm parents for the boys and so we lived at one end of the boys' dorm. The room next to us was reserved for an infirmary room, as well as the room for our own pre-school girls, Gloria and Phyllis. Of course, if any boys were put into the infirmary room because of a cold, or some other minor ailment, our girls would have to move in with us; fortunately, we never met up with that situation. When our girls turned six years of age they would then move over to the girls' dorm and both of them could hardly wait for that time. In the girls' dorm the first room was for the girls' dorm parent who was one of our single missionary ladies. There was a bathroom for each room in both the boys' and the girls' dorms. As soon as we could, we installed water pipes leading to each bathroom, as well as flush toilets, in addition to septic tanks for each bathroom; a septic tank was also installed for the kitchen in the building adjoining the dormitories; we had gone truly modern! This was the first time we had such facilities since we arrived in India in 1949. What luxury! The water pipes for each dorm ran right underneath the eaves of the roofs. In the afternoon the water would become quite hot, especially at the first bathroom. If we wanted a hot shower, that was the time to get it. On the contrary, if it was a cold shower we wanted, then we had to wait a few minutes, in order to drain out all the hot water in the pipe.

Life At A City Boarding School

During the rainy season, the system I devised for boiling our drinking water was unique. The water was pumped directly out of the Godavari River, one of India's seven "holy" rivers, which ran right through the city of Nasik. During the rainy season the water was quite stirred up and dark brown in color from the mud in the river. I had built a special place in back of the girls' dormitory, with two steel drums, lying on their sides on a stone platform. On the sides of each drum there was a 2" threaded plug; in the rim of each drum was a 1" threaded plug, to which I had installed a brass faucet. As the drums lay on their sides, the 2" plug was on top and that was where I filled the drums with the dark brown muddy city water. Under the drums I would build a fire and when the water in the drums boiled, steam would come out through that 2" hole at the top and give a loud whistle to let me know the water was boiling. In order to get the mud to settle to the bottom of the tank, so that we had clear water, I would drop a small chunk of solid alum, tied to a string, into the boiling water and leave it dangling there. I don't know the scientific principle involved in this process, but it did the trick, for the water came out of the brass faucet absolutely clear; voila! Clear, pure drinking water. It was a unique system, to say the least. I think I should have gotten a patent on my invention.

We brought back with us from the States, after our second furlough, a Maytag wringer-type washing machine. In addition, we also brought with us a large deep freeze, which would be used by the school to store food; both came in very handy during the following years we served at Sunrise School. The washing machine was used six days a week for all the remaining time we served at the school; later, when we changed locations and in a different ministry, the washing machine continued to be used for several more years without any problems. We figured that in all the years we used that machine, it had been used by a typical American family for some 75 years in all. Those Maytag machines were made to last.

Life at Sunrise School in Nasik City was quite different than what we experienced in Chikalda. In Nasik we had easy access to the bazaar, with a wide variety of fruits and vegetables. 80% of India's population were Hindu and to them the cow was considered to be holy. Because of this cow meat was not a part of our diet. On occasion, we would be able to get water buffalo meat, but this was a bit tougher and stronger in taste. It is interesting to note in comparing the butter and fat of cows to that of water buffalo, most butter from cow's milk is generally yellow, while the fat of the cow is white in color. As to the water buffalo, their butter is always white, while the fat in their meat is yellow. Anyway, our meat diet consisted mostly of goat mutton and chicken. On bazaar day, which took place one day in the week, we would sometimes be able to buy fresh fish, which was brought up from Bombay, over a hundred miles away. The fish was packed in ice and shipped by truck. One thing, which was always available in the bazaar, was *bumbeel* (commonly referred to in English as, Bombay "duck"), which was actually a dried fish, a herring-type of small fish. When the trucks brought the *bumbeel* up from

Bombay, it could be smelled from miles around, so it seemed. What a smell, but we understand it was delicious when cooked and used in the people's curry; at least, that is what we heard, though we ourselves had never eaten the fish. We simply had to take their word for it.

During our early years in India, Wilma's mother had arranged with the Fleishman Yeast Company in Canada to have packages of dried yeast mailed out to us, via airmail, which came directly from the factory. We baked most of our own bread for ourselves and for the school. One kind of bread that we came to really enjoy and still do is the *chappati* (chuh – pot' – tee), the flat whole wheat Indian bread, made without yeast. It is usually eaten, along with curried dishes as well as just alone with hot tea as an early morning breakfast. Sometimes we made scrambled eggs and wrapped it in a *chappati*, or else we would spread butter and peanut butter on the *chappati*. This made a nice snack to take along on school outings.

Speaking of outings, every school year we would have a surprise outing for the whole school, which we called "Blue Moon Day," for it happened only "once in a blue moon." The students would never know when it was to be held; but sometimes they had their suspicions, for several days prior to the event, there would be a lot of unusual activities by the staff in preparation for that day. One year, when the school was in Nasik City, we hired a small carnival to be set up on the school compound. That morning, the staff announced that there would be no school for the day, but that they were taking all the students on a hike. They did not know at the time, what the real purpose of the hike was. It was just to get them away from the school, so that the carnival people could come and set up all their equipment. How excited the children were when they got back to the school! There was a small Ferris wheel and other such things one would find at a typical carnival in India. But what was really fun for the children was the donkey ride. Now, how many children in the West would be excited about being able to ride on a donkey? From what I remember, the donkey ride was the best part of that Blue Moon Day for our children at Sunrise School in Nasik City, India. Oh, and by the way, I don't think any of us staff even thought about riding on that donkey; it was meant strictly for the students. Besides, as I remember, that donkey was quite too small for any staff member to even try sitting on it, let alone, ride on it!

Gloria's Antics At Sunrise School

One favorite piece of playground equipment, which I built for the students at Sunrise School, was a large swing. The swing set stood 8 feet tall and had two swings mounted on it. We finally had to make a rule that the students could make the swing go no higher than the upper cross pole of the swing. The swings were attached to two large ball bearings, which were inserted into the cross pole. They were never allowed to go all the way around! We had not anticipated one game they had with the swings. In fact, Gloria, who was always getting into some kind of mischief, seemed to have been the "ring leader" in this game. While one of the students sat on the swing and made it go as high as was allowed, up to the cross pole, another student would run underneath before the person on the swing came back down. Unfortunately, one day, Gloria was the one running underneath the swing; but she didn't make it fast enough, for the swing came back down as she was running underneath and hit her on the top of her head. It was a wonder she was not killed, or even knocked out. We are thankful that it only dazed her for a while, leaving a lasting "impression" on the top of her head. At the spot where she was hit, the roots of her hair must have been killed, for she has been left with a spot of white hair on the top of her head from that day to this. We are glad to say that she never tried that again. In fact, we had to make still another rule about the swings, which put a stop to that "fun" game.

At another time Gloria tried a different game. I had also put up a horizontal bar about 5 feet off the ground. One day Wilma heard Gloria calling out, "Mommy, come see what I can do, no hands." She was hanging head down, with both legs draped over the bar. As Wilma came out to see what our daughter was doing. Gloria suddenly slipped from off the horizontal bar, which was appropriately called a "monkey bar" and fell to the ground, putting her two upper front teeth right through her lip. At that time those two teeth had been protruding a bit and gave the appearance of "buck" teeth; in time those two teeth, along with her other teeth, were straightened with braces. That trick of hers left a scar just below her lower lip, where her teeth bit through the skin.

When she was much younger Gloria used to suck her thumb; in fact, when she was born, she had her thumb in her mouth. I used to tell her that if she kept sucking her thumb she would end up with her two upper teeth sticking out. Well, eventually those two teeth did begin to protrude, though we are not sure whether it was the thumb sucking that did it, or some other reason. One day I told Gloria that if she would stop sucking her thumb I would give her a *torch* (Indian word for flashlight). My bribe must have worked for I think she stopped sucking her thumb from that day on. All the students at Sunrise School had their own torches and she, a pre-schooler yet, wanted her own torch. She got her torch and no more thumb sucking!

Explosion In The Kitchen

We had a large pressure cooker, which our cook would use to cook the meat. This not only made sure the meat was well cooked with no danger of food poisoning. The pressure cooker also made the meat tender enough to chew. What meat we were able to buy in the market must have been from very old buffalos, too old to produce milk, or used to pull water from the villagers' wells. Wilma had shown Paulus, our cook, how to use the pressure cooker. She told him very clearly that when the meat was fully cooked and he removed the pressure indicator from the cover, to wait until all the steam had escaped through the vent in the cover of the cooker. One day Paulus apparently hadn't waited long enough until all the pressure had been released from inside the cooker. He had turned the cover to take it off, when suddenly things seemed to explode. Fine pieces of meat suddenly shot up from the cooker and stuck to the ceiling of the kitchen as well as on the walls. What a mess there was in the kitchen that day. It took many hours to clean up the mess. We were thankful that Paulus was not affected in any way. The explosion could have killed him, or injured him seriously. Never again did he try to remove the cover from the pressure cooker before all the steam had escaped out through the vent in the cover of the cooker.

At another time Paulus had made another nearly fatal mistake. We had a refrigerator that was cooled by a kerosene burner. Whenever the kerosene tank, which was on a shelf at the bottom of the refrigerator, needed to be refilled, we had warned Paulus to wait until everything had cooled down before pouring a fresh supply of kerosene into the tank. One day he was a bit impatient and began filling the tank with kerosene before the tank had cooled down. Suddenly, some kerosene that had spilled out caught fire. It wasn't long before we had the fire put out. We have been thankful many times that our school employees were kept from serious injuries. It was a case of their not being used to these Western conveniences.

Emergency Hospital Trips

We were thankful that we had good medical care only a few minutes away from the school campus in Nasik City, for there were a number of emergency situations that arose. With over 50 students at any given time, there were the inevitable falls from trees, resulting in broken bones, as well as scraped knees and arms from falling off bikes. Fortunately, the worst cases were broken arms. One time, one of the younger boys swallowed a five paise (pie – say) coin, which is about the size of an American nickel. The coin had lodged about half way down his throat and left him gasping for breath. I rushed him into town to the clinic of Dr. Ramdas, a Christian doctor, whom we knew quite well. The doctor was always accommodating himself to our emergency medical needs and this was one of them. When it was determined where the coin had lodged in the boy's throat, Dr. Ramdas had him put his head way back and with a long-handled pair of surgical tongs, reached down into the throat and quickly recovered the coin. When I asked Dr. Ramdas what his charge would be for removing the coin, he held up the coin and simply replied, "This much."

Before the dining room was built at our new Sunrise School campus we had to set up tables on the narrow enclosed porch on the front of the boys' dormitory. One of our daughters had been taking iron tablets, ordered by the doctor. They had a chocolate covering on them to make them easier to slip down the throat. Unless a person looked real closely at the tablets, they could have been mistaken for chocolate covered M & M's. We are sure that Phyllis, who was about 2 ½ years old at the time, must have thought that was what the tablets were. One day she discovered the tablets in a small round container sitting on one of the dining room tables and the cover had not been put on the container snugly. Phyllis must have thought the "M & M's" were for the taking, for that is what she did and she took them all. It wasn't long before we discovered what she had done and tried everything we could think of to get her to vomit up all the iron tablets she had swallowed. Finally, I did what I had never done before to our youngest daughter and that was to spank her, so that she would begin to cry and possibly then start vomiting up all the iron tablets she had swallowed. She finally began to vomit and as the tablets began coming up we began counting, for we had tried to estimate, by looking at the container as to how many of those iron tablet she had swallowed. In the meantime, we decided to take her over to Canada Hospital to be looked at by the doctor. When she examined Phyllis, she remarked that the only harm that the iron tablet would do to her, as far as any more that still might be in her, would be to give her a sore tummy and constipation for a few days. We weren't so sure about that medical opinion. Even though we did not know of the possibility of a small child dying from ingesting such a large amount of iron tablets, we made sure that from then on, all pills were kept safely away from Phyllis.

Another Furlough

Our second term of missionary service, like the first one, was 5 ½ years long. On September 12, 1961 we sailed out of Bombay for England. This time our ship landed at Liverpool On October 4th and from there we took a train to London. Our stay in London was just overnight and, as we had done in 1955, we stayed at the Ivanhoe Hotel. We can't remember, but we have wondered a number of times if the same headwaiter, the "maitre de la table", was still at the hotel and, if so, would he remember us? At any rate, we were not put into the very back of the hotel's restaurant this time, but were served up near the front of the restaurant. We flew from London to New York and on to Detroit the next day and were once again met by Wilma's parents. This furlough, like the first, would be full of new experiences and new things to learn.

During our second furlough we stayed in a house provided by our home church, First Baptist Church in Wayne, Michigan. The house was right next door to the church. When we arrived at the church's missionary guesthouse, it was late in the evening. Unfortunately, both of our watches had stopped running; that was in the day before battery operated watches. In addition, the church had not yet put a clock in the house, nor even a radio, television, or telephone. We had no way of telling what time it was. That was one of the longest nights we had ever spent in our lives. We didn't even have anything to read; that is, except for our Bibles. We've laughed about this many times, thinking at the time that it is good to read our Bibles, but read it for the whole night, however many hours that might be? Who knew, not having clock, or watch, exactly how long the night would be? We were all very much wide awake, for we had just arrived from India, where the time difference was 10 ½ hours; to us, day was night and night was day. Our body clocks had not yet adjusted to that change in time. By the time the sun finally rose the next morning, we were ready to go to bed and sleep the clock around. It wasn't long after that that we did have a clock, telephone and television in the house.

This furlough was as busy as our first furlough. We had to visit all our supporting churches in the year and they were scattered across nearly the whole country. In addition, my parents lived in Minneapolis and we drove up to see them on two different occasions. With three of our girls in school, Wilma had to stay home during much of the school year, while I did the traveling.

<u>Pussy Laid Babies</u>

During that furlough, Kathy came home from school one day to let us know that they had a stray cat in their classroom and her teacher wanted the students to find out if one of them could take the cat home and give it loving care, after getting permission from their parents, of course. Well, Kathy's wish to give the cat a home prevailed and we said, "Yes." And so, the next day Kathy brought the cat home. I am not sure at this time as to the name she gave the cat; it possibly was Tom; at any rate, he seemed very content in his new home. But then, one morning Gloria, now nearly seven years old, went down to the basement to see Tom where we had provided him with a comfortable bed to sleep in and where we kept his litter box, food and water dishes. Suddenly, Gloria ran back upstairs yelling as loudly as she could, "Mommy, Daddy, pussy's laid babies!" Well, it seems that Tom was actually a mommy and had delivered a litter of several kittens. By the time the kittens were getting bigger, we knew we had to do something about the mother cat, no longer Tom, but now Tomette, or whatever female name one would substitute for the male name of Tom. One day I told Kathy we needed to find a nice home for her mother cat and family; I persuaded her that the best place to take them was to the SPCA. She came along with me that day to make sure the cats would all be well taken care of, which the people at the shelter assured her they would do.

So much for turning our home into a shelter for stray cats.

Back Home To India

We were in the States on our second furlough for just over a year and now it was time to say 'goodbye' to loved ones and friends once again. All six of us could hardly wait to get back 'home' to India. This time we decided to accept a sailing on a P & O ship leaving from Long Beach, California. It meant visiting new places, as we sailed across the Pacific Ocean to Australia and on to Bombay. The first question on our minds, after accepting that sailing was, "How are we going to get out to California?" The cost of traveling across the country, whether by plane, or train, would have been very costly for the six of us. As it was, our tickets to sail on the P & O Arcadia were $500 per adult ticket and by this time we had to purchase three full fares, as well as three half fares. But God had it all planned out for us, so that, in the end, we would travel from Detroit, Michigan to Long Beach, California without any cost to us at all and in a very unique way. A member of our home church had a friend, who operated a 'drive-away' company, in which the company's business consisted of transporting a person's car to wherever that person wanted it to go. While that person would get to that place by flying, their car would be driven by someone else for a certain fee. They didn't want the trouble of driving their car over some long distance and were willing to pay someone else to drive their car for them. That is how we got out to California. When I went to Detroit to the drive-away office the owner of the business informed me that there was a car that needed to be delivered to a resort hotel in Santa Monica. That was close enough for us, for we could deliver the car to its intended destination and then from there get a rental car and drive down to Long Beach, south of Lost Angeles. Also, the convenient thing about leaving from Long Beach to return to India was that I had an aunt and uncle living there, my mother's older sister and her husband, Edith and Loren Blythe; we could stay with them a few days until the Arcadia was ready to sail.

"Could I drive a Chrysler Imperial?" I was asked by the gentleman behind the counter. I thought to myself, " I can drive any kind of a car and if I can't, I sure will learn in a hurry, especially if it is a Chrysler Imperial." I quickly assured the man that, yes, I could drive that Chrysler Imperial. I drove the car back out to Wayne with enough money given me by the manager of the drive-away company to meet all our expenses along the way. The car was loaded with every kind of device that was available at the time for a car in that class. It belonged to a professional golfer. In the trunk of the car was the professional golfer's set of golf clubs in his golf bag. The trunk of the car was huge enough to take, not only his golf clubs, but also all of our baggage. Larger pieces of luggage had already been shipped by freighter and would arrive in Bombay at a later date.

What a trip we had, taking about five days to get to Santa Monica along the famous U.S. Highway 66, much of which does not exist today. After delivering that Chrysler Imperial to the resort hotel in Santa Monica, we picked up the rental car and drove down to Long Beach to my aunt and uncle's home. Unfortunately, some days before we arrived at their house my aunt had suffered a stroke. My uncle informed us that she was not supposed to see visitors. But we insisted on seeing her, even though it might be for a short time. We were glad we went, for she was happy to see us and it seemed to cheer her up. We were not sure of my aunt's spiritual condition, whether she had ever trusted Christ as her own personal Savior. My uncle and aunt were not church going people though they were morally good people, with no vices at all. And yet, we knew that morality was not enough to get a person into heaven. Unfortunately, we were not able to determine her spiritual condition and it was the last time we would see both my aunt and uncle here on earth, for during this next term of service in India both of them died.

Six Weeks Of Adventure By Sea

The P & O passenger liner, Arcadia, would be our home for the next six weeks until we reached Bombay, India. Our trip to Bombay was six weeks of adventure on a luxurious passenger ship, which most people have never experienced. There are some advantages of missionary service in a foreign country. We were returning to serve once again at Sunrise School and as we were on the ship heading back to India, the school was already in session. In order to keep up with their classes each of the girls had to spend a certain amount of time in studies while on the ship, which was certainly not the favorite part of their trip. Each of them faithfully spent a certain amount of time each morning doing their studies. The Arcadia offered many interesting activities in which the girls were free to participate.

On this last trip to India, which we took by ship, our girls were privileged to get an education that went beyond their book studies. Our first port of call was Honolulu, where we spent a full day. We had to go down to Waikiki Beach, of course, as well as see some of the well-known sights of the city. From there it was on to the Fiji Islands, to the capital city of Suva. Before we arrived in Suva we crossed the International Date Line. We went to bed on the night of January 7, 1963 and awakened the next morning on January

9, 1963. Crossing the International Date Line resulted in our losing January 8; rather a weird feeling, to say the least. Not only did we cross the International Date Line, but a few days later we also crossed the Equator and went from the Northern Hemisphere to the Southern Hemisphere where we jumped from the winter season to summer. It was not until we left our last seaport in Australia and headed up toward the Island of Ceylon that we crossed back into the Northern Hemisphere. Each time we crossed the Equator our girls received a special certificate, verifying the fact that they were "hardened sailors," having crossed that invisible dividing line between the Northern and Southern Hemispheres. This in itself was quite an education for all of us.

Before reaching Sydney, Australia we stopped for the better part of a day in Auckland, New Zealand. Our stay there was long enough for us to take a city busy to a large city park at the end of the bus line. That was an unusual experience for us, being in an English-speaking country, yet, our English not being completely understood by the bus driver. Once back on the city bus to return to our ship, we told the driver we wanted to go to the 'docks.' Don't ever use that word when you are speaking to someone from New Zealand, or Australia. The driver didn't understand our American accent and thought we wanted to see some 'ducks' somewhere; he apparently couldn't think of where there would be any ducks on his bus line! When we saw the puzzled look on his face, we all laughed and finally used the word 'wharf', which he understood and assured us that he would get us to our ship in plenty of time before it was ready to sail.

Our ship was tied up for five days in Sydney for refurbishing and some necessary repairs. The Arcadia was now about half way on it's sailing between Long Beach, California and London, England, its final destination. During our five-day stay in Sydney, we rented a VW van, along with another missionary family, the Edmunds who were from Canada and were also returning to India where they served with another mission. During our five days in Sydney, we toured all over the city and into outlying areas. Every day the ship's kitchen crew prepared bag lunches for us. The remainder of our journey back was enjoyable as we stopped at several other ports in Australia and then crossed the Indian Ocean to stop at Columbo, capital city of Ceylon (now known as Sri Lanka). Our travel across the Pacific and on to Bombay was summarized in a letter, in the form of a diary, which we sent back to supporters and family members. Our experiences on that trip were summarized in the following manner:

>Dec. 28 --- A beautiful day, as we board the ARCADIA here in Long Beach.
>This is the start of our five-week (actually it was nearly six weeks) to India via the South Pacific.

>Jan. 2 --- Honolulu! Aloha! These words rang through the air, as we landed at the capital of our 50th state. We spent an enjoyable 12 hours touring this main island of Oahu by rented car. The day is not complete without a swim in Waikiki Beach, the most famous of all the beautiful Hawaiian beaches. A thrilling day for us, to say the least.

>Jan. 9 --- We went to bed on Monday night, the 7th, only to wake up and find ourselves in the 9th. We had crossed the International Date Line; and in doing so, had lost a day in our lives. How strange!

We stop in Suva, capital of the Fiji Islands and find another beautiful tropical paradise. We found many Gujeratis, who had migrated there from India many years before as indentured servants. There is a real spiritual need in this place. Little of the gospel here.

Jan. 15 --- Australia. We shall stop at all of the ports along the southern coast. But here we are in Sydney for about five days. The parks here are just beautiful. A tour of parts of the bush country is a must before we leave. A VW nine-passenger bus is available to rent, along with another missionary family.

Feb. 1 --- Colombo, Ceylon. Our journey is soon over. Today we had a lovely visit with the Rubbishes, a TEAM family on this island. They are carrying on a radio ministry via taped broadcasts coming from Manila, the Philippine Islands.

Feb. 3 --- Bombay! How thrilling to stand again and behold the Gateway of India. We were back home in India again. The Lord was with us as we cleared our things through customs. The customs duty was remarkably low.

How happy we were to be back in India and travel back up country as far as Nasik City, the day after our arrival in Bombay. We pulled into Bombay Harbor on February 3, 1963, after our six-week journey. The girls could hardly wait to see all their friends again. As far as school was concerned, well, that is another story. The welcome shown us by staff and students was beyond our expectations. A large "Welcome" sign on the front of the school building greeted us as we drove through the front gate. All the children at Sunrise School had gathered to sing us a welcome song and then garland us with beautiful flowers.

Back In The Saddle Again

It didn't take us long to get unpacked and back into our responsibilities as houseparents for the boys. Once again, I had the responsibility of teaching the $5^{th} - 7^{th}$ grade classes. We were back in the saddle again! There were always exciting events taking place at Sunrise School. Not all was "humdrum" studies and homework. There were those special Blue Moon Days, as well as birthday parties. In some months there were quite a few birthdays and at such times we always tried to have a special party. The month after we arrived back at school, there were six birthdays to be celebrated all at once. We had written in our diary, "A birthday party for all who have their birthdays this month. 6 birthdays – 6 cakes – and lots of peppermint ice cream! Our deep freezer is really appreciated by all. And no one is tired of too much ice cream, yet."

In 1963 six of our 7th grade students graduated and were ready to enter 8th grade in either the boarding school in Kodaikanal in South India, or Woodstock School in Mussoorie in North India. Three of the girls planned on attending Kodaikanal School, but were not admitted due to lack of space. As a result, our Sunrise School governing board decided to set up a special 8th grade class for these and any others ready to enter that grade. We had planned on enrolling Lily Ann at Woodstock School; in fact, she was already accepted. But with Sunrise adding the 8th grade, we decided to keep her with us and have her begin her studies at Woodstock in the 9th grade. That worked out much better and she was only too glad to stay home for another year.

One of our former Sunrise School teachers was granted a visa to return to teach the 8th grade, while I continued teach 5th – 7th grades. Graduation Day was April 9 for those six girls, including Lily; their motto was, "Not I, but Christ." It was our prayer that Christ would be made known in and through our lives as well.

A New Member Of The Family

Not long after we had returned to India in February 1963, Pal O' Mine, a purebred, black English Cocker spaniel joined our family. I had heard about a litter of pups being available in Bombay from an Anglo-Indian lady, who owned the mother of the pups. The other was a registered spaniel and so, the pups had also been registered with the Kennel Club of India. When I looked at the litter, I was especially attracted to Pal, as he eventually came to be known, and Pal seemed to be attracted to me. He was so small and at six weeks was being weaned from the mother. I took Pal with me back to Nasik where he became the star attraction at Sunrise School. Pal had a very outgoing personality and easily won his way into our hearts. That first hot season back in India, we decided to take our holiday in Mahableshwar, where we had attended the language school to learn Marathi, the language of that part of India. Whenever we went for a walk, we always took Pal with us and carried him in a *pishvee* (a cloth bag usually used for carrying home purchases from the bazaar). Pal seemed quite content to ride that way and when he did, all we could see of Pal was his little head sticking out of the top of the *pishvee*.

Our Animal Menagerie

We had all kinds of pet animals at Sunrise School. At one

time, we had a pair of white geese, which followed the children around wherever they went. Sad to say, one day a stray dog came onto the school property and attacked the female goose, leaving her with a gaping hole in her neck. We were devastated by what happened, but nothing like what her male companion experienced, we are sure. That night I stayed up most of the night, trying to save the goose, but to no avail; by morning she was dead. The male was so heartbroken over the death of his mate that soon after, he too died, no doubt from a broken heart.

We also had rabbits, parrots and parakeets, as well as a village mina bird, who liked to talk. Then there were cats; we never were without a cat all those many years we lived in India. Even though we gave special names to our cats, each one of them, somehow or other, ended up being called by the same name, puss-puss.

One year the mission held its annual conference at the school, while the students were on vacation. This made it possible for the other missionaries to stay in the dormitory rooms. At that time our mother cat was expecting her litter of kittens at any time. Wilma had prepared a special bed for puss-puss inside a floor cabinet in our bathroom, which we introduced her to so that she would know where to go to deliver her babies. One evening, while a meeting was in session over at the school building, puss-puss arrived and began making a special meowing sound letting us know it was her time. We quietly got up from our seats, trying not to disturb the conference in session any more than necessary and followed puss-puss back to our bathroom. Well, puss-puss proceeded to go into the cabinet, lie down on her special bed and delivered her kittens.

We allowed the children to bring their own pets to school,

but one time I made the mistake of telling them they could bring any pets they wanted to, with the exception of snakes! One day, some of the boys came to us, carrying several small pups. Where had they found those pups? When the boys informed me they had found the pups under a small bush not far from the school, I told them they had to take the pups back to where they had found them. "But Uncle Ken," one of the boys replied, "you told us we could bring any kind of pets to school we wanted to." While this remark left me somewhat speechless, Wilma quickly came up with a solution to the whole problem. "Do you boys realize that maybe the mother left those pups under the bush and has returned to find her babies gone and is frantically looking for them right now?" Needless to say, the boys returned the pups to the small bush, feeling quite sorry for the mother, who had apparently left them under the bush, thinking them to be quite safe there while she went off to find some food for herself.

A Difficult Decision

During our second furlough I was involved in a discussion group of the mission, with mission officials and representatives from various fields of the mission around the world. It was during that meeting that I came to realize there was a conflict of policies between the mission and what we believed were biblical principles. This initiated in our minds the decision that, perhaps, it was time to stand upon certain convictions, resulting in the possibility of resigning from the mission. We began praying about the whole matter, while deciding, until the Lord gave us very clear directions, we would return to India to continue serving at Sunrise School. Two years later we were to make another major change in our lives and ministry. After much prayer and waiting on the Lord, we had total peace of mind and heart about resigning from the mission. It was a difficult decision to make, for we had many friends serving with the mission and had been with them for over fifteen years. We had a very rich ministry and God had blessed us in so many ways. During the hot season of 1964 we traveled up to Mussoorie, located in the foothills of the Himalayan Mountains of North India. There at over 7,000 feet altitude we spent six weeks away from the intense heat of the plains. While there we met John and Cora Wilkens who were serving with Baptist Mid-Missions in the eastern state of Assam. We discussed with the Wilkens about the mission and after much prayer, became convinced that BMM was the mission that God now wanted us to serve with. It was shortly after we returned to Sunrise School in Nasik City that we began correspondence with the chairman of BMM's Assam Field Council, Fred Waldock. After some correspondence between Fred and us the decision was made to formally apply to the mission. We were accepted by the Assam Field Council on what was called a Watch-Care basis; this was necessary until we could return to the States and go through the process of meeting with BMM's General Council for their interview and examination. In the meantime, it was agreed that we would continue serving with the other mission until the end of the school year in April 1965. During all this time we are thankful there were no personality conflicts and no personal bitterness against anyone in the mission. We are happy to say that we are very good friends of former co-workers of ours during the 15 years of service we had in India with that mission. While the parting of ways was difficult in some ways, we did not regret having taken that step.

Slipping On The Proverbial Banana Peel

We were in the process of packing up all our belongings in

preparation of our move to the mountain resort of Mussoorie, located in the foothills of the Himalayan Mountains, where we would live for the next twelve years, when our oldest daughter, Lily Ann returned to Nasik during a short break at Woodstock where she was then in 9th grade. Wilma had gone to Bombay to meet her coming with a school party on the train. As she walked along the train platform, waiting for the train to arrive, she slipped on a banana peel, lying on the platform. She did not realize it at the time, but the fall had caused a fracture in her elbow. Though the pain was quite excruciating, Wilma passed it off as just a bad fall, causing a bruised elbow and so, nothing was done about the matter at the time. A few days after Wilma and Lily Ann arrived back at Sunrise School the pain was so bad we decided to have Dr. Ramdas look at Wilma's elbow. He let us know that she had fractured her elbow and that the fracture was a clean one. Dr. Ramdas was able to put her elbow and arm in a plaster cast and suggested that the cast would probably have to remain for up to a couple of months.

We had packed up all our personal belongings, including furniture, which was to accompany us when we traveled from Nasik to Mussoorie, several days' journey by train. The day we were to say goodbye to our friends at Sunrise School and get on the train Wilma decided she didn't want the cast on her arm any longer. By this time nearly a month had gone by since the cast had been put on. Surely her arm was all healed by then and would I please take it off. According to Dr. Ramdas, there were still several weeks that the cast should stay on. But Wilma insisted that I should remove it. After much persuasion, I finally cut the cast off with a pair of scissors. The arm looked just fine and Wilma felt very relieved to have that heavy plaster cast removed.

When we went to the train station to get our train to Bombay, Wilma remarked, "I hope Dr. Ramdas doesn't come to the station and see me without the cast. Would you know it, that is just what happened. Dr. Ramdas showed up at the station to see his daughter, Sheila, off on the same train. We were sitting in our private compartment in the train, Wilma sitting right by the open window, when who should come walking past, but Dr. Ramdas. Before he could see Wilma's arm, she quickly covered it. When he saw us he stopped to chat for a while and during the whole time he did not once ask about her arm and elbow. Her elbow was none the worse for my having removed the plaster cast before it was due to come off, for it gave Wilma no further problems and hasn't to this day. Dr. Ramdas had done a good job.

+ The Goal Before Us +

We leave for India on the S.S. Steel King
September 30, 1947

Our First Home in India - a 100-year-old house
made of mud bricks
The years - 1950-1952

Heading out to a village to preach the gospel in
our 1942 Ford jeep
The years -1952-1955

Our *mali* brings us water from the well
The years - 1952-1955

Co-co, our water buffalo gave us delicious milk
The year - 1953

Our church building where we worshipped at
Yaval
The years - 1952-1955

Our church congregation at Yaval
The years - 1952-1955

Our four daughters call this
their "orphans" picture
The year - 1958

Part Six: A Major Change

June, 1965 - May, 1976

God's Perfect Way

Psalm 1:3

When we commit our way to Him, it becomes His way
Then we can be sure that whether it is joy or sorrow.
Sunshine or clouds, health, or sickness, plenty or want,
His way for us Is perfect. We cannot doubt that.
He sees the end from the beginning. He sees the pattern
He is working out in our lives and will not make one
mistake.
We may not understand it, but he does. That is enough."

--- Millie Stamm in "Be Still & Know"
Daily Devotional Readings
Zondervan Publishing House

Our New Ministry with Baptist Mid-Missions

At the time we were accepted by Baptist Mid-Missions on the Watch-Care basis it was not possible for us to go Assam. There had been much tension between the Government of India and certain tribes in that part of the country. As a result, except for those missionaries who were presently serving in Assam, the government was not allowing any new missionaries to enter Assam and adjoining states on a permanent basis. Dr. and Mrs. Galen Crozier began our BMM work in Assam, India in 1936. He had no sooner arrived in the hills of Alipur than word spread amongst the people that a doctor from America had come. There waiting on the hill for Dr. Crozier saw a man with leprosy waiting to be treated. It was not long after Dr. Crozier opened a dispensary that people with leprosy began gathering at the dispensary also seeking to be cured of this terrible disease. It became evident that a special place for leprosy patients needed to be opened. Word reached our missionaries that a tea estate was for sale some distance away in the jungle. And so began Makunda leprosy hospital. Special shelters for the patients were constructed, as was a hospital building. Nurses helped in the care of the patients until Dr. and Mrs. Gene Burrows arrived with their two children, a daughter and a son, in 1958. In time God blessed the Burrows with five more daughters. Not long after the Burrows began their medical ministry at Makunda treatment of the leprosy patients was extended to surgery and more modern care as the facilities were enlarged and improved upon. As the Burrows children grew older Bette Burrows began teaching the children. But this placed an increased burden on her in addition to her responsibilities in the hospital; especially in the nursing school they were now operating. Dr. Gene Burrows had graduated from Woodstock School in Mussoorie, for his own father, Dr. L.

I. Burrows had come to Assam to serve alongside Dr. Crozier in those early days. The Burrows decided that if a boarding home could be opened by the mission they would send their seven children to Woodstock.

In addition to the Burrows, Dr. and Mrs. Quentin Kenoyer were now in charge of the hospital at Alipur. Their three oldest children, two sons and a daughter, were in high school at Woodstock, while the two younger daughters were being home schooled in Alipur. Also, Fred and Dorothy Waldock were involved in church planting ministry in nearby Silchar where they also had begun a Christian bookstore. The Waldocks had three sons studying at Woodstock and their two youngest children, daughters, were also being home schooled.

Woodstock was operated by a number of missions, including well-known old line denominations, along with a number of evangelical missions. Baptist Mid-Missions had one missionary serving on the school board at the time. Because of the fact that we could not get permission from the Indian government to live in Assam, it was decided that we should be assigned to serve on the staff at Woodstock. The school had been looking for teaching staff in both the elementary and high school departments, as well as residence supervisors. Paul and Genella Versluis were some of our other missionaries serving in Assam, but Genella eventually was asked to be supervisor of the elementary girls residence, which was located in the main part of the school campus. Wilma was asked to serve as supervisor of the high school girls' residence, Midlands, while I began teaching high school algebra and geometry. We had a lovely apartment on the main floor of Midlands with our three daughters, Kathy, Gloria and Phyllis. It was an ideal situation. By this time, our oldest daughter, Lily

Ann, had graduated from high school back in the States and had begun her first year of Bible college

Life At Woodstock School

Life at Woodstock School certainly was not boring. Our responsibilities kept us busy nearly round-the-clock. As supervisor of the high school girls' residence at Midlands, Wilma had a multitude of duties. Not only did she have to see to the comfort of each resident, but also felt a responsibility toward their safety and welfare. With upwards of 85 high school girls to care for, it was not all that easy to keep everyone contented. Internal conflicts had to be resolved, not always to the satisfaction of all involved.

Every morning, after the girls left for their classes, Wilma would check each room for neatness. It was not unusual for our black cocker spaniel, Pal, to go around with her to each room, sometimes making pretence of inspecting the rooms for himself. One morning he found a piece of paper lying on the floor; picking up the crumpled-up paper in his mouth, he gave it to Wilma, as though to say, "See what you missed!"

It wasn't long after we settled into our apartment at Midlands when Pal discovered a female cocker, belonging to another couple on the staff at Woodstock School and who lived in staff quarters just below Midlands. One afternoon the lady of the house arrived home from school to find Pal at their apartment. With a stern-sounding voice, she told Pal to go home. With his tail between his legs, he turned and headed around the corner of the staff quarters on his way back to our apartment. He never made it. We were told later that immediately after Pal went around the corner, there was a sharp noise and then all was silent. When our fellow staff member went to see what had happened, she found no sign of Pal, but there were leopard pug marks on the ground; nothing else. We had been aware of the fact that there was a female leopard, with one crippled paw, which was known to hang around the area. The only thing we could conclude was that Pal became supper for one hungry crippled female leopard. We were to meet that leopard later on.

Crisis At Midlands

A crisis arose one night when it was discovered that one of the high school girls had left school and simply disappeared. No one seemed to know where she had gone. Had she been abducted, attacked, was she still alive? What happened to her? It was about eleven o'clock that night when the phone rang; it was the high school girl, calling from the railway station in Old Delhi. She had fled to Delhi for reasons unknown to us at the time. We did not ask her what her reasons were for running away to Delhi. Our immediate concern was to see to her safety. There was a desperate tone to her voice and she needed help fast. We told her to stay just where she was and there would be someone who would come to her rescue. We quickly hung up, got our clothes on and raced up the hill to Canon Burgoyne, the school principal's house. It didn't take long to rouse him and tell him that we had located the runaway student. Canon Burgoyne quickly got on his telephone and rang a number in New Delhi, to friends of the school. Somehow they heard their phone ring, even though it was located outside their bedroom where they had the air conditioner running. It wasn't long before they made it to the train station to find one desperate and lonely high school student. Taking her home with them to stay the rest of the night, arrangements were soon made to get her back to Woodstock the next day. Needless to say, she was a very repentant young lady, who made a rash decision only to find herself alone in a city very much foreign in culture, amongst strangers and whose language she did not understand.

Friday Evenings At Midlands

Friday evenings at Midlands were always an exciting time for high school students. The girls knew our apartment was open to them for informal social times. The boys would come over from their residence and bring cake mixes they had received in parcels from home. What a time we had as two or three cake mixes were baking almost at the same time. We cooked with a propane gas hot plate and put a portable oven on top to do our baking. We seemed to go through one tin of hot chocolate every Friday evening. We enjoyed having the students in our apartment and tried to make it a home-away-from-home for any who showed up at our doorstep.

Spit Wads On The Ceiling

I was on the teaching staff at Woodstock, where I taught 9th grade algebra and 10th grade geometry. In addition, I was asked to teach a junior high shop class in woodworking. The school had a large and well-equipped workshop with a fine array of power tools. It was fun teaching that class and enjoyed having access to all the tools so that I was able to do some personal projects. One of my algebra students was quite a challenge and loved to carry out pranks, which one day, sad to say, would be his final undoing resulting in his tragic death. During one algebra class, the last class in the day, the student in question was shooting spit wads, which stuck on the ceiling of the classroom. I knew early in the class hour just what he was up to and decided to see how long he would keep up his prank. It continued through most of the class period. When the last bell rang I asked my "challenging" student to wait behind until the rest of the students had left. I revealed to him that I knew what he was up to and that he had to remove every one of those spit wads that had stuck to the ceiling. The classroom was located at the back of the school auditorium, Parker Hall. Fortunately, a tall stepladder was leaning against a wall nearby. With the use of the ladder, he was able to reach the ten-foot high ceiling and undo all the fun he had during the algebra class that day. We didn't say anything about the incident to anyone else. You can be sure, he didn't try that prank ever again, at least while he was in my algebra class.

Life In Mussoorie

Mussoorie is located in the foothills of the Himalayan Mountains of North India, at about 7,000 feet above sea level. Some of the students would prepare their backpacks with supplies and hike back into some of the higher mountains to the north for the weekend; they would leave right after classes were finished on Friday afternoon, returning to school Sunday afternoon.

One place we liked to hike to was a village about eight miles away from school on the road to Tehri City. We especially liked to hike out there on a full moon, which took us nearly two hours each way, all for the purpose of waking up a tea stall owner to have him brew a kettle of delicious hot tea. We came to enjoy, not only Indian food with all its spices, but also Indian tea. Tea is prepared with full cream milk and lots of sugar, all boiled in together with the tea. Then there are added certain spices, such as cardamom seed and whole cinnamon. How delicious it is! The eight-mile hike was well worth the effort to pay a few pennies for a delicious cup of *chai* (tea).

One challenging hike would be to take a 'bee line' down the mountain to the market town of Dehra Dun, which was 22 miles by way of the serpentine road; straight down the mountain was only about half the distance. Walking down the mountain was enough of a challenge, for it would take us at least 5-6 hours to hike that distance. We always took the bus back to Mussoorie.

Winter Holiday In Assam

All of the buildings at Woodstock School were of stone, with most of the ceilings ten feet high. There was no way to heat the buildings during the coldest time of the cold season. Because of this, the school's long vacation was during the coldest time of the year, with "Going Down Day" being in November. School would begin again near the end of February. As mentioned already, we had been accepted by Baptist Mid-Missions on a provisional basis until it was possible for us to meet with the General Council of the Mission. During our first winter in Mussoorie we traveled to Assam, where our BMM missionaries were serving in various ministries. There we would meet most of our fellow missionaries for the first time.

Assam is located in a part of India that lies between what was then known as East Pakistan (now the independent nation of Bangladesh) to the west and the Indian tribal states of Manipur and Nagaland. To the east of these two tribal states is Myanmar (formerly Burma). Assam, along with several tribal states lying to the east of Bangladesh, is joined to the main part of India by a narrow corridor of some 20 miles. The only way to get to Assam is by flying from Calcutta, India's largest city. On our trip to Assam that winter, we took a train from Delhi to Calcutta, where we stayed overnight at the YMCA Guest House, located in the very heart of the city. The next morning we went out to the airport by taxi and there caught one of the old Dakota (DC 3) planes. At that time, everything that went onto the plane had to be weighed. Not only the baggage, but even the passengers and crew had to be weighed. Our flight took us across East Pakistan, with a stop at the jungle village of Agartala; from there it was but a short hop to our journey's end at Silchar, head town of Cachar District where some of our Baptist Mid-Missions ministries were located.

During the two months we were in Assam, we stayed out at Banskandi, which was quite some distance from the town of Silchar and across a small river. The only way to get across the river was by a small ferry, which the ferry driver pushed across to the other side with the aid of a long bamboo pole. The ferry was just large enough to contain two small vehicles and several foot passengers. While we were staying in Banskandi, I became very ill and had to return to Alipur, where Dr. and Mrs. Quentin Kenoyer served as medical supervisor and nursing school director, respectively. Dr. Kenoyer ran a number of tests, which showed that I had a severe case of nephritis, a kidney disorder. After several days of rest and treatment, I was able to return to Banskandi, where we remained for most of the rest of our time in Assam. During my time of recuperation from nephritis, I received daily injections of penicillin, which eventually caused an allergy reaction to the drug that remains with me to this day. I'm thankful that the infection in my kidneys cleared up before it was time for us to return to Mussoorie.

Jaundiced!

Shortly after having arrived back at Woodstock School and classes had begun, I once again took ill. This time it was much more serious than the problem with nephritis. I had come down with infectious hepatitis, commonly referred to as "jaundice," because of the yellow appearance of the skin and whites of the eyes. I had gone down to Dehradun on my motor scooter to do a bit of shopping and brought back with me a box of fresh eggs, which I had tied onto the back rack of the scooter. Midlands, the high school girls' residence, where we had our apartment, was located at a lower level from the main school campus. Because of that I had to always leave my scooter at the upper level of the school. That day I parked the scooter and proceeded to carry the small box of eggs down to our apartment at Midlands. The box seemed so heavy and my pace down the steep path was much slower than normal. Little did I realize at the time what the real problem was.

A day or two later, we were sitting at the dining room table having our lunch, when Wilma looked at me and remarked that I looked yellow. My reply was that it must be a reflection of the yellow plastic table cloth' "No," she answered, "You really do look yellow; go look at yourself in the bathroom mirror." Sure enough, my skin was yellowish in color and so were my eyes. I was jaundiced! Wilma suggested that I should have a *dandee* take me up to the hospital. A *dandee* is a boat-shaped, canvas covered seat, which had a yoke in front and one in back, so that four coolies could carry the *dandee* and its passenger. I begged off the *dandee*, telling Wilma I would walk up to the hospital; it wasn't that far, really. But the walk up the hill to the hospital was much farther and slower than what I thought it would be. A walk that ordinarily took only about fifteen minutes ended up taking nearly hour. Upon arriving at the hospital I asked the receptionist to see the doctor. I was told to sit in the waiting room and the doctor would come to look at me shortly. When he walked into the room and looked at me, he knew at a glance what my problem was. His only remark was, "Ken, stay away from me; sit down in that chair. You have jaundice!" I was admitted as soon as they were able to find a bed for me. I stayed at the hospital for nearly three weeks until I had gained enough strength to stay in bed at home with Wilma as my nurse.

During six weeks of bed rest at the hospital and home a substitute had to be found to teach my classes at school. I was still very weak from my bout with jaundice, but was anxious to get back to my classes. I knew that at the beginning it would not be wise for me to walk up to school. For the first week I was taken up to school in the morning and brought back down to Midlands in the afternoon in a *dandee*. The following week I rode up to school in the morning in a *dandee* and after my last class in the afternoon I was able to walk back down the hill to Midlands. By the third week at teaching, I was able to walk up to school and then back down in the afternoon. But it would take me nearly an hour to walk up that long hill to school and about half an hour to walk back down. It was a slow process, but gradually, I was able to carry on a regular schedule as I did before those two illnesses of nephritis and hepatitis hit me. I was thankful, most of all, that there had been no damage to both my kidneys and liver, which could have happened, had I not received the medical attention I did. That walk up to Landour Community Hospital could have damaged my liver permanently resulting in other still more serious complications. It took me about six months from the time I came down with the infectious hepatitis, until I felt like my old normal self and able to walk up and down the hills of

Mussoorie like a healthy person, acclimatized to the altitude and up and down walking. Everything in Mussoorie is either up, or down. Nothing is on the level there, except the main part of the Mussoorie bazaar. By this time I had had my share of sicknesses in a land where my mother, so many years before had told me that I would get sick and die from some disease if we persisted in going to India. She was nearly right about that possibility. There were yet other illnesses and other crises that both of us would experience, while still in India.

War in India

In 1966 we saw the first of two wars between India and Pakistan, all over each one's claim to Kashmir, to the far north. Kashmir borders on China and Tibet to the north, with part of it controlled by India and part by Pakistan. The concern to us at that time was that Mussoorie was well within striking distance of the Pakistani air force and one of India's main communication centers was located on a point above the school. As the war began, we were under strict orders to make sure not even one sliver of light should be seen from any window at school. The problem we had with covering up the windows at Midlands was that there were many windows in the building. The school bought up every piece of black paper available in the local market and even then there was not enough black paper to cover up every window on the school campus. We had to devise other means to prevent that one sliver of light to be seen. One night we received a phone call from an observer in the bazaar a short distance away, who told us that he could see light coming from Midlands. We located the spot from where the light had been seen and in no time had it covered. During those tense days of uncertainty, there was concern about the few students we had from Pakistan who were children of missionaries serving in that country. There was no way we could communicate with their parents. There had been some discussion as to whether we should evacuate those particular students to the States, but in the end, it was decided that everyone should stay right there and hope that we would all be safe. We had hoped that somehow or other the school could get messages through to the missionary parents in Pakistan assuring them that their children were safe. Fortunately, the war did not last very many days and we were soon back to living normal lives with the windows all clear of any black paper, allowing the sun to shine through the windows once again. We were also glad we could get back to a normal school schedule once again.

Tibetan Refugees in Mussoorie

The Chinese had claimed "suzerainty rights" (sovereignty) over Tibet for many years. It was in 1949 that the Chinese army marched into Lhasa, Tibet's capital, and took over control of the government. Pressure was brought to bear on the Dalai Lama to yield to the Chinese any rights he claimed and having the Tibetan people recognize the Chinese authority over their land. The Dalai Lama is the spiritual head of all Tibetan Buddhists and is highly revered by Tibetans, whether living in Tibet itself, or the many, who now find themselves as refugees in India, as well as many other countries of the world. Ten years later, in 1959, there was an uprising by the Tibetans in the capital city of Lhasa, at which time the Dalai Lama, under advice of his cabinet, fled Lhasa in the middle of the night. There fled with him many other Tibetans, both young and old. They managed to elude the Chinese army and find their way through a number of mountain passes and finally, into India, eventually ending up in Mussoorie. The Dalai Lama was not allowed to remain in Mussoorie because of the friendship pact India had with China at the time. He was allowed to settle on the plains of North India at a place called Dharmsala. A large Tibetan community remained in Mussoorie and with the gold that the fleeing Tibetans had brought with them, were able to get settled in Mussoorie, set up businesses and build a private school for their youth, who had trekked those many miles out of Tibet with the women and old men.

Reaching Tibetans for Christ

Irma Jean Wessells, a single missionary lady with TEAM, became burdened to reach Tibetans for Christ and began an outreach amongst them, especially the teen-age girls. In time, she opened a hostel for the girls and, in time, saw a number of them come to trust Christ as their own personal Savior. There were others also, who began to witness to the Tibetans and among them were Elcho and Millie Redding. God blessed their efforts as they saw numbers of young men also place their faith in Christ.

During our second summer break at Woodstock School, I taught a class of Tibetan children at a camp at Deodars Conference Center, directed by Olaf and Helen Dubland. One evening, as I was getting a group of young boys settled in for the night and reading to them from the Bible, one little lad, who was sitting on my lap, looked up at me and said, with much feeling, "Uncle, I love Jesus, but I love the Dalai Lama too." Oh how my heart ached for that little lad, as I did for each and every boy in that room. How could I make them understand that only through Jesus could they ever find everlasting life, while, at the same time, get them to understand that this one they revered so much, was not a god, but just an ordinary person like they were. Yes, revere him as their national leader, but not as a god. The only one to whom they should give their love and devotion to was to the Lord Jesus Christ, Who alone is God. I have often wondered where those boys are now, grown into manhood. Have any of them come to a saving faith in Christ and Christ alone?

During the following winter vacation, we were asked to keep two Tibetan teen-age girls. This was a new experience for our whole family. Our girls were in agreement that we should open our home to these two girls from Tibet, who were refugee students at the nearby Wynberg Allen School, another Christian boarding school on the hillside and about an hour's walk from Woodstock. Ngawang and Tsimchung came to stay with us during the winter break. In the meantime, we had planned on taking a trip that winter back to Nasik City and visit all our friends at Sunrise School. And so, it was that eight of us traveled for two days on the train, some eleven hundred miles. It was an enjoyable trip and quite an experience for Ngawang and Tsimchung, who had fled with many other Tibetans from their country in 1959 to escape the Chinese army that invaded Tibet.

We had come to find out that these two girls had never had a bath or shower, as most Tibetans do not. And so, it was Wilma's job to teach them about bathing and keeping clean and smelling nice. Tibet is generally a cold country and the people wear heavy long robes the year round. Water also seems to be scarce in that mountain country and so; the people would confine their bathing to only the exposed parts of their bodies, their faces and hands. It was not long before Ngawang and Tsimchung fitted right into our family life and participated in all our family activities. We were glad for the short time they were with us, for they heard the gospel message, as they must also have heard it during those years they were students at Wynberg Allen School, a school mainly for Indian and Anglo-Indian students.

Ministry Opportunities in Mussoorie

During the second semester of our first year at Woodstock School, I was not only teaching up to five hours a day at Woodstock, but on Sundays I was visiting pastor at the Northern Railway School for workers' children. Every Sunday morning I went down to Oak Grove School on my scooter. During the hot season I was also teacher of the adult Sunday school class at Kellogg Church, where many missionaries, who were in Mussoorie to escape the heat of the plains, attended. The local officials in Mussoorie closed the road through the bazaar after 9 a.m. and with the service finished at 8:30 a.m. at Oak Grove School, I had to hurriedly drive back up the mountain and through the bazaar before the road closed to vehicular traffic. I was very glad for those opportunities to preach and teach, especially at Oak Grove School, for I was sure that even though the staff and student called themselves Christians, most of them were really not saved.

Meeting the General Council

We decided that we should go on furlough right after the second semester classes were finished in the second week of July in 1967. We had been back in India just over four years at the time. Our plans were to meet with the General Council of Baptist Mid-Missions at the July tri-annual conference to be held at Emmanuel Baptist Church in Toledo, Ohio from July 11-17. What a time we had winding up affairs at Woodstock School. I had final exams for my students to prepare and administer. Wilma had to turn over responsibilities at the high school girls' residence in Midlands. There was packing up of things we would be storing while gone on furlough, selling of things we didn't want to keep, arranging booking of our flight back to the States, getting our No-Objection-to-Return endorsements in our passports by the Indian officials and a myriad of other things too numerous to mention. July 12, 1967 found us back in the States after a 24-hour flight from New Delhi to Detroit, Michigan.

This was a difficult time for Lily, in that she had just completed her 11th grade at Woodstock and had to say goodbye to friends of many years and goodbye to her first home, India, possibly never to return to India again. She would be doing her last year of high school in the States and then going on to college. It turned out that she would return to India later on, that time to get married.

Wilma's parents had sold their home of many years in Belleville, Michigan and moved to Oak Ridge, Tennessee, where Wilma's sister and husband, Sylvia and Bob Rice, lived. Bob worked for the government at the Oak Ridge center for atomic research and development. My in-laws had moved there to be near at least some of family, inasmuch as they couldn't be near us in India. They had driven up from Oak Ridge to meet us upon our arrival from India, so that they could keep the girls, while we attended the BMM tri-annual conference in Toledo, Ohio.

Upon arriving at the conference, we met with an examining committee of the General Council, in order to answer questions as to our joining Baptist Mid-Missions. We thought they would ask us questions having to do with our beliefs, that is, doctrinal questions; but we were surprised by their interest in us as to why we had resigned from the other mission and wanted to become a part of the BMM family. From what I can remember, they did ask Wilma a couple of doctrinal questions, one of which she had hesitated in giving her answer. At the time one of the members of the committee said that they wouldn't be very concerned about it, because "Ken would straighten her out if she was in error." We had a wonderful time during the hour we sat with the council members and later were informed that we had passed with flying colors and accepted into the mission. After the tri-annual conference we traveled down to Cedarville, Ohio to attend two weeks of orientation at the BMM candidate seminar, which was held on the campus of Cedarville College. There were many younger couples and single men and women attending the seminar, who were also appointees. In fact, Wilma and I were the "senior" couple, having already served on the mission field for some fifteen years. One part of the seminar was that we had to take a test to see if we had the capability of learning another language, other than our mother tongue of English. Needless to say, we both passed the test. But then, we had learned the Marathi language and used it for those years we had been in India. When we moved up to Mussoorie, to serve at Woodstock School, we took an intensive course of study in Hindi, the national language of India.

The following months, after candidate seminar was finished, there was much travel, visiting family and supporting churches. We had obtained a vehicle to use during our furlough time and the Lord provided a comfortable place for us to stay on furlough. An older couple in our home church in Wayne, Michigan had a basement suite, which was very adequate for our family. By September we had arranged for the girls to attend local public schools. Lily was in 12th grade and would graduate from high school the following June. Kathy was in 9th grade and attended a nearby junior high school, as did Gloria, who was in 7th grade. Phyllis attended the elementary school, which was only about two blocks away from where we were staying and was in 5th grade. School life in the States was very different for our girls; it was not India, for one thing. Also, they were not used to going to a public school. When we returned to India the following year, Lily remained behind to begin her first year of studies at Bryan College in Dayton, Tennessee. Kathy, Gloria and Phyllis were only too glad to go back "home", back to India and back to Woodstock School in Mussoorie. That was their real home, as far as they were concerned.

While the girls were in school, Wilma did not travel with me in meetings, for she had to be at home for the girls. I didn't enjoy traveling by myself, but knew it had to be done. We were far short of the support amount set by Baptist Mid-Missions, for when we were to return to India for our first full term of service with our new mission. It was necessary for me to arrange as many meetings as possible, hoping to raise the needed support. Most of my travel was by car and during our year on furlough, I drove many miles.

Mother's Homegoing

During those first two years we were on the staff at Woodstock School in Mussoorie, my mother was not well. News came to us on more than one occasion that she had suffered a stroke. Little did we know at the time that the Lord would take her to heaven at the beginning of 1968. I happened to be home with the rest of the family at the time a phone call came from my older brother, Warren. "Ken, I think you had better come as soon as possible. Mother is in the hospital and I don't think she has much longer to live." I was able to catch a flight from Detroit to Minneapolis the next morning and shortly after arriving in Minneapolis, I rented a car and drove right to Northwestern Hospital, where Mother had been taken. She looked very pale and weak, and though she recognized me, it was difficult for her to speak. In fact, I had to put my ear close to her to hear what she was saying. She was actually not saying anything to me, but, rather, was trying to say Romans 8:28. Her pastor, Dr. Richard V. Clearwaters had been trying to get her to memorize Scripture and she had, apparently committed this verse to memory. Dr. Clearwaters was my pastor when I came to know Christ as my own personal Savior on that cold Saturday night in January, exactly twenty-six years before. As I listened, Mother began to say in a very weak and hesitating voice, "For I know that all things work together for good to them that love God..." That was all the farther she got, for she seemed to have slipped off into a coma. Those were the last words I heard from Mother. The rest of the family was not there at the time. How precious that memory has been to me over these many years. Knowing that she had not been in agreement with my going to India as a missionary, I believe that at the end of her earthly life, she had surrendered her second son to the Lord. She was happy with that surrender, as eternity will one day reveal it to us.

The next day Mother slipped away from our presence and into the very presence of the Lord she had first come to trust as her own personal Savior that Sunday morning in 1942. She is buried in the military cemetery at Fort Snelling on the far south side of Minneapolis, for Dad had been in the army during World War I. He was to be buried beside her nearly seven years later. It was very hard on Dad, for he had come to depend on Mother in many ways. There came into my possession some years later something that Dad had written about Mother. At the beginning he wrote, "Before I review almost forty-five years of married life with my darling wife, I might explain that since she left her earthly home to be in her heavenly home, I would be cruel and without love to wish her back with me, when our Lord wanted her to be with Him. Although I miss her and I cry so much when I see so many things around the house that remind me of her, I am happy that the one I loved so dearly is in her heavenly home, waiting for me." What a happy reunion that must have been when God took Dad in December 1974.

Mother was one who always saved things about her sons, of whom she was very proud. Because of that, much of what I have been able to write about my early life, I have been able to do so, because of what she kept stored in boxes in her closet. We found many letters I had written home from my college days, even a letter I wrote as a small boy while at Boy Scout camp. Those prize-winning essays I had written, while in high school were found in one of the boxes. While going through all her things, after Mother's funeral, I came across pictures, which I never knew existed. They all tell a story and some of those pictures are included in these memoirs.

Another Mother's Surrender

A few days after my mother's body had been laid to rest in the Fort Snelling military cemetery, I said goodbye to Dad and left to return to our furlough home in Wayne, Michigan. Not long after, I had meetings at our supporting church in Gary, Indiana, Grace Baptist Church. That Sunday morning I preached a message entitled, "The Cost of Discipleship." I gave testimony concerning my mother, of her struggle to let me go to India, where she thought I would die from a terrible disease, or be killed by some wild animal. I challenged mothers in the congregation, who might be holding onto their sons in a selfish manner, not wanting God's will to be done in their lives. At the end of the message, I gave an invitation for such mothers to come forward, in testimony that they were, right then and there, surrendering their son to the Lord. There were several mothers who came forward, in response to the invitation. They came, tears flowing down their faces, publicly confessing their sin of selfishness. Little did I know at the time what relationship the son of one of those mothers would have with our third daughter, Gloria a few years later. But that is another story that will have to wait, a story, which would end, humanly speaking, with tragic results.

A New Ministry Assignment

While we were on furlough, just prior to our return to India in July 1968, we received a letter from our India Field Council, telling us of their plan to open a private boarding for our BMM children who were studying at Woodstock School. This is just what the Burrows and our other missionaries had felt was needed for several years before. The missionaries in Assam were willing to also take in students from other missions, which would help to pay the expenses of operating such a boarding home. Arrangements were made with the Assembly of God Mission to rent Claremont, a large house on the hillside which that mission owned, but was not using at the time. We prayed about the matter and God gave us total peace and assurance that this was what He wanted us to do during our next term of service. When we eventually arrived back in Mussoorie, we came to find out there were a lot of renovations which needed to be done before we could begin BMM's boarding home at Claremont.

More Travel Adventures

There was never a time in all our travels to and from India, but what we were caught up in one unusual situation or another. On July 20, 1968 we flew from New York to Rome, Italy on a Trans World Airlines Boeing 707 jetliner. Our flight across the Atlantic went smoothly and it was not until the next day, when we arrived in Beirut, Lebanon on a plane of Italy's national airline, Alitalia, at which time we discovered one of our suitcases was missing. The suitcase had arrived in Rome, along with our other baggage; but something happened to it in Rome. Whether it was stolen, or missing for some other reason, it did not arrive with us in Beirut. We immediately lodged a complaint and filed a claim in writing, with Alitalia authorities in Beirut; but we received no reply, or satisfaction at that point in time. It was not until many months later that Alitalia made payment for our loss. In the meantime, there was nothing we could do but continue on with our journey from Beirut to New Delhi, India. We felt very badly about the loss of the suitcase, for it contained a number of personal things of our daughters, things which could not be replaced for any amount of money. In addition, we had packed into the missing suitcase a single bore 12-gauge shotgun, which we were taking to India for a special purpose. Wilma's uncle, Ivan LaVoy had given us the shotgun to take with us to India to give to some villager in exchange for his old muzzleloader shotgun. Uncle Ivan had been looking for such a shotgun to add to his collection of old guns. With the loss of the suitcase, that hope of his was not to be fulfilled. As far as our trip back to India was concerned, the loss of the suitcase was not the end of our adventures; there was more to come.

The parents of one of our boarding students, Keith Joyce, were living in Beirut at the time. Ray and Mona Joyce had a literature ministry to the Muslims in the Middle East. We stayed with the Joyces for a couple of days flying from Beirut to New Delhi, India on a newly established route by Japan Airlines (JAL). But when we called the JAL office in Beirut to confirm our flight, we were informed that JAL was intending to fly that route, but had not yet started. Someone had certainly made a mistake in setting up our travel arraignments. Now what were we to do? It seemed as though we were stuck in Beirut, Lebanon for a while. Ray Joyce suggested that we should consult with a Lebanese Christian friend of theirs, who was a travel agent in Beirut. What an answer to our prayers! There was great relief, when the Joyces' travel agent friend was able to transfer us over to a Middle East Airways flight from Beirut to Karachi, Pakistan the next morning. From Karachi we would then catch a Pan American flight to New Delhi, arriving there not long after we would have, had we flown directly from Beirut to New Delhi. Ah, but our adventures were still not finished. There was more to come!

We made the MEA flight to Karachi with no problem. The connection between flights was very close. In fact, upon landing in Karachi, we found that the Pan Am plane was already on the tarmac, ready to take off. The captain of that flight, received word that there was an American family coming in on a MEA flight from Beirut and he consented to wait until we arrived. As soon as we disembarked from our MEA plane, we were rushed by coach out to the Pan American 707 jet, along with our baggage. We found that we had to climb up a long flight of steps to get into the plane waiting for us. As soon as the five of us were in the plane, seated and belted up, ready for the plane to take off and our baggage loaded into the plane's baggage compartment, the pilot began to start all four engines. Here is where the next trouble happened. One of the engines would not start. Before long the other three engines were shut down and there we sat, a plane full of passengers, wondering what was happening. No lights, no air conditioning, nothing. There we sat for several hours, while someone was deciding what to do next. Eventually the captain announced to us over the loudspeaker as to what happened and told us that we were to all get off the plane. They would take us into the city to a hotel, there to wait until the engine was repaired and we could fly on to New Delhi. We were all bussed into the city and given rooms where we could rest. Later on we were given a very delicious meal in the hotel's dining room. Several hours later we were informed the plane was ready to fly and were taken back to the airport to reboard the plane for the last leg of our journey. I am happy to note here that our flight from Karachi to New Delhi went without any further hitch and we arrived at the capital city of India some eight hours later than what we should have. Soon after we cleared through customs, we were on our way to Mussoorie. It was a long day for us and we were tired and dirty, but glad to finally arrive back "home" in India once again.

Life at Claremont

There were many things to do as soon as we arrived back in Mussoorie. The mission had already taken possession of Claremont from The Assembly of God Mission. We got settled into our new home without delay. We had acquired a cook and a cook's helper and soon would have some fifteen or more students descend on us. In time, we would not only take care of our own Baptist Mid-Missions MK's, but also some from other missions.

It wasn't long before we had a request from the school to

take an Indian boy from Bombay. Nauzer Daruwalla was a Parsee by religion. His father worked for an Italian corporation and made a very good salary. Nauzer was not able to cope with the school boarding situation; and so, the school asked us, "Would you be willing to give him a try?" Nauzer was a challenge to be sure. He was an only child of a Parsee couple, who came from the upper middle class. It was not long before we found out some of Nauzer's problems. He was not accepted by the other boys in school boarding for two reasons. First, he never took a bath, which is unusual for anyone of the Parsee religion. His other problem was that, coming from a well-to-do Indian family, Nauzer had a monthly allowance of 100 rupees, which would be like having an allowance in the States of 100 dollars. This was far more than any of the other boys had as a monthly allowance. Nauzer also seemed to have a great liking for candy, especially chocolate candy bars. When he came into our Claremont boarding, we asked his parents to cut down considerably on his allowance and we explained the situation to them. They were very gracious about the whole matter and agreed to our suggestion. The biggest challenge was to get him to take a bath. I told him one bath day that if we found out he was not taking a bath, I would come in myself and give him a good scrubbing; that seemed to do the trick. Another problem Nauzer had was that he never changed his underwear or socks from day to day. No wonder he didn't have many friends in school boarding; they couldn't get near him to become his friends! To solve this problem, every night, when he got ready for bed, he had to drop his underwear and socks down at the foot of his bed. I would then collect and drop them into the basket where the dirty clothes were kept for the daily washing.

Cannibalizing Two Washing Machines

When we returned to India from furlough in 1963 we brought with us a wringer style Maytag washing machine. For those two years we were still with the other mission and were at Sunrise School in Nasik, that washing machine was used six days a week to wash clothes for upwards of sixty people, including students and staff. When we moved up to Mussoorie and joined the staff at Woodstock School, we used the washing machine for our own personal use. At the time we went on furlough in 1967 the machine was put into storage, along with all our other personal belongings. But then, when we opened Claremont boarding in 1968 the washing machine was once again used six days a week to wash clothes for all of us living at Claremont. That Maytag wringer-type washing machine was used for another eight years that we served as houseparents at Claremont. Even after we left India in 1976, our BMM boarding at Claremont continued for another few years and the washing machine continued washing clothes of some 15-20 students and houseparents, again, six days a week. We had figured that during all those years, the washing machine had washed clothes, equivalent to a family of four children, for some 75 years! I probably should have written the Maytag Company and told them the story and maybe they would have given us a new machine. Maytag was a machine built to last forever. Well, not exactly.

One day that machine broke down and I wondered what I had to do to get the machine working again. We needed that machine; otherwise, our Indian lady helper would have to wash clothes by hand, an almost impossible task, considering all the other responsibilities she had. One day I happened to walk into a shop about half way down Mullingar Hill, in which I found an old Maytag washing machine, exactly the same model as ours. After some hard and long bargaining with the shop keeper, he was glad to get rid of the machine, for who else would have use for an old machine like that? That was when I got the idea of taking the two machines, ours and the one I bought from "Junkeedas", the shopkeeper, and using the best parts out of both machines, put them together. I would then have a "new" machine, ready to wash clothes for possibly many more years. I hired a Nepalese coolie to carry that old Maytag washing machine back up the hill to Claremont and then I began to "cannibalize" the two washing machines. Once again we were in business, washing clothes six days a week.

Life in the Himalayan Mountains

We enjoyed our life in the Himalayan Mountains very much. There was always something interesting and unexpected that would happen. Though Woodstock School closed down during the winter months, we stayed right at Claremont, living mostly in the sitting room on the east, or sunny side of the house. We had counted all the rooms on the upper level of the house, including bathrooms, kitchens (we had two of them), storage rooms, bedrooms, etc. and found there to be a total of 27 rooms in all on just that upper level. There was a lower level apartment with three more rooms, besides the lowest level of the house, where were located servants quarters, as well as five storage rooms. It was a large house, large enough for our boarding. The largest number of students we had in boarding at any one time was 25. That was quite a big family.

Trying to decide what to do on a free day was not hard to do. There were weekend hikes with small groups from school, going back into the higher elevations. Gloria was not one for much outdoor activity, as well as Kathy, but both Lily and Phyllis enjoyed hiking with others from school carrying backpacks, which weighed up to 16-20 pounds. We enjoyed hiking down to Kempty Falls, which was on the far side of Mussoorie, a hike that would take up to two hours each way. It was a long way down to the falls and felt like much longer on the way back up. Some of the children would wear their bathing suits under their outer clothes and when we arrived at the falls, they would take off their outer clothes and slide down the falls to a deep pool below. Oh, what fun that was!

Friday evenings were always a special time for our family. We usually set aside that time as our family time to play games, while munching on a big bowl of popcorn. That tradition was carried on at Claremont. The children were not allowed to do any homework, or anything else on their own on Friday evenings. Everyone was required to put everything else aside for "game night." We were fortunate that popcorn was available in one of our provisions shops in Mussoorie bazaar and so, we enjoyed popcorn while playing games. What fun we had!

Birthdays were also a special time at Claremont, not only for the one who had a birthday, but also for all the boarders. The birthday person was allowed to choose their special meal on that day. One of the boys decided to have a chocolate birthday party; everything was to be chocolate. We decided in that case that such a meal was quite impossible and we persuaded the boy to confine his chocolate birthday to having a chocolate cake, with chocolate flavored icing on the cake. He readily agreed to that arrangement.

Speaking of popcorn, somehow or other, we had

"inherited" a black and white spotted mongrel, to which the children decided to give the name, "Popcorn." I think they chose that name for the dog, because he was always jumping around, full of energy. But Popcorn had one failing. On any given school day he managed to get out of our fenced in yard and follow the children to school. When he was discovered by one of the teachers to be in their classroom, the teacher would call a coolie and have him return Popcorn to Claremont. Each time it happened, which was quite frequently, we had to give the coolie a rupee for his efforts. We soon found that Popcorn was getting to be too expensive to keep. Popcorn had to go; that was all there was to it. We gave him to our general helper, who had a relative in a nearby village and who would take good care of Popcorn. It was a sad time for the children to see their four-legged friend go. How could we justify to their parents that part of the boarding accounts read: "Paid coolie 1 rupee for bringing Popcorn home from school." I certainly wasn't going to take that rupee out of my own pocket and there was some doubt that any of the children would be willing to pay the rupee out of their own monthly allowance. In the end, the children agreed that it was best that Popcorn find a new home.

The Pumpkin Man

One day an old man came to our back door at Claremont. When I went out to ask what he wanted, I saw that he had a large pumpkin in a rope bag slung over his shoulder. He asked me if I would like to buy his pumpkin. This is the way the conversation went that day, all in the Hindi language:

"Sir, would you buy my pumpkin?"
"Old man, why should I buy your pumpkin?"

"Because I have carried it a long way."
"Where did you come from, old man?"
"I came from over there."

And with that last remark, he gestured with his nose, pointing backwards, letting me know he had come from a village far away, from over several mountain passes. Well, at that point, any resistance I might have had in buying his pumpkin disappeared. I bought that old man's pumpkin and took it into the kitchen to give to our cook. For the next meal the cook had cooked up some of the pumpkin and served it. Pumpkin was not a favorite food for some of the children; but they knew they had to eat at least some of it. The ruling at Claremont was that the children had to eat something of every kind of food served at our meals, even if it was a small portion; that is, unless a child happened to be allergic to some kind of food. From time to time, whenever we had pumpkin served in one form, or another, one of the children would remark, "Uncle Ken felt sorry for the pumpkin man."

Pumpkin Pie and Other Such Things

Speaking of pumpkins, one day Wilma asked our cook if he knew how to make pumpkin pie. Lest he be thought to be ignorant about making any kind of a dish, he replied, "Yes, memsahib, I know how to make pumpkin pie." Wilma then directed him to make pumpkin pie for dessert for the next meal. This time I was not responsible for buying the pumpkin. When it came time to serve the pumpkin pie, the cook brought it out and put it down in front of Wilma to cut into the required number of pieces. What appeared on the table left Wilma with an open mouth. We all suddenly began to laugh. You see, he thought that pumpkin pie was made just like you would make apple pie, cut the pumpkin up into small pieces and put into the pie shell, like you would do with apples and then bake the pie. Needless to say, we didn't have pumpkin pie for dessert that meal. Later Wilma showed the cook how pumpkin pie really was made and we did have pumpkin pie at a later time. It was very delicious and believe it or not, the children asked for more.

Life was much easier in Mussoorie than it had been on the plains. We had available in the bazaar most of any kind of vegetable and fruit you could think of. In fact, we were able to even buy rhubarb at our favorite vegetable stand from time to time. Not long after we returned to Mussoorie in the summer of 1968, Lily Ann sent us a package of rhubarb seeds. I had never heard of rhubarb being grown from seed. In fact, I had never heard of rhubarb seed before, but I decided to give it a try. I planted a row of rhubarb seed along the shady side of the house. Later that year the rhubarb sprouted and in time on we were able to pick our own rhubarb. I think the children at Claremont decided that Uncle Ken's rhubarb was a lot better than the pumpkin I had bought that one time from the pumpkin man.

<u>Sports at Woodstock School</u>

One of the special days at Woodstock School was the annual Sports Day. Everything else at school was set-aside for this day. Many of our Claremont children participated for their classes. Our own Kathy loved to run and on Sports Day she was there to run. She had a pair of running shoes, but on one of the Sports Days, she was getting ready for her race and decided it was easier to run barefoot!

In addition to Sports Day at Woodstock School, there was always competition with several other boarding schools in Mussoorie. The big day for Mussoorie was the annual

Mussoorie Olympics, which was usually held on the playing field at Woodstock School. One year, though, it was held at Wynberg-Allen School. Our Woodstock students usually ran off with most of the trophies at the Mussoorie Olympics. Several years our students lost out to other schools and had to learn to eat "humble pie" at such times. They found out that they were not so invincible after all.

Basketball was a favorite sport at Woodstock. The basketball court at that time had a concrete floor and the hoops were on wooden backboards. One time, cadets from the Indian military academy in Dehra Dun came up to play our boys. Most of the men from the military academy stood head and shoulders above our students. Many of them were Sikhs, who were quite tall. But the men from India's military academy were not used to the altitude at Woodstock School, which was a bit over 7,000 feet above sea level and Dehra Dun was only at about 2,000 feet. As a result, the military soon ran out of breath and, in the end, lost to our Woodstock boys.

First Wedding in the Family

Shortly after Lily began her first year of studies at Bryan College in Dayton, Tennessee, she met Terry Yoder, who was from West Liberty, Ohio. Terry came from a dairy farming family, though he had no interest at all in being a dairy farmer, or any other kind of a farmer. It wasn't long before their friendship developed into a "budding" romance and plans began to develop for marriage. We were not happy about their desire to get married before they both graduated from college, but we gave a grudging approval for Lily to get married before she turned 21. It was always our rule that if our daughters wanted to get married, the prospective husband-to-be, was required to seek our approval for the marriage. All four of the girls are married and before each wedding took place, I was asked for the hand of my daughter in marriage. In only one case was there any kind of doubt in our minds about the match. Lily and Terry did continue through their second year of college studies and then decided to get married by the fall of 1970. When they wrote us about getting married, they said they wanted to come out to India for the wedding and have it at Union Church in Mussoorie. We thought that to be a good idea and gave our approval. Plans began to develop for their trip out to India and it wasn't long before we had made arrangements for them to stay in a lovely little "honeymoon" cottage on the hillside for a few days after the wedding. After that they would then move on into the downstairs apartment in Claremont just below the main part of the house. I wrote to Terry, telling him that on the way out to India Lily was ours and that we would pay for her way to come out to India; but on the way back she was "all his." He agreed to that arrangement. They bought tickets on Pan America Airline's round-the-world flight #1. They dropped out of school for the fall semester of 1970-71 and spent four months in India after the wedding. We bought pure silk from a cloth shop in New Delhi and Wilma sewed all the dresses for Lily, her three sisters and Laura Carter, Murray and Florence Carter's daughter, who was to be Lily's flower girl. The colors for the wedding were to be moss green and a pretty shade of yellow for the attendants and white, of course, for Lily's wedding dress. Lily sent out the measurements for her dress, as well as her footprints she had traced on a piece of cardboard. With the traced out footprints, we had a local shoe maker make a pair of shoes for Lily, covered in white silk, the white silk used for her wedding dress. When Lily and Terry arrived shortly before the wedding all that had to be done with her dress was to sew up the hem; it fit her perfectly, as did the shoes.

The Band Plays On!

Lily and Terry's wedding was to be held at 4 p.m. on Sunday, October 10, 1970 at Union Church in Mussoorie. The church had moveable heavy wooden pews, with an aisle going down on either side. In order to provide a middle aisle for the wedding, the pews had to all be moved to one side and the other. All of this, plus the decorating of the church and setting up for the reception to follow, had to be done in less than four hours, beginning immediately after the morning service was finished. We had counted on about 150 guests to be served at the reception, which was by RSVP only. Unfortunately, Charlie Warren, pastor of Union Church, had announced the wedding during the morning service and invited one and all to both the wedding and reception to follow. Our hearts sank when we heard the announcement. Who doesn't like weddings and wedding receptions? In India weddings and their receptions are put on with great flourish. Lily's wedding was expected to be no less! The wedding went off very well, until the exchanging of vows. Just as this part of the ceremony began, there was a great noise, which began just outside the church on the road going past. Down the road had come a brass band, playing typical Indian brass band music. That day there had been a sweepers' caste festival and the brass band was playing for the sweepers. Sweepers in India are street cleaners and clean the latrines, as well. The church, as a result of Charlie Warren's announcement about Lily and Terry's wedding to be held that afternoon, was filled with people, so many that some had to watch through the open windows of the church from the outside. Because of all the activity at church, the brass band stopped right outside the church. Finding out that a wedding was going on inside the church, they must have decided to honor the bride and groom with their special music. It was their contribution to the wedding! Needless to say, inside the church Charlie stopped what he was about to say, wondering what he should do, continue with the ceremony, or wait until the brass band had passed on down the road. He decided to continue and by shouting, so that his words would be heard by Lily and Terry, proceeded with the exchanging of vows. Because of all the noise outside, Lily and Terry had to shout their vows. There is no doubt that all within the church were able to hear the vows being exchanged between our daughter and her soon-to-be husband. It was quite a unique ending to an otherwise very beautiful wedding.

One special guest at the wedding was Paulus, our cook at Sunrise School in Nasik. Paulus was now the cook at another mission boarding home in Landour, which had been started about a year after we opened ours at Claremont. Paulus had known Lily from the time she was very small and watched her grow up to adulthood. He was very special to her and was Lily's very special guest at her wedding. Paulus must have been thrilled to be considered so.

Needless to say, having planned for 150 guests at the reception, we soon found that with well over twice that number of people, possibly even as high as 400, we had to do something very quickly in order to serve that many people. It was Sunday and provisions shops in town were all closed. But I found a pharmacy near the church that was still open. When I dashed into the pharmacy, I found all they had that I could buy for the reception were some bottles of concentrated fruit juice, called *squash*. In the meantime, the women who were serving refreshments began cutting the wedding cake into smaller and smaller pieces. Somehow or other, we managed to get through the wedding and the reception to follow. From the beginning, we should have expected the unexpected.

Gloria's Continuing Health Problems

Ever since Gloria was young, she had been having problems with her kidneys. We couldn't find out what the problems were and they continued to get worse, so that by the time she was in the 11th grade, she had lost a lot of class time. She was in and out of the hospital a number of times and finally ended up having to stay in bed at home, but she continued with her studies at home and managed to keep up with her class. We knew that something serious was wrong with Gloria and needed to be taken care of. I had already taken her to India's two prestigious Christian medical colleges to Ludhiana in the north and Vellore in the south. At both places they were unable to find the source of her problem. Ultimately, we knew we would have to take her back to the States to get to the bottom of the whole problem.

A situation happened at the hospital in Vellore, which caused me to make a quick decision to remove her from the hospital and take her back home to Mussoorie. One day an orderly began to give Gloria an injection; but when I noticed bubbles of air in the syringe, of which he made no attempt to remove, I told him to stop, sent him out of the room and quickly informed the hospital authorities as to what happened. I decided to remove Gloria immediately from the hospital. After quickly packing up my suitcase at the guesthouse where I was staying, I had Gloria get dressed, packed up her suitcase and we left the hospital. We took a taxi to the train station in order to catch the next train to Madras. From there we were able to get a flight on India's internal airline to New Delhi and then to Mussoorie by private taxi. The distance from New Delhi to Mussoorie was about 175 miles by road.

One thing happened while we were at the hospital in Vellore, which made it very difficult for Gloria to travel as we did. She suddenly came down with infectious hepatitis. In addition to her kidney problem, there was now the jaundice to deal with. She was one sick girl and I had to make a decision, whether to allow her to stay at the hospital in Vellore, or take here home, even though she was sick with jaundice. It was a judgmental call and I made what I felt was the best decision for her, considering all the circumstances. We were able to get a first class compartment out of Vellore for Madras, which made it possible for her to lie down during that part of our trip back to Mussoorie. We had no problem getting seats on the flight to New Delhi, but it was not easy for Gloria to have to sit up during that nearly three hour trip by air. And then, of course, the taxi ride was much harder on her. Finally, after finally arriving back in Mussoorie, there was still a long way up the mountain to our home at Claremont; but I had four coolies carry her in a *dandee* up to Landour Community Hospital, where she was immediately admitted. Gloria remained in the hospital for three weeks until she had gained enough strength to recover fully at home. We were thankful that no complications followed from the long trip we took from Vellore to Mussoorie. There was still the kidney problem to deal with.

War With Pakistan Again

The year was 1971 and tension between India and Pakistan continued to grow. The question was not whether another war between these two countries would take place, but rather, when it would take place. War seemed inevitable. By the end of November, Woodstock School was getting ready for Going Down Day. This was the time when students returned to their homes for the long winter break. There were many uncertainties about conditions in regard to India and Pakistan. It was felt wise for the students to leave for their homes without delay.

None of our BMM missionaries in Assam were able to come and take their children back into Assam. I volunteered to accompany them all the way to Assam, while Wilma and the girls remained behind at Claremont. At the same time, while I was to be in Assam for only a short time, I was invited to speak at the annual Bible conference for both missionaries and national believers in the Fellowship of Baptist Churches in Assam, along with churches in the nearby tribal states of Nagaland, Manipur and Mizoram. That part of India was mostly restricted to foreigners and in order for me to be able to go to Assam I had to apply for a special permit, which was eventually granted, allowing me to be in Assam for a maximum of fourteen days.

Not only was there great tension between India and Pakistan, but also there were disturbances in what was then East Pakistan. The people demanded independence from Pakistan. It was almost a ludicrous situation with Pakistan being made up of two territories, West Pakistan and East Pakistan, separated by nearly two thousand miles of India. As the tension in that part of the Indian subcontinent continued to grow, Pakistan closed its air space to Indian planes. As a result, all Indian Airlines flights into Assam had to go through the narrow corridor of some twenty miles between East Pakistan and Nepal.

Our Assam group of students traveled from Dehradun to New Delhi by an overnight train and then transferred to a fast train to Calcutta. From there we were to catch an Indian Airlines flight to Silchar, the main town in Cachar District in Assam. Because of no flights being allowed over East Pakistan, our plane had to go through that narrow air corridor up to North Assam and then on down to Silchar, which was in the southern half of the state. We had one stop to make at Gahauti in the north. As we got closer to Gahauti, the pilot of our plane received a message that we could not land at Gahauti. The airport was closed to passenger flights because of the Indian Air Force making flights along the border with East Pakistan. We had to continue on to a very small airport in the far northeast corner of India, close to the China border. There we waited for some time until the all-clear signal was given and we could return to Gahauti to disembark a few passengers before going on to Silchar. There certainly were some tense moments, as we wondered if we would ever make it to Silchar. The Lord was certainly with us and protected us along the way, even though we were several hours late reaching Silchar. What a relief it was to see our plane finally touch down at the Silchar airport and put our feet on solid ground once again.

About the time our conference with missionaries and national brethren began, war finally broke out between India and Pakistan. We were close to the border with East Pakistan and at any moment we could be bombed by a Pakistan fighter jet; or Assam could be invaded by Pakistan ground forces. We had to come up with some kind of plan to avoid being caught up with such a conflict, for the sake of our Indian national brethren. We missionaries met together one day and decided that if worse came to worst, we could each pack up one small case of belongings, along with important papers and trudge through the jungle into Manipur and from there head for the Burmese border. I am thankful we did not have to take such a drastic course. One day I decided to take a taxi some 30 miles away over to where Dr. Gene and Bette Burrows were serving at our leprosy hospital at Makunda, along with Jim and Joyce Garlow. On the way we heard a loud noise in the sky; it was a fighter jet, without doubt. Was it friend or foe? We couldn't tell; and so, we left the taxi in a hurry to find some place to hide. We soon found out it was an Indian jet and with that, all of us who were passengers in the taxi, along with the driver, decided it was safe to return to the taxi and complete our journey to where each of us was going. Again, those were tense moments, knowing that, in the end, we would be at the mercy of any enemy plane that might fly over.

During the time fighting continued between the two countries, I was unable to communicate with Wilma in the normal manner of either calling on the telephone, which was hard enough even in normal times, or by mail. No mail was being transported from Assam to the rest of the country. All passenger planes were grounded during the war. The son of one of our Indian national leaders was in the Indian army, stationed in Calcutta as a communications officer. We were able to get word through to him by means of military channels and through him, to call Wilma on the telephone to let her know I was safe.

Gloria's Problem Solved

With Gloria's ongoing kidney problem and no solution being found in India, Dr. Kenoyer advised me to take Gloria back to the States as soon as the war ended and I could get back to Mussoorie. He had a friend at Mayo

Clinic in Rochester, Minnesota, who was a kidney specialist and would arrange by correspondence, for us to take Gloria there. Five days after the war broke out, India had destroyed all of Pakistan's fighter jets and the next day India started up its commercial flights again. I was able to catch a flight back to Calcutta and then from there to New Delhi. Within two days from the time I left Assam, I was back in Mussoorie with news about taking Gloria back to the States for medical attention. We had many things to take care of in the following days, including making arrangements to fly from New Delhi to New York and on to Detroit; from there we would drive back to Cleveland and our mission home office. At our mission home office we would be able to make arrangements to take Gloria to the Mayo Clinic. There were exit permits to obtain, as well as fresh No-Objection-to-Return endorsements in our passports. Everything was in readiness and we left New Delhi with special return air ticket having to be back in India within four months. The total cost of our tickets was still a lot of money for five adult tickets, but the Lord provided for this emergency trip to the States. Did He not promise in His Word that He would supply all our needs according to His riches in Glory by Christ Jesus? (Philippians 4:19)

We left New Delhi on December 24, arriving in New York at Kennedy International Airport on Christmas Eve. We had to transfer over to LaGuardia Airport in order to catch our flight to Detroit and were given two choices as to how we could go from Kennedy to LaGuardia, either by ground transport, or by helicopter. We chose to go by helicopter. What a flight we had, as we seemed to just skim over the rooftops of the buildings. It was a thrilling sight, as we looked out of our 25-passenger helicopter and saw all the Christmas lights shimmering in the night sky. There couldn't have been a prettier sight to greet us on that Christmas Eve of 1971. We had been away from the States for 3 1/2 years. Wilma's parents were at the airport to meet us upon our arrival in Detroit and we had a precious few days with them over the Christmas and New Year's Holidays. Early in January we made the trip to Cleveland, where we met with our field administrator to talk over plans for taking Gloria to the Mayo Clinic.

When a call was put through to the Mayo Clinic and Dr. Kenoyer's urologist friend was contacted, he advised us to stay right there in Cleveland and take Gloria to the Cleveland Clinic. According to the specialist, Cleveland Clinic had as good facilities to handle Gloria's problem as at the Mayo Clinic. Praise the Lord that we were able to get Gloria into the Cleveland Clinic right away and were able to find out within the day what her problem was, along with the source of the problem, as well as its solution. On March 13, 1972 we were back in India, less than three months after leaving and less than a month after the students had arrived back in Woodstock from their winter break. Our girls had a little bit longer vacation than the rest of the students, but were able to get caught up to their classmates with little effort. While Gloria's kidney problem continues to this day, she is able to deal with it and keep it under control. As the years progressed, she would be diagnosed with more serious medical problems.

The Nest Gets Smaller

The following July Kathy graduated from Woodstock School and we sent her back to the States with friends who served in TEAM (The Evangelical Alliance Mission) and were returning to the States. Kathy was registered to begin classes at Los Angeles Baptist College in Newhall,

California that September. Until her classes began, she stayed with our friends, Dr. and Mrs. Al Holt, whose home at the time was in Lake Arrowhead, in the mountains east of Los Angeles. Al had been TEAM doctor at Chinchpada, a small village in the northwestern part of the state of Maharashtra, India. He had delivered Phyllis and also had done major surgery on Wilma, when we had been in that part of India many years ago. It was not easy sending a daughter all the way back to the States, but we knew she was well taken care of. Besides that, she was in the Lord's hands. When our girls were born in India, we had perfect peace about sending them to the States, or leaving them there, after our having completed a furlough time. We were later to do the latter for both Gloria and Phyllis, as we had done earlier with Lily Ann. Kathy was the only one of our girls who returned to the States from India without our being along.

Crises Over London, England

Except for the brief time we were in the States, when Gloria's serious kidney problem was diagnosed at the Cleveland Clinic in January 1972, we had not had a regular furlough since 1967. Nearly five years had passed; it was important that we spend some time with family and supporters. On June 26, 1973 we left for what was to be our last furlough from India. We had with us Mary Seefeldt, who was in the same class as Gloria and whose parents, Ralph and Nellanne Seefeldt, served with TEAM in Mussoorie. The girls had just graduated from high school at Woodstock and were returning to the States to begin their college careers.

Little did we know when we took off in that Boeing 747 jumbo jet, that we would have the ride of our lives upon arriving over London, England. Until then our flight had gone smoothly and without incident. The plane was not completely full and Gloria and Mary decided to sit by a window. Wilma, Phyllis and I were in the middle section. As we approached London, getting ready to go into a landing pattern, our plane suddenly shook violently. What happened? Were we struck by lightning? There were no storm clouds in the sky at the time; it couldn't have been that. Had we been hit by another plane? The violent shaking took place just as we were beginning to descend and go through a heavy cloud that was in the area. Just then a yellow light by a young woman attendant's telephone began flashing. As she picked up the phone to hear what the captain had to say, she turned so pale the freckles on her face stood out sharply. Then we heard a message from the captain. We had been bombarded by large hail as we went through the cloud moments before we were to begin our descent to the airport runway. The hail had caused massive damage to the plane's large windshield and the captain and co-pilot were unable to see out of the windshield. We had been told that for a jumbo jet, the captain lands it visually; that is, he must be able to have a clear vision through the plane's windshield. Such was not possible with the captain of our jumbo. We were in a crisis situation.

For the next hour we flew in circles above London, while all other planes in the area were diverted to other airports and our plane dumped most of its fuel it had taken on during our brief stop at Frankfurt, Germany. We were also instructed as to what to do at the last moment before our captain attempted to land the plane on an emergency runway. All eye glasses, false teeth, watches and shoes were to be removed. We were all given pillows, while babies were wrapped in blankets. We were then told to lower our heads towards our laps as we approached landing. All the time this was going on and until our plane actually touched down on the runway, we heard the drama going on between the captain of our 747 and the control tower; we heard it all. Control tower literally talked our plane down, for the flight crew could not see anything through the severely damaged windshield. What a cheer went up by all of us on the plane when the wheels of the plane hit the runway and we finally came to a full stop. We were safe on the ground. Ground crew had lined up fire fighting equipment and ambulances, ready for any eventuality. But we were all safe, thanks to the skillful handling of the plane by our capable crew. After arriving at the terminal, we were invited to go up to the flight deck to view the damage; we were astounded by what we saw and wondered how it was possible to keep the plane under control and bring it safely to the ground. We were praising the Lord for His control of that 747 jumbo jet.

Because of the extensive damage to the plane, we were delayed several hours in London, while another plane was made available for all of us who were flying on to New York. While we waited, we were served a large and delicious dinner at the airline's expense. Besides that, when we finally reached New York we had to be put up at a hotel until the following morning, for we had missed our flight to Detroit, due to the accident in London. In the meantime, Mary Seefeldt was met at Kennedy International Airport by relatives, for she was going no farther. It was the end of the line for her. What additional surprise awaited us as we opened our suitcases at the hotel, to find most of our clothes were very damp. Colors from one of Wilma's silk saris had run onto other clothes, ruining them completely. We did not make any claim on our ruined clothes. We were just thankful to have arrived safely.

Furlough in Grand Rapids, Michigan

Our furlough was spent in Grand Rapids, Michigan, where I was signed up to take courses at Grand Rapids Baptist Seminary. We stayed in the home of an older couple who lived in St. Petersburg, Florida in the winter, where they were volunteer workers at the D & D Homes. They had a comfortable home right next door to a state-operated detention center for wayward girls. During our furlough time Wilma was able to get a job at the center and make enough to supplement our limited income through the mission. As September approached, Gloria made plans to fly out to Lost Angeles, where she had agreed to take one year of Bible college studies at Los Angeles Baptist College in Newhall. After that one year she would then begin her training at West Suburban School of Nursing in Oak Park, Illinois, a suburb on the near west side of Chicago. The year at Los Angeles Baptist College went very well for Gloria. With Kathy also studying at LABC, the two girls were of help to each other. Phyllis began her 11th year at a high school not far from where we were living. Close to the high school was Berean Baptist Church, which we made our furlough "home" church. Phyllis was very active in the youth program at the church and became close friends with the youth sponsors, Bob and Vicky Rehkopf. Bob and Vicky had a daughter the same age as Lily's oldest son, David, with the same handicap as our grandson. Phyllis enjoyed playing her clarinet in the high school band and had the opportunity of not only going with the band to Niagara Falls, New York to march in a special parade, but the band also got to welcome President Gerald Ford, who was returning to Grand Rapids, his home city, for a special event. That was quite an honor for our youngest daughter.

India Comes to Canada

In the spring of 1974 I attended Baptist Mid-Missions' triennial conference, which was held in Hamburg, New York. During the conference I was approached by our field administrator for North America, Dr. Denzel Osburn. He discussed the need of missionaries, who would be willing to go to British Columbia, Canada to reach East Indians with the gospel. Would Wilma and I pray about the possibility of our going? I told Dr. Osburn I would talk it over with Wilma and we would certainly pray about that possibility. It would mean, of course, our changing fields from India to North America, as well as having to apply to the Canadian government for landed immigrant status.

In the spring issue of HARVEST magazine, BMM's quarterly publication, there was an article written by Mrs. Merle Richardson, who had served with her husband in church planting ministry in Merritt, British Columbia. Merritt is in the interior of the province and about a four-hour drive from Vancouver. There were several thousand East Indians living in that small mill town, almost all of them being from India's state of Punjab; thus, they were, by religion, Sikhs. The title of Doris's article was "India Comes to Canada." That article, along with Dr. Osburn's request for us to pray, was a challenge for us to do just that, pray. I called Wilma on the phone from Hamburg and told her what Dr. Osburn had discussed with me. We left it at that until I got back to Grand Rapids. Our decision at the time was to return to India, for we still had a commitment to Claremont boarding. At the same time, we would continue to pray for the Lord's guidance in the matter.

Changes in Our Family's Lives in 1974

There were a number of changes that took place in our family's lives in 1974. In September Kathy returned to LABC. Instead of flying back to Lost Angeles, she decided to go by bus, in order to save money. We agreed to let her do it, but were still concerned, for she would be traveling on the bus by herself. There would be other passengers, of course, and the trip would take three days for her to reach L.A. She made it out there safely and later on we came to find out that all she had to eat, or drink during the whole journey was milk. Kathy told us later that she wanted to save her money for school. What a girl!

Gloria, in the meantime, had enrolled in the nursing program at West Suburban School of Nursing, located in Oak Park, Illinois, on the west side of Chicago. As for Phyllis, she was ready to begin her final year of high school. The question before us that summer concerned what we should do, whether to let her remain in the States for that last year of high school and, if so, where would she stay? Or should she return to India with us and finish her schooling at Woodstock School, then return to the States after graduation? We were surprised one day when we approached by the Rehkopfs, telling us they would like to keep Phyllis with them, so that she could complete her schooling there in Grand Rapids. When we asked Phyllis about this, she thought it would be a good idea and so, we agreed to the plan. It meant signing a legal document, giving authority to Bob and Vicky as though she was legally theirs. We had done that one other time, when Lily had stayed with Wilma's sister and husband, Sylvia and Bob, after she graduated from high school in 1968 and before her first year at Bryan College. We had returned to India that summer of 1968. The arraignment for Phyllis worked out very well and we were at total peace about leaving our youngest daughter back in the States. We committed her, as we had done with each of the girls, to the Lord's keeping. We knew that each of them was safe in the Lord's hands.

We were home on furlough for over a year and it was time to get back to India and our responsibilities at the BMM boarding home at Claremont. During the year we were on furlough, friends serving with the Free Will Baptist Mission, whose two sons were in our boarding, volunteered to be houseparents while we were away. The wife carried on most of the responsibilities, for her husband had to go back and forth to India's state of West Bengal where their ministry was located. This arrangement was approved by our Assam missionaries. But then, the wife needed to get back to their station by some time in September. What were we to do? We still had support to raise before the mission would allow us to return to India. The decision was made for Wilma to return to India by herself, while I remained in the States to seek further support. I stayed for an additional seven weeks after Wilma left for India on September18[th]. I flew to New York with Wilma to see that she had gotten on her direct flight to New Delhi and then flew back to Cleveland, where I stayed at our mission's guesthouse.

During our furlough time the mission had given us a used vehicle to use. It had been a gift to the Mission from an elderly couple, who decided it was time for both of them to stop driving. To make the transaction legal, for the car had to be put in my name, I paid one dollar for the car. The condition on the whole deal was that when I returned to India, I would turn the car back over to the mission. No, I didn't get my dollar back. During the next seven weeks I was in the States by myself, I was able to raise the additional support needed before I could return to India.

My Last Goodbye

Before I left the States to return to India, I flew out to Lost Angeles and spent a few days with Kathy. From there I flew back to Minneapolis to spend some time with Dad. He had moved out of the apartment on the north side of the city where my parents had lived since moving back into the city from Crystal Village in 1942. He was then living in a highrise apartment building on the near south side of downtown Minneapolis. Dad was comfortably situated and enjoyed living there very much. I had a good time with him during those days, not knowing that a little over one month later he would be gone.

An amusing thing happened while I was with my father those few days. He had only one bedroom and I suggested that I could sleep on the floor in the living room. It was not the best of arrangements, but comfortable enough for me at the time. I had slept in far worse situations than that many times in India. Dad always liked the temperature in his house to be hot. One night I awoke with beads of perspiration on my forehead. Why was it so hot? I got up to look at the thermostat and saw that Dad had set it at 85 degrees! I turned it down to a comfortable 70. When I woke up in the morning, I noticed that the thermostat was back up to 85 and Dad was still asleep. He had apparently awakened in the night feeling cold, gotten up and turned that thermostat back up to his comfortable 85. I didn't say a thing about it to my father, but simply had to accept the fact that he needed a higher temperature than I did. Besides, it was his apartment, not mine. I just had to endure the heat during the remaining nights I was there. After my time with Dad, I caught a flight back to Chicago and then on to

Cleveland, back to the mission guesthouse. That was the last time I would see my father alive, not knowing at the time it would be my last goodbye. From Cleveland I flew on to New York, where I caught a direct flight back to New Delhi. Wilma and I decided that we would never allow that kind of set up to happen again. When we traveled, we would travel together.

<u>Dad's Homegoing</u>

I arrived in New Delhi on November 2, 1974 and took an overnight train from the Old Delhi railway station, which would arrive the next morning at its final stop and my destination by train, Dehradun. Before the train got to Dehradun, I began a letter to Dad, telling him a bit of my trip and from where I was beginning that letter. The train arrived in Dehradun before I could finish the letter and so, I had to wait until the next day, the 4th, to finish the letter and send it off to him. It was the last letter I was to write Dad, for a month later the Lord called him home to heaven.

My letter said, in part, the following:

> "It is early morning on the train, as I near Dehradun and the end of the line; expected arrival of the train is about 9 a.m. After arriving in New Delhi yesterday morning I managed to get through a long distance call to Wilma and, believe me, in this country making a long distance call is a real trial - and she said that she would be down to meet me. One of our high school boys has his driver's license and so, they'll be down in our jeep to meet me. I'll be glad to finally arrive back home in Mussoorie and also be able to get a nice warm bath in our large oval Indian tin bathtub!

> Well, here the train sits in the station at Hardwar, which is a place very sacred to Hinduism. Many Pilgrims come here and there are many temples. Just a few moments ago a whole tribe of red monkeys came by, unmolested by hundreds of travelers, each quite oblivious of the other. I'm back in India with all the yells, bells and smells."

In the end, I had to take a taxi up the mountain to get to Mussoorie. Wilma had gotten word to me that the battery in our jeep was not working properly; in fact, it was dead and they were unable to meet me, as planned.

I finished the letter to my father after arriving back in Mussoorie, with the following words:

> "Monday – November 4, 1974
>
> It was 25 years ago tomorrow that Wilma and I first set foot on Indian soil. Now, here we are back again. The time is 4:30 a.m. I've had my sleep and so I decided that I had better get up and finish this letter and others that I started while on the train yesterday…It's good to be back, though I must say that I'm tired from the trip and will be glad for a few days' rest before I get into the thick of the work again."

I had earlier written that there was 10-½ hours difference in time from where I had started my trip back to India, from New York, and New Delhi. No wonder I was wide-awake at 4:30 a.m.

On December 12th, the day of my 49th birthday, I received a telegram from my older brother, Warren, letting me know of Dad's death the day before. I did not realize it at the time I was with him in late October, before my departure for India that he was suffering from a large ulcer. He himself probably did not know it, though he must have been in much pain at the time. He never said anything about his discomfort and pain; but that was much like my father.

Dad had a younger brother, Harold, who never married and lived by himself on the south side of Minneapolis. Uncle Harold called Dad quite often to check on him and see how he was doing. One day Dad did not answer the phone when my uncle called which was a matter of concern to him. He decided to call my brother, Warren, who lived in Chippewa Falls, Wisconsin, about 100 miles due east of the Twin Cities. Warren left right after getting this message and drove over to see what may possibly have happened to our father. Warren had a key to get into the apartment and when he got no response from inside, he opened the door to find Dad slumped over, unconscious, on the floor. How long he had been in that condition, no one could tell, of course. I'm surprised that my uncle had not called the police before calling my brother. But that is something we will never know. As soon as my brother saw Dad lying on the floor an ambulance was summoned immediately and Dad was rushed to the hospital. Besides the stomach ulcer Dad's kidneys failed at the last. Two days after being admitted to the hospital Dad had a triumphant entrance into heaven. Both Dad and Mom are buried in the Fort Snelling military cemetery on the near south side of Minneapolis. Mom was able to be buried there because Dad had been in the army and fought in France during World War I.

<u>Phyllis's Special Care on Pan Am Flight #1</u>

During the following two years, we had an enjoyable

ministry, caring for upwards of 25 students from grades 1 through 12. Phyllis had graduated from high school in Grand Rapids, Michigan. As a graduation present, we paid for her to fly out to India and spend several weeks with us. We were concerned about her making that long trip on her own half way around the world. Because of that concern, we made contact with a friend of ours, who had been a chief pilot with Eastern Airlines, but now retired. He was a member of our largest supporting church in the Washington, D.C. area and knew personally the head stewardess with Pan American Airlines, by which Phyllis was to fly to India. The end result was that Phyllis flew from Detroit to New York and met the head stewardess in her office at Pan Am's terminal at Kennedy International Airport. It was set up that during every stage of Pan Am's flight from New York to New Delhi, the head stewardess on that leg of the trip would see to Phyllis's comfort. What an arrangement! Not only that, but when Phyllis arrived back in New York, she spent five days in the home of the head of Pan Am's stewardesses. Phyllis was able to see much of the city, as the stewardess's father, who lived with her in her uptown apartment, became our Phyllis's chaperone and tour guide in the "Big Apple." Praise the Lord for His wonderful provision for our daughter.

Kashmir

While Phyllis was with us the summer of 1975, the three of us went to Kashmir for a very delightful holiday. Kashmir has been disputed territory claimed by both India and Pakistan, with part of the mountain territory controlled by each of the two countries. We traveled from Delhi to Amritsar by train and then from there flew up to Shrinagar, capital of the part of Kashmir controlled by India. Amritsar is located close to the Pakistan border and site of the Sikh's most sacred temple. The Golden Temple is to the Sikhs what Mecca is to the Muslims and the Vatican is to the Roman Catholics. To a true believer in the One True God and His Son, Jesus Christ, he (the believer) is the temple of God, the dwelling place of the Holy Spirit. "Know ye not that ye are the temple of God and that the Spirit of God dwelleth in you?" (1 Corinthians 3:16; note also verse 17, as well as 2 Corinthians 6:16)

During our first week we were in Kashmir we stayed on a typical houseboat on Kashmir's famous Dal Lake. That was quite an experience in itself. Every houseboat comes with its own cook. Our cook prepared delicious meals for us, menus which were almost fit for a king. One day I happened to catch the cook dipping the water pitcher into the lake to get our next meal's supply of drinking water. And all the time we thought we were drinking boiled water. Who knows, up until that time, what germs from the muddy Dal Lake, were going into our bodies. We were thankful for the Lord's protection and that we did not come down with some kind of intestinal infection. During the second week of our holiday in Kashmir, we stayed in a small cabin, situated right on the edge of a mountain stream and in a beautiful wooded area in the higher reaches of the Himalayan Mountains of Kashmir. The sound of the cold water flowing past, hardly five feet from the cabin, seemed to lull us to sleep at night. We found it hard to leave that tranquil place and return to Mussoorie, but we knew we had to come back to the realities of life. We also knew we had our responsibilities at Claremont. It would soon be time for the students to all return from their summer break. It was also time for Phyllis to return to the States, where she would soon begin her first year of studies at Clearwater Christian College in Clearwater, Florida.

Decisions to Make

During our second year back in India Wilma began to have some physical problems and we decided that she should go to Ludhiana, a city in the Punjab, to the north of us about a day's journey by train from Delhi. Ludhiana Christian Medical College and Brown Memorial Hospital were located in Ludhiana and operated by the Presbyterian Mission. Upon arriving in Ludhiana Wilma consulted with a woman specialist. The hospital was not unfamiliar to me, for it was there I had taken Gloria a few years earlier, to try and find out the source of her kidney problem. As for Wilma, the advice of the specialist was that she should seriously consider making a change in what she was doing. It was suggested that she turn over responsibilities at Claremont to someone else, who was younger and could take much better the strains of such responsibilities. I too saw the wisdom of this and thought that maybe this was the Lord's way of telling us to make a change in our ministry, that maybe this was the Lord's timing and way of telling us to go to Canada to begin a ministry amongst those thousands of immigrants from India. Had we not been praying about this, as we had, when we were asked to do so by our then field administrator for North America two years previously? There would soon be some major decisions we would have to make.

+ Life in the Himalayan Mountains +

Road to Mussoorie in the Himalayan Mountains Nine hairpin turns in one-mile distance

A coolie bringing us 200 lbs. of charcoal

Wilma washing clothes in our Maytag washer

Mussoorie's taxi service

Part Seven: A Call to Canada

June, 1976 - December, 1990

"God help me make Thy highest choice;
Let others have the rest.
Their good things have no charm for me;
I want thy very best."

--- copied from the private diary on prayer
of Greg Gay, Vienna, VA

Certainly I Will Be With Thee!

Certainly I will be with thee!
Father, I have found it true;
To Thy faithfulness and mercy
I would set my seal anew.

All the years Thy grace had kept me,
Thou my help indeed has been,
Marvelous Thy loving kindness
Every day and hour has seen.
Certainly I will be with thee!
Let me feel it, Saviour dear,
Let me know that Thou art with me,
Very previous, very near.

Certainly I will be with thee!
Blessed Spirit, come to me,
Rest upon me, dwell within me,
Let my heart, Thy temple be.

     --- Francis R. Havergal

Is It The Right Decision?

In the spring of 1976 we made the decision to go on a special furlough. We sold most of our things in India, including furniture and anything else, which we felt could not be shipped back to the States, in case we did not return to India. I packed down all my study books and a few other personal items.

There was an uncertainty that began to settle upon us, as though it were a heavy cloud. Were we doing the right thing? Were we mistaken in making the decision to even return to the States at that time? We knew of the difficulty of relocating to a different part of India and to a different type of ministry. The government of India did not easily grant such permits to foreign nationals, especially Christian missionaries at that time. When we prepared to leave the country for whatever reason, we had to obtain a "No Objection to Leave" permit. Before leaving India to go on furlough, to be sure that we would receive a visa to re-enter the country, it was also necessary to obtain a "No Objection to Return" endorsement in our passports. Every year we had to apply for a residential permit; sometimes the permit would be granted about the time we had to apply for the next year's residential permit. Also, while living in India, if we left our particular district of residence to travel to another part of the country, we were supposed to report to our local police and then to the police in the place where we were going.

On the last Sunday before we left India, we walked into a back room of Union Church. There we found sitting on a small desk a plaque with part of Exodus 3:12, "...certainly I will be with thee..." Was that God's way of telling us He would show us His way, His plans for us for the future? If

He said it, it must be true. We took courage in that promise and then and there told the Lord that we would trust Him completely regarding the future.

When one of my professors at Grand Rapids Baptist Seminary in Grand Rapids, Michigan, heard of our return to the States, he invited us to stay in their home until we could make our own housing arrangements. He and his wife would be away at the time for a brief vacation. It would be a help to them if we could house sit for them. We accepted the offer, not knowing that in their home was a further confirmation of the Lord's leading in our lives. As soon as we walked into their bedroom, what should we see on the wall, but a plaque, with those same words in Exodus 3:12, "...certainly I will be with thee..." Well, praise the Lord! At that moment the heavy cloud of doubt that had been on our hearts before we left India and before we saw that same verse in the back room of the church in Mussoorie, just a few days before, vanished completely. Total peace flooded our souls. We were confident that God brought us home at that time for a special reason and, further, that he wanted us in Canada to begin a gospel outreach to those thousands of immigrants from India. As to that special reason, we would soon find out it had to do with a sudden tragedy that would happen to Gloria a few weeks later.

Several things were to take place that year. First, Kathy was getting married. She had met and fell in love with Bruce Callison while a student at Los Angeles Baptist College. Kathy was about to graduate from LABC, while Bruce had completed just two years of studies at the college.

Bruce had written us, asking for the hand of our second daughter in marriage. Though we had not met Bruce personally, we felt perfectly comfortable about his marrying our daughter. Their wedding was planned for July of 1976. In addition to the wedding, I wanted to do some more work on my master's degree at Grand Rapids Baptist Seminary. With one more year of concentrated studies, I could nearly finish my degree requirements. We bought into a cooperative townhouse complex, which we later sold, when the Lord finally took us to Canada. We arrived back in the States on May 27, 1976 and shortly after that I took a special summertime course that was being offered at the seminary.

While Gloria was studying at West Suburban School of Nursing, she would often drive down to Gary, Indiana and stay with friends of ours, who lived across the road from our supporting church, Grace Baptist Church. Roland and Lola Arbogast made Gloria feel at home and a part of the family; it was an ideal situation. At that time, she met Tom Wilson, son of one of those women, who had come forward at the close of the message I preached at the church, not long after Mother's death in January, 1968. Tom would sometimes drive up to Oak Park, whenever he had the opportunity, to spend an evening with Gloria; he always drove his car to see her and was a very careful driver. It was not long before they fell in love and, no doubt, thoughts of marriage. When we left India we had flown into O'Hare International Airport near Chicago that day in May 1976. Who should be there to meet us, but Gloria and Tom. They seemed to be so happy. Tom was dedicated to the Lord and we were convinced that Tom would be a good match for Gloria.

Tragedy Strikes

God had other plans for Tom – and for Gloria, as well. It

was just five weeks after meeting Tom at the airport, when he and Gloria came to greet us upon our arrival back in the States from India, that God called Tom Home to Heaven. It was a tragic accident on a freeway south of Chicago, which took Tom's life. He had gone up to see Gloria on his motorcycle, the only time he had done that, for he always drove his car. Tom's mother was quite concerned about Tom driving in heavy traffic on Chicago's freeways on his motorcycle and urged him to take his car instead; but Tom assured her he would be careful. Gloria had permission from the nursing supervisor to go with Tom to a nearby ice cream parlor. Their conversation that evening centered on things of the Lord, talking about heaven and how wonderful it must be. During their time together Tom showed signs of fatigue and Gloria suggested that he could rest in the lounge at the nursing school; she would get permission for him to do so. But Tom was anxious to get back home, for he had to get up early the next morning to get to work at the steel plant in Gary where he and his father worked. Saying goodbye to Gloria, he headed for home and hardly half an hour later, with little traffic on the freeway at that time of night, Tom was apparently sucked into the back of a semi-truck. He died instantly and was so disfigured that at his funeral a few days later, his casket was kept closed. I was just finishing the last class of that summer session at the seminary in Grand Rapids, when I was called out of class to answer a call on the telephone; it was from Tom's father, who told me of Tom's accident and death. I immediately left to tell Wilma and we decided then and there to hurriedly pack up our things and drive to Gary, Indiana.

We were prepared to go from there, after Tom's funeral, to California for Kathy and Bruce's wedding. Gloria had already been brought to Gary by the pastor of the church, who had gone up to Oak Park to break the news to her of Tom's tragic death. We were convinced that God brought us back to the States to be with Gloria at that time. God certainly makes no mistakes and He didn't when it came to Tom's death. Gloria was supposed to drive out to California with us, along with Phyllis, for Kathy and Bruce's wedding; but she decided that she would rather stay on there for a few more days and then fly out to Sacramento in time for the wedding. Phyllis was home from Clearwater Christian College for the summer and so; she went with us in our car.

Kathy and Bruce were married on July 10 in a little white church in Citrus Heights, California, where the Callison family were members. The wedding was quite unusual in that they both stood at the front entrance to the church to welcome all the guests as they arrived. After everyone had been seated, Kathy and Bruce walked together down the aisle to the front. I was seated with Wilma on the front seats and, as is the custom at most weddings, the pastor asked, "Who gives this woman in marriage?" I stood and replied, "Her mother and I do," at which time the pastor then turned over the rest of the ceremony to me. I was thrilled to have this privilege of being the officiating minister at my own daughter's wedding. It was at the very end that I announced to the congregation, "I now present to you, Mr. and Mrs. Bruce Callison." Kathy and Bruce had both written their own vows given to each other. Gloria had flown out to California in time to be part of the wedding and be there for our support during this time of grieving for the loss of one whom she had planned to marry. One day we will understand it all. Until then, we only "...see through a glass darkly..." (I Corinthians 13:12.)

Spying Out The Land

After the wedding, we headed north to British Columbia. Gloria flew back to Chicago and Phyllis went with us to "spy out the land." Our purpose in going to British Columbia was to see firsthand possible places of ministry in pioneering a gospel outreach to the East Indians in Canada's westernmost province. Several places had been suggested to us in other parts of Canada, as well as in the States. This included Toronto, Ontario, which had the largest concentration of East Indians, but we soon ruled that out as a place that God would want us to serve. While we recognized the need to reach the many thousands of East Indians living in Toronto, the challenge presented to us in that spring issue of *Harvest* in 1974 was for British Columbia, not Toronto. Also, we could have gone right away to Yuba City, California, where John and Cora Wilkens were having an effect ministry. They were seeing fruit from their efforts in reaching the vast numbers of Punjabis living in the Sacramento Valley. Yuba City is only about 40 miles from Citrus Heights, where Kathy and Bruce are still living. But, again, it was the appeal that Doris Richardson had given in her article in our mission publication for British Columbia. We knew that was where God wanted us to be, rather than in Yuba City, California. From California we drove up to Abbotsford, which is about 100 miles north of Seattle.

We stayed in one of the summertime workers' quarters at a raspberry farm operated by Henry and Mary Stobbe, a Mennonite couple, who also had a great burden for East Indians and had been praying for someone to come to give them the gospel. Most of the workers the Stobbes usually hired to pick their raspberries were Punjabis, who come from the Indian State of Punjab in the northwestern part of the country. The Sunday we were in Abbotsford, which happened to be Wilma's 51st birthday, we went with the Stobbes into Vancouver to attend a Hindi service. The Stobbes told us that the Hindi service, which was held in a basement room of a Mennonite church, was, to their knowledge, the only effort being made at the time to reach East Indians with the gospel in the Greater Vancouver area.

By early August we were back in Grand Rapids, Michigan, after having traveled some 8,000 miles, including our trip out to California for Kathy and Bruce's wedding, our trip up to British Columbia and back to Michigan, as well as some deputation meetings. A few days after arriving back in Grand Rapids, we packed up our suitcases again and headed for Toronto, Ontario. While we had made our decision to move to British Columbia to begin our new ministry amongst the people of India, who had settled in that part of Canada, we felt it important to do some kind of a survey of the East Indians in the Toronto area. We stayed in the home of Ray and Mona Joyce, parents of Keith Joyce, one of our former students at Sunrise School; at the time that Keith was at Sunrise School, the Joyces were missionaries in Abu Dhabi in the Arabian Gulf. The Joyces had a literature ministry to Muslims worldwide. They were suppliers of gospel literature to other missionaries reaching Muslims for Christ. They were our very dear friends with whom we had stayed in Beirut, Lebanon back in 1967. During the two days we were in Toronto, we tried to get as much information about East Indians in Greater Toronto as we possibly could in that short a time. While there were more East Indians living in Greater Toronto than in any other part of the country, we were still convinced that God wanted us to move to British Columbia. This decision was finally made when we attended BMM's tri-annual conference being held in Upper Marlboro, Maryland the second week of August. We had driven there directly from Toronto. While at the conference, we came to know that our transfer to the North America Field was made official. We were now ready to press forward with plans for applying to the Canadian government for our landed immigrant papers.

A Diary Of Events - In Regard to Applying for Canadian Landed Immigrant Status

1976

September 10 - Applications for landed immigrant permits are sent to the Canadian Consulate in Detroit.

September 21 - A letter to the Canadian Consulate from our BMM Canadian representative, certifying that we had a guaranteed job in Canada and that our salary will be paid in U.S. funds, is forwarded to the Canadian Consulate.

November 6 - We write the Consulate in Detroit to find out what has happened to our application.

November 9 - A reply from the Consulate informs us that they never received the mission's letter of guarantee.

November 23 - A fresh letter of guarantee is sent. All we can do now is wait and pray.

1977

January 25 - We have our interview with the Canadian Consular officer in Detroit. His reception of us doesn't seem to be all that encouraging. Two demands are made of us, which we feel we cannot keep. What should we do now?

February 15 - A letter to the Canadian immigration office in Detroit from our BMM Canadian representative arrives in the mail.

February 16 - On the spur of the moment, I decide to drive down to Detroit and hand deliver the letter to the Canadian Consular officer with whom we had our interview in January. I am told by the receptionist in the outer office that I would need to have an appointment. My request for an appointment at that time for just 5 minutes is eventually granted. I am well received by the immigration official. His reception this time was quite in contrast to the earlier meeting we had with him in January.

February 19 - A draft of what our purpose would be in going to Canada as landed immigrants is mailed to the Consulate in Detroit. The paper is entitled, "A proposed strategy for establishing a new ministry of Baptist Mid-Missions of Canada in the Province of British Columbia."

February 26 - A letter, dated February 23, is received from the Canadian Consulate in Detroit, along with medical forms to be filled out by an examining physician. Our application this time for landed immigrant papers has apparently been approved.

May 5 - Praise the Lord! Our immigration papers are granted. They are valid until September 29 by which date we must be "landed" in Canada.

Watch God Work

In a newsletter to our supporters, dated January 1977, we

wrote the following:

"Praise the Lord! We have just heard from the Canadian Consulate in Detroit with the following: 'This is to inform you that your application for permanent admission to Canada has been reviewed and is being processed.' We are to appear at the Consulate on Tuesday, January 25 at 10:30 a.m. for an interview. At that time we are to present certain documents as proof of citizenship, personal assets, job guarantee, educational qualifications and local police certificates. Following the interview we are to have a complete physical examination and present the doctor's report on their special forms. We have been informed that processing of the medical reports will take at least another four to six weeks."

On January 25th we appeared before the consular officer with great expectations that we would be well received and receive assurance that our permits would soon be granted with no problem at all. As soon as we entered his office at the specified time, we knew the official was not as friendly as we thought he would be. He was cordial in a business-like manner. What was asked of us in the course of our one-hour interview left us a bit dismayed. In a special bulletin to supporters, written after we arrived home from the interview, we wrote the following: "While he (the consular officer) recognized our bonafides and our sincere desire for a spiritual ministry amongst the people who had immigrated to British Columbia, Canada from India, he informed us that our case was most unusual; the Canadian Government had apparently never had anyone before us apply for a permit to work amongst a foreign ethnic group, as well as by established, recognized Baptist churches, or organizations."

We went on to write in our special bulletin to supporters the following: "Both of these conditions, if required to be carried out, will make it almost impossible to obtain the needed permit for Canada. Those requirements were: 1. that we receive the endorsement of Baptist churches in the province and 2. that we receive the endorsement of the East Indian community in the province. As soon as we got back home we contacted Rev. Leigh Adams, our North America Field administrator, for consultation. He was surprised to hear that the Consulate had made such conditions in granting us our landed immigrant permits, for none other of our missionaries who were working in Canada at the time, were required to provide such endorsements in order to obtain their permits. Brother Adams decided to contact the Canadian Consulate in Cleveland for their advice in the matter. They informed him that inasmuch as the mission is the second agent and not the ethnic group to which we are going, no mandate or invitation from that group is needed. There seems to be a conflict of opinion between the different Canadian Consulates."

Continuing in that newsletter to supporters, we wrote, "A fresh letter from our Mission's Canadian representative to the Canadian Consulate in Detroit will be sent to us as soon as possible. That letter will simply state our case and ask that the permit be granted us on the same basis as has been previously granted to our other missionaries working in Canada. Ken will take the letter right away to the Consulate in Detroit and at that time make an effort to get a fresh interview. If the consular officer still does not recognize the mission's request, then we will seek an appeal to a higher Canadian government official."

And so it was that on February 16, 1977 I made that quick and unannounced trip to Detroit. I went with the intent of speaking with the same official, with whom we had our interview on January 25th. Upon my arrival, I was told by the receptionist that I would need an appointment and the soonest that would be possible would be in one month. In another month I was to be in the southern part of the States for meetings. When I informed the receptionist of this and that all I needed was just five minutes with the official. I was willing to wait in the outer office as long as necessary. When she heard this, the receptionist excused herself, informing me that she would see what could be done. A few minutes later the receptionist returned to say that the official would see me at exactly 12 o'clock noon for five minutes. It was 10 a.m. when she told me this. I had two hours to wait. I came prepared for such an eventuality and had my briefcase with me with a number of things to take care of. Time seemed to drag by, but promptly at noon, I was beckoned by the receptionist to follow her, which I did.

The five minutes granted me stretched into over half an hour and my meeting with the same official was as different as day is from night compared to our first meeting with him in January. I was greeted very cordially and invited to sit down and share with him what was on my mind. The letter from our Canadian representative was presented to him and in the course of our conversation, nothing was mentioned at all about the two requirements we would need before our permits could be granted. Instead, he asked me to submit to him, in writing, details of our expected church planting ministry and how we would go about getting such a work started. I promised him to have those details in his hands within a week. After our meeting ended, I drove back to Grand Rapids, going over in my mind what I was hoping to put down on paper. By the end of the week I had prepared that paper and sent it off in the mail. Within one week following my meeting with the

Canadian consular officer a thick envelope arrived from the Canadian Consulate in Detroit containing forms to be filled out by a doctor. We were making progress in our application for our landed immigrate papers for Canada and just that one step left to take, our physical exams by a doctor, along with chest X-rays. At the end of our prayer letter to supporters in January, we closed with the following, "Hanging on the wall over our desk is a motto with these words, **WATCH GOD WORK**." This is actually the motto of the D & D Homes in St. Petersburg, Florida, a place where missionaries who are home on furlough can stay during the time they are in the States. Present directors of D & D Homes are Colonel and Mrs. Phil Fogle. Phil served with our U.S. army for many years and retired with the rank of colonel. Phil also serves on the General Council of Baptist Mid-Missions. We have known Phil and his wife, Betty for many years and also count them as very dear friends. Well, we did watch God work. He was bringing to pass His will for our lives that we might enter Canada as landed immigrants in order to reach other landed immigrants, people from India, with the gospel. Our permits, dated May 5, 1977, were actually in hand four days after our medical papers had been sent to the Consulate in Detroit.

Near the end of May we made a quick trip to Abbotsford to locate a house to rent. Our plan was ultimately to buy our own house as soon as was practical. We were told of a house, which was available to rent. It was owned by a missionary couple serving in Borneo under an interdenominational mission. They were relatives of former co-workers of ours in our early days in India. They were looking for someone to stay in their house while they were on the field in Borneo and were asking only $300 rent per month, considerably less than what a house of that type would rent for in Abbotsford. The house was located in a part of the city where there were numerous East Indians. In fact, one family, the Narangs, lived right across the street. Returning to Grand Rapids, we began preparation for our move to Canada. We had to be out of our townhouse apartment by June 30, at the latest.

God Provides…But Never Too Soon

Another motto of the D & D Homes has hung on the wall in our office, which states the following:

> "In a work of faith one soon learns to try to look not too far ahead. God, you may be sure, will provide, but…never too soon."

It wasn't long before God also proved this to us.

We were ready to move to Canada, though we had no furniture of our own. What furniture we had at the townhouse in Grand Rapids, was loaned to us by a number of friends at our home church in Wayne, Michigan. That furniture was returned to them at the time we left for our new home in British Columbia. We came to find out about a family at Berean Baptist Church in Grand Rapids, where we attended during the time we lived there, who owned a furniture store on the north side of the city. When these folks heard about our need for furniture for our new home in Canada, they invited us to come in to their furniture store and look around. Our interest was in burying a sofa bed, so that we would at least have a place to sit down during the day and sleep on during the night. What we would do about other furniture, we hadn't even given it a thought. When we arrived at the store, we were told to look around throughout the whole store and pick out enough furniture to fill five rooms of a house. Well, we decided, even if we didn't have the money, it wouldn't hurt just to look; and so we looked. We picked out enough furniture to fill five rooms of a house, just as the owners of the store told us to do. After we had walked through the whole store and picked out those five rooms of furniture, we were told by the owners that they would sell the furniture to us at their cost, tax free and we could pay them whenever we had the money, just as the Lord provided. God did provide and within six months of our arrival in Canada, we had the furniture all paid for. God even provided so that we were able to ship all our things by commercial moving van and had enough money on hand to pay for that major expense. Yes, God did provide, just at the right time. Philippians 4:19 proved to be true in this case; and so did that motto hanging on the wall.

Welcome to Canada

"Welcome to Canada! We hope your stay will be a happy one."

With those words, we were welcomed to British Columbia, Canada as landed immigrants, by the immigration official who processed our papers. We had entered Canada at the Canadian Port of Entry in Huntingdon, just on the south edge of Abbotsford. It was about 7 p.m. on July 2, 1977 when we crossed into Canada, less than five days after we left Grand Rapids, Michigan. It was also our oldest daughter's 27th birthday. We had traveled over 2,600 miles, averaging 600 miles a day to get there. The Lord watched over us as we drove across the country, through bright sun, rain and dust storms, along with high winds. Months of waiting, praying and unwinding of bureaucratic red tape were finally over and we had reached our destination. Welcome to Canada!

It was late Saturday evening when we arrived and local stores were all closed, but we found a small grocery store still open and were able to buy a few things to tide us over until Monday. At that time, all stores were closed on Sunday, except for a few gas stations. Our household goods were still on the way, but with some forethought, we had brought with us a few bed sheets, blankets and pillows. After spreading them on the floor, we "climbed into bed" and dropped off into a heavy and much needed sleep, even though our bed was a bit hard.

The next day, Sunday, we attended a local independent Baptist church, which was to become our first home church in Canada and later became active members of the church. After the morning service and a simple meal at our new home, we went out calling on Indian families in the neighborhood, as well as in some nearby communities. It was quite interesting how we found out where many of the East Indians were living. We, first of all, searched through the telephone directory, looking for names that were distinctly Indian and Punjabi, in particular. We also went out into the countryside, looking at all the mailboxes until we found one with a Punjabi name on it. We were amazed to find out how many of these people were living in the Greater Abbotsford area. They seemed to be moving into the area by the hundreds every month. As time went on, the people began to flood Abbotsford and its surrounding communities. We came to find out that by the 1990's the East Indian population in Abbotsford had reached over 10% of the total population.

The first family we met when we went out calling our first Sunday in Canada was the Chahal family. Mr. Chahal had professed at one time to having become a Christian, but, sad to say, continued holding on to some of his Sikh religious practices. He was being taken to Vancouver General Hospital in Vancouver for tests, later to receive treatment for a bone condition in one of his hips and legs. We were sorry to have eventually lost contact with the family and never had the opportunity of finding out for sure if Mr. Chahal had truly placed his faith in Jesus Christ as his own personal Savior and God. One day, as we are ushered into the presence of Christ, we will find out if Mr. Chahal was saved or not; we can only hope that he was.

Right across the street from us on Debreen Crescent lived the Narang family. It wasn't long before we made a special call to meet the whole family, including two grandfathers, a grandmother, an aunt and others, all living in the same house, which was a mirror image of our house. At that time the Narangs had only one child, a young daughter by the name of Swaran. Swaran came to spend a lot of time in our house. In time the Narangs had their one and only son, Jesse and later on two more girls were born. We met other families in the neighborhood, who would all come under the hearing of the gospel.

The Beginning Of Our Bible Club Ministry

Three months after our arrival in Canada we held our first Bible club for East Indian children. At the time we called it our JOY (Jesus, Others and You) Club. Later on we came to find out that there was a copyright on that name by another mission and, therefore, we had to use another name. Nancy Knopf, of our mission, had begun a Bible club program; called Bible Seekers, and that is the name we gave to our Bible clubs. Our first club was held on October 13, 1977 with ten children in attendance. In time, we began to average 22 children per club time and soon had to divide the club, going to two different club meetings per week.

We did a lot of driving in our six-passenger car, bringing children who lived some distance away. We held our clubs right after school was out in the afternoon and would wait near the schools to pick up the children as they came out. I don't believe that would be possible today. At any rate, we were able to reach many East Indian children with the gospel in this fashion, with permission of their parents.

In time, the Lord provided an 8-passenger station wagon, in which we would often bring up to twelve children at a time, sometimes more. There is a strict seat belt law in British Columbia, which states that every person riding in a vehicle must be in a seat belt. One day I went to see our local chief of police and asked him what the law called for in regard to hauling people in a vehicle. I asked him how many people I could legally transport in our 8-passenger station wagon. His reply was that I could transport as many people as I could comfortably fit into the station wagon, but on two conditions; every person must be in a seat belt and I should be able to see clearly through the rear view mirror, in addition to the two side view mirrors. Well, we never broke the law, for every child we brought to Bible club in our vehicles was in a seat belt. Many times there were two children to a seat belt.

That first October we invited many Punjabi families to our home for a time of refreshments and to meet Pastor Daniel Abraham, a longtime friend from India. Brother Daniel had been chaplain at the Christian Medical College in Ludhiana in the Punjab. Daniel was visiting in the States and speaking in regard to a new ministry he had been developing in Ludhiana, which was a Christian private school for Punjabi children. Having Daniel in our home presented a golden opportunity to present the gospel to those who came to our home, which was filled with people we had met since arriving in Canada.

Sowing Seeds Through Friendship Evangelism

One of those who came to our home that evening was Sukhdev Saran. Sukhdev very seldom visited the local Sikh temple, except for special occasions. Since coming to Canada he had shaved his beard and cut his hair, while also not wearing the traditional Sikh turban. One day we stopped at the Saran home and when the door was opened to us, we began speaking in Hindi. We were welcomed into their home as though we were relatives from India. Hindi is very close to the Punjabi language, spoken by the overwhelming number of East Indians in the Abbotsford area. We were invited to stay for tea, which turned out to be a small meal. The Sarans' married daughter and her husband were living in the basement suite of their home. In addition, there were two sons who attended a local high school. That initial meeting was the beginning of a longtime friendship with the Sarans, which eventually led to Sukhdev coming to our Sunday afternoon Bible studies in our home. In time, we began to have English tutoring classes with the son-in-law, who had only recently arrived in Canada. He still had his long hair tied up on top of his head and covered with the Punjabi turban. It was not long after that he cut his hair and beard and no longer wore the turban.

We befriended the Sarans in many different ways, which ultimately gave us the opportunity of giving them a clear witness about our living, loving God, Who sent His Only Begotten Son, Jesus Christ, into this world to die on a cross in order to provide eternal life to all who would accept Him. It was not long after we first met the Sarans that the wife had an accident at a local factory, which processed vegetables grown in nearby farms. She had to meet with the Workmen's Compensation Board to prove that she was worthy of a fair compensation for the injury she had sustained in the factory. I went with her to give her confidence and to interpret for her what was being said.

About two years later Sukhdev had been arrested for DUI (Driving Under the Influence of alcohol). He had run into another car after drinking at a friend's house and had to appear in court a few days later to give answer to his offense. Sukhdev came to see me a few days after the accident and told me what had happened. He confessed how ashamed he was of himself, how he had disgraced his family, even disgraced me and disgraced God. Would I help him when he appeared before the magistrate? My immediate reply was that I felt like letting him "stew in his own juice", that he had to work himself out of this problem on his own and pay the consequences for his foolishness. But then I told him I would go with him and stand beside him when he stood before the magistrate. I did just that and even pled on his behalf, reminding the magistrate that this was Sukhdev's first offense and deserved some mercy from the court. Well, the end result was that he had his driving privileges taken away for three months and had to pay a fine of just $450, which could be paid in installments. Ordinarily, the penalty could have been a suspended license for up to two years, a two thousand dollar fine and possible jail time.

In time, after befriending the Sarans in other ways, Sukhdev asked me one day, as we stood out in front of his house talking, "Ken, why are you doing all this for us?" Well, praise the Lord again! That was just the opportunity we were praying for. My reply, as I looked Sukhdev in the eye, was, "The reason why we are doing all this for you is this. We want you to come to know and love the one and only God there is and come to trust His Son, Jesus Christ, as your own personal Savior." It was not long after Sukhdev had asked that question of me and I had given him my answer, that he did make a profession of trusting Christ alone as his God and Savior. After we had moved into our new home on Magnolia Crescent, our friend from India, Dr. Daniel Abraham, came to visit us a second time. As we had done on his first visit we had a special meeting in our home for all our East Indian friends in the Abbotsford area. While Daniel was with us, we made a call in the home of the Sarans. It was actually a pre-arranged visit, for we had all been invited to their home for a special meal. Sukhdev was happy to see us when we arrived at their home and urged us to come with him right away into a room in the basement. He quietly told his son-in-law to go upstairs and tell Mrs. Saran to hold up on serving the meal until we came back upstairs. There were more important things to take care of than eating. Daniel Abraham had thought of bringing with him a Hindi language Bible and there in the basement of their house, as we three men bowed our knees before a long sofa, Sukhdev once again heard the gospel story and in a simple prayer, acknowledged his sin and accepting of Jesus Christ as his own personal Savior. What a great time we had upstairs at their dining room table, feasting on a delicious Punjabi meal that Mrs. Saran had prepared for us. That was the second meal we had experienced that evening, for just a short time before, we three men, Brother Daniel Abraham, Sukhdev Saran and I, had feasted on the Word of God which brings new life to all who believe in Christ. It is our prayer and hope that one day we will see Sukhdev in heaven, along with many others whom we had reached with the gospel over the many years of our lives and ministry.

A Lost Sheep Is Found

December 4, 1977 was a momentous day, when Gurdeep Dhillon bowed his knees with me in my office and gave his heart to Christ. Later that morning, after the service at our church, he made a public profession of his faith in Jesus Christ through believer's baptism. In the December edition of our newsletter, *From Our Desk,* I quoted from Luke 15:7, "...joy shall be in heaven over one sinner that repenteth, more than over ninety-nine just persons who need no repentance." This verse was a testimony of Gurdeep's victory over a life gripped by alcohol, which had left him a derelict, a wandering bum. Realizing his desperate need, he tried fleeing to the Salvation Army, as he cried out for deliverance from his terrible habit.

On October 5, 1977 there was a long article in our local newspaper, the Abbotsford, Sumas and Matsqui News, entitled, "Stewards ministering to East Indians." It spoke of our Bible club outreach to East Indian children, of our attempt to reach East Indian families with the gospel and of our being available "day or night to any other needs in the East Indian community." The day after this article appeared in the newspaper we received a call from one of the workers at the Salvation Army Rehabilitation Centre in Miracle Valley, northeast of the town of Mission, which is just across the Fraser River from Abbotsford. We were informed that there was a young Punjabi man, who was an alcoholic and had come to them for help, trying to get rid of his terrible drinking habit. But they didn't seem to have the answer to his need, not knowing exactly how to help him. Would I be willing to drive out to Miracle Valley to meet him? The next morning I made the hour's drive to meet Gurdeep. His appearance was of one who had fallen about as low as a person could fall. He was dirty and smelly, bleary eyed, but with a pitiful look on his face, which seemed to cry out, "Help me!" I informed Gurdeep that if it was agreeable with my wife, he could come and live in our home.

As I drove back home with a heavy heart, I cried out in prayer, "Oh Lord, You are the only One Who can help this young man get deliverance from his habit. But if You can use us to bring him to Christ and give him deliverance, we are willing to do anything to bring that to pass." When I told Wilma of Gurdeep and my desire to bring him home to live with us, she was in perfect agreement with me. The following day I drove back out to Miracle Valley and told Gurdeep of our willingness to give him a home. He had to agree to certain conditions, which included eating with us, sitting at the table when we read the Bible and prayed. On Sundays he would have to go to church with us. He would be under our total care and authority. Without hesitation, Gurdeep agreed to those conditions and I took him home with me.

I am sure he had not had a bath in a long time and had never slept between two clean sheets in a warm and comfortable bed. Aside from the short time he had been at Miracle Valley, he certainly had not eaten nourishing food in many days. But beyond all we gave him in a physical sense, the most important thing was that he found love in our home. Outwardly, he had an astonishing transformation. He was now clean and wearing clothes I found in my closet that fit him. He smelled clean and had a bright look about him. Outwardly he had become a different person. But it was the spiritual change that took place, which caused us to rejoice. What Gurdeep needed was an inward transformation of a new life in Christ. And that was what happened that first Sunday morning in

December 1977, when Gurdeep came into my office to tell me that he was now ready to trust Christ as his own personal Savior. Would I show him how to do it? Would I? I could hardly wait to open God's Word that Sunday morning.

Gurdeep's Struggle, But Final Victory

Victory over alcohol did not come easily for Gurdeep. On more than one occasion, he succumbed to drinking and each time he would seem to stop. What seemed to be the catalyst to eventually give him total victory was what happened one day when I went to see him in Vancouver, where he was then living. He had left us some time before and moved into Vancouver, where he had a job. It didn't pay much, but it was at least a job. Our concern was that he faithfully attend a Bible teaching church every Sunday morning. Of that we couldn't be sure, but all we could do was to encourage him, pray for him and commit him to the Lord.

I had found out where he was living at the time and was not happy regarding that situation. He was living in a room on the second floor of a cheap hotel on East Hastings Street in Vancouver. East Hasting Street was known as Skid Row, the place where all the "winos" and drug addicts hung out. I drove into the city one day and found the hotel. When I parked my car nearby, I could only hope that it would still be there and nothing would be stolen from it when I came back out. As I walked up the stairs to the second floor, the smell was almost overwhelming. Holding my breath as much as I possibly could, I found the room where Gurdeep was supposed to be staying. Could this possibly be his room? It reeked of alcohol, and when I called out the voice that answered was quite unintelligible. The slurred voice from within, of one completely drunk, cried out "Come in," which I did. As I walked into the room I had to literally kick aside all the wine, beer and whiskey bottles that littered the floor. I was totally shocked by the appearance of the room and of Gurdeep lying on the rough steel cot in a drunken stupor. I had come unannounced, for Gurdeep had no prior knowledge of my coming to see him and I was glad it was so. When Gurdeep saw me, he was shocked to see me standing there before him. If ever there was such a thing possible, he seemed to have been shocked into instant sobriety. He could not believe at first it was me. But his look told it all and, sitting up, he began to weep. I could only unashamedly weep with him and pray with him. He was a broken man. But that is what God needed in order to deal with his alcoholic problem and give him victory once and for all.

God got hold of Gurdeep's life and gave him total victory. When that happened, whenever we saw Gurdeep, he would testify of the victory God gave him over alcohol and unashamedly testified before other family members and friends of his faith in Christ. Gurdeep later moved to Toronto, where he had a responsible job with a company, manufacturing plastic shopping bags. He was faithful in attending a small Baptist church on the west side of the city where he lived in a small apartment. We visited him there and when we saw a calendar on the wall with marks beside every day, we asked him about it. He then told us the story. Every morning, upon waking to a new day, he would put a mark on the calendar and say, "Another day of victory for Jesus." Gurdeep could have made the song, "Victory in Jesus" as his very own testimony. While Gurdeep was living in Toronto, I would receive a phone call from him from time to time at around 9 p.m. our time. When I would remark, "Gurdeep, why are you calling so late? It is midnight where you are and you should be in bed." His only reply was always, "Well, I just wanted to call you and let you know how I am." He was always rejoicing in the Lord and relating of God's blessings in his life. He eventually moved back to Vancouver where he found a good job and a respectful place to live. He had struck up a close friendship with another Punjabi man, who was also a Christian. One day Gurdeep came to visit us with a nephew, who lived in Victoria on Vancouver Island. While sitting at our table enjoying a meal Wilma had prepared for us, Gurdeep said the following, "I cannot understand how people can live in this world without knowing Jesus Christ as their own personal Savior." He nephew was a follower of the Sikh religion that Gurdeep had once been a part of. That statement of Gurdeep was cause for much rejoicing, knowing that Gurdeep was not ashamed of the gospel of Christ, for it had become, in his life," the power of God unto salvation." (Romans 1:12)

A few years later Gurdeep was again in our home with his friend from Vancouver. We had an enjoyable time together, as we talked about the things of the Lord. Upon leaving us that day, Gurdeep assured us he would make contact with us again in a few days. The time went by and there was no word from him. What had happened to him? Why had he not called us as he promised to do? Something was not right. We knew that he had a married sister living in Abbotsford in another part of the city from where our home was. We decided to locate her and see if she knew about Gurdeep. We found her house and found her at home and some other women with her. Her husband must have been at work. When we asked Gurdeep's sister if she knew of the whereabouts of Gurdeep, for he had promised to give us a call on the phone, her reply was simply, "Oh, didn't you know? Gurdeep died suddenly a few days ago from a heart attack." What a shock that was to us. We didn't know what to say. The family had probably given Gurdeep a typical Sikh funeral, including cremation of his body. We felt that something was not right about this whole situation. Could it have been that Gurdeep had been killed, possibly poisoned, by a family member because of his open confession of Christ as his Savior and God and that he was now a baptized Christian? We will never know the true story of his death until we get to heaven. This much we are sure of, Gurdeep had truly placed his faith in Jesus Christ as his own personal Savior on the Sunday morning he walked into my office and told me, "Mr. Steward, I am now ready to trust Christ as my Savior; please show me how." One day we will surely meet Gurdeep again, along with all the saints who have gone before us. Had Gurdeep been the only result of our years of service for the Lord in British Columbia, it would have been worth it all. But there were others, as well, who came to trust Christ as their own personal Savior. Eternity will one day reveal the extent of that ministry.

Purchasing Our First Home in Canada

After arriving in Canada on July 2, 1977, we lived for eight months in a house owned by a couple who were missionaries to Borneo. We could rent the whole house, except for one room in the basement where they had stored their household items, for a very small rent, well within our budget. It was there on Debreen Crescent that we began our Bible club ministry and there where we reached Gurdeep with the gospel. Also, while living in that house we had our first opportunity to have a gathering of our many Punjabi friends, when they heard a Christian message from our friend from India, Dr. Daniel Abraham. We knew that, in time, we would have to find our own place to live, whether to rent or to buy. The missionaries to Borneo were soon to return to Canada on furlough and would need their house. And so, we began to pray about buying our first home. We came to find out through friends of ours in Abbotsford that there was a Christian family who had decided to sell their home that had become too small for them with their growing family. They were willing to rent their house to us for just $250 per month. If we decided to go ahead and buy the house, any moneys we had paid for rent would be applied toward the final purchase price of the house.

On April 1, 1978 we moved into our new home and a few months later we stepped out on faith and approached a local bank for a loan in order to buy the house. We were informed by the loan officer that early the following week the mortgage rate would go up a few points. He was willing to have us sign a letter of intent, which would hold the mortgage at the present rate. The loan officer told us that he probably should not have told us of this increase in the mortgage rate, but, for some reason, which he could not explain, he had to tell us. He then told us that we would have a number of days to raise the down payment. We went home, somewhat in trepidation as to what we had agreed to. The letter of intent did not bind us to a contract, which would demand a down payment by a certain date and even require us to take out a mortgage on the house. And yet, we still wondered about the step we had taken. Despite any possible doubts, which may have been in our minds, we soon found out that God would provide the funds we needed for the down payment, set at $10,000. As we thought more about the whole matter, we felt that the down payment might as well have been $100,000, or even a million dollars! But God brought to our attention the motto tacked to the bulletin board in our office once again, "In a work of faith, one soon learns to try to look not too far ahead. God, you may be sure, will provide, but...never too soon." God would soon prove that to us again.

A few days after our meeting with the bank loan officer, we were invited to the home of Simon and Lucy Hoogendoorn, friends from the church in Abbotsford where we had become members. In the course of our conversation, Simon stated that they felt we should buy that house we were living in at 2519 Magnolia Crescent. He then told us they wanted to loan us $6,000 interest free to be paid back whenever we had the money! Having said that, he wrote out a check for that amount and handed it to us. It was the beginning of the down payment we needed to take out the loan at the bank. A few days later the doorbell rang and who should be standing at the door, but the son of other friends in our church in Abbotsford. He was holding in his hand a check for $2,000 and told us that it was a tithe of the commission he had made for selling a large commercial building in town. There were no conditions placed on the check, as he told us it was a gift to be used toward the down payment we needed on our house. We had no idea how he had come to know of our decision to buy that house. Praise the Lord! Now we had $8,000 and all we needed was the remaining $2,000. We remembered that we had that amount of money in a retirement investment, which had accumulated over a number of years. We decided to cash it in to make the total amount we needed for the down payment. We arranged to meet with the loan officer at the bank and present him with a check for $10,000. We were able at that time to sign the papers for the loan and the house was ours. Mortgage payments came to less than $200 a month, which was $50 less than what we had been paying the former owners for the monthly rent. And, on top of all that, they came through with their offer of applying what we had paid, up to that point in rent toward the price agreed upon for the house.

We now had plenty of space for our Bible club ministry and held most of our meetings in a large room in the basement. There was also a large back yard where we had picnics and other activities when the weather permitted. There was also space for a good size garden to grow some of our own vegetables in the summer. We loved it! For several summers we had Bible college students come to help us in our ministries. In addition, we were thankful for people from our church in Abbotsford, who helped us in a large literature outreach. There were also friends from across the border in nearby Everson, Washington, from Nooksack Valley Baptist Church, who came to help. We thank the Lord for each and every one, too numerous to name here; but who are known by the Lord and will one day receive their reward for their part in our efforts to reach East Indians and others with the gospel of Christ.

A Major Literature Outreach

In 1978 God gave us a burden to reach thousands of Punjabi-speaking East Indians throughout much of British Columbia with the gospel by means of the printed Word of God. We began gathering together a sizeable mailing list, which would ultimately reach nearly 7,000 households in numerous towns and cities throughout the province. We obtained telephone directories from the telephone company and from those directories we culled out the names and addresses of many people. It was quite an undertaking and took many hours of work searching every page of every directory, typing out the names on our electric typewriter and printing envelopes, one envelope at a time. How much easier and less costly would it have been if, at the time, we had the technology and computer system we have today.

A young German lady, who had immigrated to Canada

from South America, was a talented artist and she designed for us the cover to the Gospel of Mark in Punjabi. She did a beautiful job and from her master copy we were able to print 5,000 copies of that Gospel by a local Christian printing press. I then prepared a special letter, which was mailed with the gospels, explaining what the booklet was about and also inviting the readers to enroll in a special correspondence course we had prepared; enrollment cards were also enclosed. The course we offered had been used for many years in India. During those years we had been in Mussoorie, as houseparents at Baptist Mid-Missions boarding home for our MK's who were studying at Woodstock School, I served on the editorial committee of *Jiwan Jyoti* (Light of Life), a Bible correspondence ministry, which reached many thousands of people in India. I was given permission to use the course in connection with our ministry and to use the same name, **JIWAN JYOTI** Bible **Correspondence Centre.** As we prepared the materials to send out through the mail, friends from our church in Abbotsford helped us to stuff and seal the envelopes. Our deep gratitude goes to Bob Jones University, though their missions fund, for a grant that met the expense of printing the Gospels of Mark in Punjabi. The total cost of the project was over $3,000 Canadian. At that time it cost us only 18 cents for postage, with the weight of each packet of material coming to 3 ounces. It was quite an undertaking.

Though we did not receive a huge response from this literature outreach, we did hear from many. There were people who wrote, regarding our message. In one case a person tore up the gospel and returned it to us in the envelope we had used to mail it to him. We have no idea who it was, for he obliterated his name from the envelope and managed to return it to us without paying any return postage.

One positive response we had from the project was a young man by the name of Prem Singh Sidhu. Prem enrolled in our correspondence course, completed the whole course and received his special certificate. In the fall of 1979 we met Prem in his home in the Vancouver suburb of Surrey. What a joy it was to hear of his new-found faith in Christ. He and his wife and three small children lived only three blocks from Temple Baptist Church, which was pastored at the time by Gordie Hagen, a Bob Jones University graduate. I had preached at the church on a number of occasions and was able to direct Prem and his family there. In time he was discipled by Brother Hagen in preparation for believer's baptism. In January 1980 I had the joy of baptizing Prem at that church. What rejoicing there must have been in heaven over one sinner, who repented and chose to leave behind his old religion and openly confess Christ as his own personal Saviour. Unfortunately, over the years we lost contact with this young man and can only hope that he went on with the Lord and that one-day we will see him in heaven.

Our Adopted Indian Family

In February of the same year we saw Richard and Zarina Ling baptized. We had first met Richard shortly after our arrival in Canada. At that time he was not married, but soon after, he returned to India to marry Zarina whom he had met at a church party in Calcutta where both of their homes were. Richard's people were South Indians with a Hindu background. Zarina's people had been Muslims and came from North India; and so, this match was quite unusual, even for Indian Christians. Zarina's father had been pastor a Methodist church in Calcutta.

In the fall of 1979 Richard and Zarina asked if we could have a Bible study with them on Sunday afternoons in our home. We agreed to this eagerly and began the very next week. At the same time, we invited Sukhdev Saran to come for the study. He lived only a ten-minute walk from our house and was faithful in coming most Sundays. This proved to be the seed that resulted, along with another Bible study I was having in the nearby town of Aldergrove, in our planting Calvary Baptist Church of Aldergrove beginning the following year.

One Sunday, after our Bible study, Wilma was out in the kitchen preparing some refreshments. Zarina had also gone out to the kitchen so that she could reveal to Wilma her exciting news. "Mrs. Steward; I think I'm pregnant." To that, Wilma replied that she thought it would be a good idea if Zarina would consult with her doctor and see about getting a pregnancy test. It was not long after that Zarina was assured that she was carrying their first child. In time, Richard and Zarina were blessed with the first of three sons. All three of the boys, Zubin, Aaron and Ravi, have known us only as Grandpa and Grandma Steward. They had no other grandparents, for Richard and Zarina's parents had all died before Zubin was born. We were only too happy to accept them into our family and we were as family to them.

The Birth of Calvary Baptist Church of Aldergrove

By the end of 1980 there seemed to be enough interest on the part of a number of people to begin a new Baptist Church in Aldergrove. We were aware that there was already a Baptist Church in that town of some 15,000 people; but its doctrinal and ecclesiastical positions were such we could not agree with. As we prayed about the possibility of planting a fundamental Baptist church, which held to a pre-millenial, pre-tribulation position on the return of Christ, we saw the need for such a church. We consulted with our North American administrator at the time, Rev. Leigh Adams, who recommended that we should go ahead and begin such a ministry.

In early January, 1981 I put an ad in the local paper in Aldergrove, telling of our proposal to begin a Baptist Church, which was fundamental, pre-millenial and held to the pure Word of God. The ad revealed that a special meeting would be held in a local restaurant in Aldergrove, to explore the possibility of beginning such a church. There were some 25 people, who attended that informal meeting. When I explained to them what I had in mind for a church, 23 of them signed a paper, telling me that they were interested and wanted to become part of such a church. The following week I put another ad in the paper announcing our first meeting to be held at the Old Age
Pensioners' hall in Aldergrove on Sunday morning, January 11. I arranged with the O.A.P. people to rent their hall each Sunday morning and evening for just $25 a Sunday, with the agreement that if, at any time, they had some function that would take place on a Sunday evening; we would have to meet somewhere else. In the 2-½ years we rented the hall for our meetings, there was not one time in which we had to meet somewhere else.

On that first Sunday there were 19 in attendance at Sunday School, 20 who came to the morning service and 21 who were there for the evening service. From that first week we had prayer meeting on Thursday evenings in the home of one of our young couples, who lived just a few blocks from the O.A.P. hall. John and Susan Fehr were enthusiastic supporters of the work. From the beginning, prayer meeting attendance almost matched our Sunday services. In time, the church began to grow and it was not long before we began to see attendance reach into the 50's. On September 13th we had a rally day and called it, "Let's Go Over The Top!" Our goal for that Sunday was 50; there were 51 people in attendance that day. One of our supporting churches, Calvary Baptist Church of Gulfport, Florida, on the near south side of St. Petersburg, sent us songbooks they were no longer using. They were old books, but they were our first hymnbooks and we made use of them until we could purchase our own.

In March of 1981 we had an organizing service at which twenty-one baptized believers, signed a covenant and became charter members of Calvary Baptist Church of Aldergrove, B.C. We met one Sunday afternoon in the auditorium of Nooksack Valley Baptist Church in Everson, Washington for the special service at which we had the signing of our covenant; in addition. We also held our first baptisms. One of those who began attending church almost from the beginning was Ursula Borchert, who had come to Canada from what was then East Germany. She had grown there during World War II. When Ursula saw our ad in the Aldergrove paper, she decided our church was just what she needed. In time, Ursula became burdened to call on people in the community and invite them to our services. Ursula was not yet baptized, for that was to come later that year.

Calvary Baptist Church's First Convert

One Saturday afternoon Ursula began ringing doorbells at a nearby housing development. When she came to one door and rang the bell, a young mother opened the door. Ursula began telling the mother about Calvary Baptist Church and invited her to come to the service the next day. That young mother, Pamela Martin, seemed to react with great joy and her face lit up when she told Ursula that she would be very happy to come to our church the next morning. You see, just before her doorbell rang, Pamela had been trying to call several other churches to find out about their services. She hadn't received an answer to any of her calls. The next day, Sunday morning, Pam loaded up her two-year old daughter and infant son into the baby stroller and pushed them two blocks to the hall to attend our services; she never missed a Sunday after that, unless she had to be out of town. Unfortunately, to this day, her husband has rejected the gospel. At first, he was very hostile toward us, but in time, warmed up and occasionally would come out for a special function at church. Pam faithfully prays for her husband, as have the people at Calvary Baptist Church.

Pam heard the gospel every Sunday and the Lord began to bring her under deep conviction. And then, one Saturday evening, God finally got hold of her. It was October 12, 1981 when a well-known youth evangelist, Jack Wyrtzen sent his Word of Life Collegians, along with his associate, Harry Bolback, to Abbotsford for a citywide meeting. The meeting was held in the gymnasium of a large private Christian high school in Abbotsford. Most of our members at Calvary Baptist Church were there for the meeting, along with Pamela. Throughout the whole meeting, which was based on the Book of Revelation, Pam seemed to be under great conviction. Sitting beside her was Phyllis, our youngest daughter. Pam and Phyllis were about the same age and had struck up a warm friendship. When an invitation was given at the end of the meeting for anyone who wanted to be saved to come forward, Phyllis looked over at Pam and whispered to her, "Pam, if you want to go forward, I'll go with you." Praise the Lord, Pam could hardly wait to get out of her seat and rush forward to the front, so that she could let someone know of her desire to trust Christ as her own personal Savior. We are so thankful that Phyllis had gone forward with her as an encouragement and that she saw Pam's need and was willing to do that. In a very special way, Phyllis had a part in Pamela Martin coming to Christ.

The Blessings Continue at Calvary Baptist Church

In February 1982 we held a Sunday School contest. The theme was "Cruise for Christ". We had posters depicting two teams heading out for a cruise to Alaska, which eventually would take them to the small village of Iliamna, where our BMM missionaries, Bill and Carol Bursell, were serving. It was an exciting time as every Sunday we saw the small ships inching their way up the coast on their way to their destination. Every Sunday we saw new people coming and our overall attendance at Calvary Baptist Church began to grow even more.

In time, we saw the need to have our own church facilities. We learned that the local United Church of Canada congregation had built their new church. Their old church, which was located directly across the street from the post office to the south and Aldergrove Credit Union to the west, was up for sale. Our congregation voted to negotiate for purchase of the building and, as a result, the building was offered to us for what was considered to be a reasonable price. Yet, the amount was way beyond our church's ability to pay. The United Church allowed us to move in and take possession of the old church with no down payment and monthly mortgage payments of $800. It was an almost overwhelming challenge for our people; but they rose to the challenge and every month the Lord provided for the funds needed to make those payments. Attendance continued to grow and it was not long before it went into the 60's. At one time, for a special occasion we had at church, there were some 90 people in attendance.

We had our first wedding in our "new" church, as well as our first funeral. As a matter of fact, I had the joy of marrying two of our young couples. As for the funeral, one dear old lady, who had faithfully come to our services as her health permitted, suddenly died and we had the funeral in our church.

By 1983 we were joined by another BMM couple, John and Doreen Lacy, who had served in Liberia; but health conditions of John, resulted in their having to leave their field and seek a ministry in the States or Canada. They were a great addition to our ministry. Later on, the Lacys left us to take over a church in Hawaii. They remained there until it was discovered John had recurrence of a brain tumor, which brought them back to the States, where John soon went into the presence of the Lord while in a hospital in Bellingham, Washington, some 20 miles south of Aldergrove. John is buried in the cemetery in Lynden, which is about halfway between Aldergrove and Bellingham. John and Doreen were dearly loved by our people at Calvary Baptist Church of Aldergrove.

Physical Testings

Almost from the day we arrived in Canada to begin our ministry among the growing East Indian population, we were tested with one physical problem after another. After my heart attack in India in the spring of 1973, I continued to have angina attacks from time to time. It wasn't long after we had moved into our new home on Magnolia

Crescent that I came home from doing some shopping in town, only to find Wilma lying on the couch in our living room and our dog, Pema, lying beside her. Wilma seemed to be in much pain and replied almost casually, when I asked her what had happened, "I think I broke my foot." Nothing more; just that. I managed to get her into our car and off to emergency at our local hospital we went. X-rays showed she really had broken some bones in her foot. She had been up on the top step of a small footstool arranging curtains on a window in our dining room, when her feet slipped from under her and she went crashing to the floor. Needless to say, that put her out of commission for a while.

On Sunday, April 29, 1984 Wilma was coming down the steps from the church nursery, which was in the building adjoining the main part of the church. A children's class was meeting near the steps and Wilma, not wanting to disturb the class with her shoes making noise on the carpet less steps, slipped and fell down the last two steps onto the concrete floor. I was teaching the adult class in the church auditorium at the time when someone came in to inform me of what happened to Wilma. I quickly dismissed the class and informed someone to take charge, as I ran in to find her lying on the floor. With the help of one of our members, I managed to get Wilma out to our car and off to emergency we went. X-Rays showed that she had fractured her left pelvis in two places. There was nothing that could be done about that except for her to have complete bed rest and let the injury heal itself. One day I came home from town to find Wilma down in the basement. When I asked her how she got down there, she replied, "Oh, I sat down and bumped myself down, one step at a time!"

Burning My Candle at Both Ends

By late summer of 1984 I was having continuing angina attacks and when I consulted with our doctor, he very wisely suggested, "Ken, you are trying to burn your candle at both ends. You had better make a choice." We were giving nearly full time to our various ministries to the East Indians, including a large literature outreach, Bible club program, calling in homes of the Bible club children, plus other efforts to reach the East Indian community in our area. At the same time, we were giving many hours to our church-planting ministry at Calvary Baptist Church. Listening to what my doctor had told me, the first Sunday of September I handed in my resignation as pastor. It was a very hard decision to make, for I loved the pastorate. I loved the people and God was doing a great work in the hearts of the people. But, for the sake of my health and our ministry to the East Indians, I had to make the choice to burn my candle at only one end. I could not have an effective ministry in both places.

When I resigned my position as pastor of Calvary Baptist Church of Aldergrove, we felt it best to attend church elsewhere. We knew of Nooksack Valley Baptist Church in Everson, Washington, and eventually became members of the church. It was not long before we were involved in various ministries of that church, while still being able to give nearly full time to our East Indian ministries. Eventually, the church we had planted in Aldergrove called as their pastor a young missionary with Baptist Mid-Missions, who had served with his wife on our mission's Alaska Field. Chuck and Irene Brocka (they told people how to pronounce their name by saying "I'm Broke - eh!"). did a fantastic job in that ministry. One day we received a call from Chuck. Would we be willing to come back to

Calvary Baptist Church and help them on a limited basis in a teaching ministry? We agreed to come and help them for just two years, under certain conditions. I would only have teaching responsibilities with no administrative responsibilities. Most important of all, after consulting with our supporting churches, if this arrangement met with their approval, we would come and help. Our supporters gave their approval and we helped the Brocka's for those two years. Here I was, old enough to be the Brockas' father and the founding pastor of the church, but now serving under the leadership of Chuck. It was a very wonderful relationship we had with the Brockas and with our folks at Calvary Baptist Church during those two years

After our two years were up and we returned fulltime to our East Indian ministries, another couple came to work with the Brockas. John and Aloha Vance had been serving with Baptist Mid-Missions on the Big Island in Hawaii. After a year another change took place at the church when the Brockas, resigned as pastor and moved to Hawaii to reach the Mormons on the Island of Oahu. They served for a time at Gospel Baptist Church in Pearl City, a church where we too would later serve as interim pastor for three months. When the Brockas left for Hawaii, John Vance became the full time pastor of Calvary Baptist Church in Aldergrove.

Calvary Baptist Church had its struggles over the next few years and, in time, it sold the church buildings, put the money in the bank to earn interest, while they met at a local community hall every Sunday. By that time church attendance had fallen way off and there were only about as many people coming to the services as we had when we first began the church in 1981. John and Aloha had a great ministry and the church slowly began to build up again. In time, the Lord led them to purchase several acres of wooded land with a house on the property, which was located on the very western edge of Abbotsford, bordering on the town of Aldergrove. It was an ideal location and God continued to bless the work. The Vances moved into the house, while, at the same time, after doing some major renovations of several rooms, a small auditorium was opened up where the congregation could meet. Later on we came back to Calvary Baptist Church, became members and had an enjoyable time helping in the ministry.

Through Deep Waters

We had other physical testings, other than what we have already written about. But none had tested our faith so much as to what happened while I was still pastoring Calvary Baptist Church of Aldergrove. During our ministry there we received a shocking letter from our longtime home church in Michigan. Wilma had grown up in the church, where she had come to trust Christ as her Savior at the age of seven. I became a member of the church when we were married in 1947, or soon after. When we first went out to India, the church took on a large percentage of our support. A letter we received from the chairman of the church's missions committee stated that they did not believe I should be pastoring a church, that there was no need for such a church, inasmuch as there were many other churches in the area. The letter went on to say that we should be giving our fulltime to holding Bible clubs for East Indian children. The letter concluded that they would be giving us less toward our support and that this was a kind of "punitive" action. In addition, we would be given one year to leave our church-planting ministry. Twelve months later I was still pastoring the church. As a result, our longtime home church in Michigan cut off the remaining amount of support, just as they said they would. It was a devastating blow to us and we wondered what would happen to our total ministry. This action possibly played a part in the increased stress that happened to me and ultimately led to my resigning as pastor of the church. We never had full support during all our years in Canada, yet God met our needs, as He did in this case. We lost over $500 a month in mission support and the months ahead were a great struggle for us. There were major decisions we eventually would have to make. The deficit in our account at our mission's home office began to grow and it became a matter of great concern. As we look back on this whole situation, we believe the Lord was allowing us to go through these deep waters to test our faith in Him and His ability to see us through such a crisis in our lives and ministry. One day the Lord gave us the following promise: Isaiah 43:2-3 --- 'When thou passeth through the waters, I will be with thee and through the rivers, they shall not overflow thee…for I am the LORD thy God; the Holy One of Israel, thy Saviour…"

As our deficit continued to grow, it got very much out of hand and grew to the extent of $23,000. We wrote to our field administrator to say that something had to be done to reverse the situation. It was suggested that we should sell our house, leave Canada and move down to Yuba City, California, to work in a team ministry with John and Cora Wilkens. As already mentioned, the Wilkens were having a fruitful ministry amongst the many Punjabi people, who were living in that part of the Sacramento Valley. But, believing that God had called us to British Columbia to work amongst the East Indians in that province, we did not feel our ministry there was finished. It would have been great, in one sense to move down to Yuba City, for we would have been only forty miles away from Kathy, Bruce and their family. But that was not where God had called us;

we were convinced of that. We sold our home on Magnolia Crescent in 1985, as well as our second car, which we were also using in our ministries. We still had our eight-passenger station wagon, which we used like a school bus, to bring in children for Bible club. When we sold the house, it brought us a capital gain on the sale that was enough to pay off our deficit and still have $5,000 left over to use as a down payment on another house. We put the house up for sale on a Wednesday and three days later I happened to be home when a real estate agent came by with a couple, who were interested in purchasing the house. They had no sooner walked in through the front door when the wife asked me, "How much are you asking?" I gave her the price we wanted and she then remarked that the amount was agreeable with them and that they liked the house. They had come only into the front entrance of the house, barely stepping into the living room when they told me they wanted the house. Sold! Within three days!

Knowing that we had to find another place to buy, and soon, we went around town looking at various houses. We came upon a doublewide mobile home on a permanent foundation and on its own lot, a large lot. The mobile home also had an addition to it. The couple who owned the mobile home let us know their asking price and when we offered them 5,000 less, they said, "Sold." There was the 5,000 we had as a down payment. We were able to take out a new mortgage on our new home and within a few days we moved from our old home on Magnolia Crescent to our new home on Lombard Avenue. To add to all this, within a year our support level was back up to where it had been. In fact, we gained additional support beyond the previous amount. More than that, God began blessing our outreach to the people of India, whom we were seeking to reach for Christ. God had called us to British Columbia in a church-planting ministry and to pioneer a work among the growing East Indian population of Canada's westernmost province.

The Gospel Rejected

Not everyone who received a gospel witness from us accepted that witness, for it was rejected by many, both East Indian and white Canadian. In early November 1979, we received an urgent letter from a woman in St. Petersburg, Florida. She had apparently heard of us through our supporting church, Calvary Baptist Church, which was located in Gulfport at the time. Her request was for us to meet her brother, who was dying of a decaying muscle disease, possibly Lou Gehrig's Disease. He was unsaved and had long resisted the gospel, having turned a deaf ear to his sister's witness. We drove into Vancouver two days after receiving the woman's letter and met her brother, who was lying in a private hospital. Though we gave a very clear witness to him of Christ, we could see the hardness of his heart. While he knew that he was dying, he did not want anything to do with the Christian religion and he let us know this. He wanted nothing to do with his sister, or her attempts to get him converted. We came away from the hospital very disappointed that he had openly rejected our message. Before we left him, we told him that "it is appointed unto man once to die and after this the judgment." When we repeated this verse from Hebrews 9:27, it left him speechless. He had nothing to say. He did not speak to us again and we left him with a heavy heart, knowing that in his present spiritual condition, he would go out into a Christless eternity and to hell. We could but hope, at that point in time that somehow the Holy Spirit would bring such deep conviction to his soul that he would see his helpless, hopeless spiritual condition and come to trust Christ as his own personal Savior. Only eternity will reveal to us what his final decision was.

The Gospel Received

Though there were many who rejected the gospel, as did the man in the hospital in Vancouver, there were others, as I have already related in these memoirs, who did receive the gospel. One such one was a woman in the nearby town of Mission. One day she called us in great desperation. Would we please come to her home, for she knew that she needed to be saved, but didn't know how. What a joy it was to meet this woman, who had a ready heart to hear the gospel and trust Christ as her own personal Savior, right there in the living room of her home. There were others, as well, for which we give God all the glory.

There were many other victories and there were many other testings. But in and through them all, we knew that God was with us as we were reminded from time to time His promise given in those two different places, in Mussoorie, India and in Grand Rapids, Michigan, some ten thousand miles and less than two weeks apart, "Certainly, I will be with thee." (Exodus 3:12)

In the early part of the 1980's I was away from home on deputation meetings, seeking to raise more funds for our ministries in British Columbia. It was a discouraging time, for I raised little support. In fact, it cost me more to make such a trip than I gained in support; it was a case of one step forward and two steps backward. While I was away from home, Wilma, knowing the situation, sent a card that had printed on it, "I Miss You." Inside the card she included some comments from the current issue of "Our Daily Bread." She wrote the following,

"If we would let our hearts rest in the certainty that God's mighty hand is extended in preparation, provision and protection for us, we would not worry and fret."

At the time her card reached me with those words, I must confess that I was certainly worrying and fretting. At the end of the devotional for that day were the words,

"Those who see God's hand in everything can best leave everything in God's hand."

+ A Call To Canada +

Old Age Pension Hall in Aldergrove where
Calvary Baptist Church had its beginning

Calvary Baptist church's first church buildings in
Aldergrove

Our congregation at Calvary Baptist Church of Aldergrove, BC
The year - 1983

Gurdeep Dhillon. Our first East Indian convert

Part Eight: Retirement Years

January, 1991 -

Go Labour On!

Go, labour on! spend and be spent,
Thy joy to do the Father's will:
It is the way the Master went;
Should not the servant tread it still?

Go labour on! 'tis not for naught
Thine earthly loss is heavenly gain;
Men heed thee, love thee, praise thee not;
The Master praises: what are men?

Go labour on! Enough while here,
If He shall praise thee, if He deign
The willing heart to mark and cheer:
No toil for Him shall be in vain.

Go labour on while it is day;
The world's dark night is hastening on;
Speed, speed the work, cast sloth away;
It is not thus that souls are won.

Toil on, faint not, keep watch and pray,
Be wise the erring soul to win;
Go forth into the world's highway,
Compel the wanderer to come in.

Toil on and in thy toil rejoice!
For toil comes rest, for exile home;
Soon shalt thou hear the Bridegroom's voice,
The midnight peal, "Behold I come!"

----- Horatius Bonar, 1843

"Cast me not off in the time of old age;
forsake me not when my strength
faileth…O God, be not far from me:
O my God, make haste for my help.
I will hope continually and will yet
praise thee more and more."

                      ----- (Psalm 71:9, 12, 14)

"I have been young and now am old;
yet have I not seen the righteous
forsaken, nor his seed begging bread."

                      ----- (Psalm 37:25)

Is There Life After Retirement?

Wilma celebrated her 65th birthday on July 18, 1990, and the following December 12^{th 1} turned 65. It was the age of retirement. Retirement? That thought seemed the farthest from our minds; it seemed to be a "nasty" word. But we had to face the reality of it and a decision had to be made, whether to apply to the mission for retirement status and make some possible changes in our lives or to continue on in the ministries God had given us there in Canada. We finally made the decision to go on retirement status and by the end of the year the mission office informed us that we were now recognized as being on emeritus status. Emeritus? That means something about serving with merit, or having served well. As for that, our only desire has been that one day, when we meet our Savior in heaven, He will be able to say, "Well done, good and faithful servant; thou hast been faithful over a few things, I will make thee ruler over many things; enter thou into the joy of thy Lord" (Matthew 25:23). We applied to both the U. S. and Canadian governments for both countries' social security benefits and those benefits began from January 1, 1991, when our official "retirement" began.

Retirement? We weren't quite ready to call it "quits" yet. Our health was fairly good and we had a determination to just keep going for the Lord. As an old friend used to put it, we decided to just "keep on keeping on," as long as the Lord gave us good health and clear minds.

We praise the Lord for the many churches and individuals, who have faithfully prayed for us and given financially for our ministries over many years. It was time that we gave something back to them. We made it known to the churches that we wanted to serve them and if they were willing, we would like to give time to working in the church, doing anything, whether it was cleaning the church, helping in the nursery, working in the church office, going calling on shut-ins, doing whatever there was that needed to be done. All the churches had to do was provide us with a place to stay, while we were serving in the church; we asked nothing else. We served in two of our supporting churches in this way and thoroughly enjoyed our times with them. I had the privilege of teaching Sunday school, as well as preaching on a number of occasions.

Near the end of our first year of that type of ministry, we received a call from our field administrator, Rev. Leigh Adams. Would we be willing to go out to Pearl City, Hawaii for three months that summer to serve as pastor of the Gospel Baptist Church? The church was struggling after a sad situation, which happened in regard to the recently resigned missionary pastor. We agreed to go and had a wonderful time with the people. My ministry was one of pouring oil, so to speak, on hurting hearts. God blessed our ministry and we saw people begin to come together. On July 4, which happened to fall on Sunday that year, we had a special service, recognizing all the military service people, past and present, who attended the church. It was a very colorful service, as veterans and those presently in the various branches of our country's military, especially Army and Navy, came in their dress uniforms. After the morning service we went to the home of one of the church families where we had a picnic. At that time, I had the joy of baptizing a young female Navy officer in the swimming pool. Gospel Baptist Church met every Sunday in a local elementary school gymnasium, which meant that all the church's equipment used for the Sunday services had to be brought and set up each Sunday morning. The equipment was being stored in the back of the church van. Our only means of transportation to get around the island was that church van. And so, whenever we went anywhere on the island of Oahu with the van, we had to take all that equipment with us. What a sight it must have been to the islanders!

But then, we were also able to travel by the island's bus service. By paying a fee of fifteen dollars, as retirees, we could ride the bus anywhere on the island by showing the driver a special pass with our pictures on it. You can be sure we used the church van only when we absolutely had to. It was hot that summer we were in Hawaii and the van had no air conditioning in it. As a result, we had to always drive with the windows rolled down, bringing in hot air from the outside. We enjoyed those three months of ministry in Pearl City.

While we were in Hawaii, Sylvia and Bob, Wilma's sister and husband, flew out to spend a week with us. We had an enjoyable time with them touring the island of Oahu, including a trip out to see the sunken battleship, Arizona, which had been sunk in Pearl Harbor by the Japanese on December 7, 1941. It had been the second time we were able to visit this memorial to our servicemen, who gave their lives for the cause of our freedom so many years before. It was very interesting to note that oil continued to come to the surface of the water from the Arizona, lying on the bottom of the harbor. There is much that lends to the beauty of the island, including the many varieties of orchids being raised commercially. In contrast to the beauty of the island is the great amount of commercialism that attracts tourists by the thousands. One place we did not visit that time and had no desire to visit was Waikiki Beach. We left that to the lovers of sand, surf and sinful display of the flesh. But then, we were there for a spiritual ministry and not for pleasure.

On December 6, 1995 we left our home in Abbotsford and drove across Canada to Kenora, Ontario to serve there for five months. We had been asked by our field administrator to fill in for Garth and Margaret Roberts, who were in desperate need of a furlough. We arrived in Kenora to be greeted by cold weather and lots of snow. Kenora is located at the very northern tip of Lake of the Woods, most of which lies within the State of Minnesota. We enjoyed our ministry among both the white Canadians and First Nations People, the Ojibway. It was not easy living, for we stayed in the Roberts' mobile home a short distance out in the country. A number of times the water pipes froze and we had to bring in buckets of snow and melt it over the kitchen stove to get water for cooking and drinking. We heated the mobile home with a wood burning stove and that meant chopping wood and hauling it by a large plastic sled up to the house. Every evening, before settling in for the day, we had to connect the car's in-block heater to an electrical outlet on the side of the house; this was to ensure that the next morning we would be able to start the car's engine. One evening I forgot to do that and the next morning I couldn't start the engine. The temperature had dropped to a minus 40 degrees. As a matter of fact, for most of January we didn't see the temperature get much above minus 40. One morning the temperature was down to a minus 53 degrees C., with the wind chill factor registering at minus 90! That day we had gone for a walk with the snow up to our knees. We were well covered to keep out the cold air. Our faces were covered with woolen scarves, leaving only our eyes uncovered to see where we were going. Every breath we took froze as icicles on the scarves; it was that cold. We didn't see bare ground that winter until early May.

Also serving at Kenora with Garth and Margaret Roberts at the time was Carrie Thompson. It was a delight to work with this fine single missionary lady. Carrie is very talented musically, and had a warm heart for the people. She literally gave herself to the ministry at Kenora. We enjoyed our time working with Carrie, especially in the children's clubs. Each month we went to the local jail with Trapper John, the oldest member of the congregation, to preach in the city's jail. Trapper John, who was 96, did most of the preaching.

We left Kenora the end of May 1996 and drove down to Spartanburg, South Carolina, where Lily and family live. Our granddaughter, Katherine Jean, had met Matthew Bolton at Bob Jones University and were engaged to be married. Katherine had just completed her master's degree at BJU in the field of speech education. They had a lovely wedding in her home church in Spartanburg on June 8. What a joy it was for me to officiate at Katherine's and Matthew's wedding. Leaving Spartanburg the following day, we started heading back home. It was good to be home again and sleep in our own bed. We had been away for over six months.

The following spring we traveled across the States by Amtrak train and visited five of our supporting churches. Our travels took us all the way back to South Carolina and to Tennessee. During the times we weren't traveling on Amtrak, we rented a car to get from place to place. After spending some time with Wilma's father, along with her sister and husband in Oak Ridge, we brought Dad LaVoy back with us by train to our home in Abbotsford, BC. He enjoyed traveling by train very much and had his own private bedroom on each train we were on. He was with us for the celebration of our 50th wedding anniversary on

August 22, 1997. We made plans for him to stay on with us and live out the rest of his days in Canada. But God had other plans for him less than four months later.

We had a wonderful time with our family, as most of them were there for that special time in our lives. We rented a 20' x 20' tent top and set that up in our back yard. Invitations went out to family and friends, inviting them to our home to help us celebrate 50 years of marriage. That day we had over a hundred guests and what a time it was. We had received over a hundred cards from family and friends, including one from our then president of the United States, Bill and Hillary Clinton! We have often wondered who actually signed the card and hand wrote our name and address on the envelope. After our wedding anniversary, Gloria returned to her home in Round Lake Heights, Illinois. John, then only eight years old, and James, about two, were with her. Dave was not able to come with them, as he was still in the army and on duty. Wilma's father flew back with Gloria and the boys as far as Chicago and from there he was on his own to Knoxville, where Bob and Sylvia met him to take him back out to Oak Ridge. It was not long after that that he took ill and was admitted to the hospital. On December 28 God took Dad LaVoy home to Heaven. Wilma's mother was already there, having gone to be with the Lord in early December seven years earlier. She had suffered much for a number of years with Alzheimer's disease.

On The Road Again

In March of 1998 we drove back down to Oak Ridge, Tennessee, to help Wilma's sister and husband dispose of their father's personal belongings, as well as sell his house. Things went very well, though it was left to Wilma's sister,

Sylvia, to take care of final settlement of his estate. We returned home by April and once again were involved in the ministry at Calvary Baptist Church in Aldergrove, working along with Bob and Aloha Vance.

In the summer of that year I received a request to fill in for John and Cindy Burrows, who were home on furlough from Guyana, South America. In the meantime, I received a call from Paul Johnson, pastor of Grace Baptist Church of the Comox Valley, in Courtney, on Vancouver Island. Could I come over and preach for him in October, while he and Cindy and the children were away on a brief vacation? Little did we know at the time that less than four years later we would sell our home in Abbotsford, move over to Comox and become a part of that church in Courtenay. I enjoyed the week I was in Courtenay. Paul is Canadian, from Edmonton, Alberta, while Cindy is American from Michigan. They had met, as we had, while students at Bob Jones University. During my free time in Courtenay, I spent my free time preparing for my upcoming trip to Guyana, preparing Bible messages as well as courses I would be teaching in the Bible college.

I was in Guyana for three months in the early part of 1999 and stayed with Leon and Nancy Willover, resident missionaries in the village of Bush Lot. Bush Lot had no electricity, no running water, no telephone system, and no sewer system. It lay right on the main highway running from the capital city of Georgetown west to the border with its neighboring country, Surinam. I enjoyed my time there preaching at a small church each Sunday in #53 village. I traveled by bus every Sunday morning and returned back to Bush Lot in the evening, in the same way. The buses in Guyana were Japanese vans that had been licensed to take up to about 12 people, but usually there were at least 15-18 people squeezed in. It was quite a trip that took up to 45 minutes to make the distance that ordinarily might take half the time. I found out real quickly how to hail the Guyanese bus to stop and pick me up. The custom was to simply stand by the edge of the road and when the bus was approaching, simply point the hand down toward the ground; that meant "stop." I also enjoyed teaching in the Bible college, which met every weekday in the back of the church building across the road from where the Willovers were living. The only problem about staying at the Willover's house was that right next door was the cinema and every night the cinema would start up its movies, with the sound turned up to full volume! I managed to fall asleep from sheer exhaustion from the day's activities.

When I left Guyana to return home, I went by way of Nassau, Bahamas. John and Sheryl Hoogendoorn were working in Nassau amongst the hearing impaired Bahamians. They were part of a small and fairly new Baptist church, which was being pastored at the time by another American missionary. It was my privilege to preach nine times in the seven days I was there in Nassau. This was my third trip to the Bahamas, having gone the first time a few years before to preach one week of revival meetings at the Nassau Christian Academy. I returned the following year to attend the graduation exercises of the Academy. The valedictorian of the class was a girl of Indian origin living in the Bahamas, Jennifer Bandhu. She had expressed to me the previous year I was in Nassau for the week of revival meetings, of her desire to become a pediatrician and wanted to take her studies at Bob Jones University. I promised her I would make contact with Dr. Bob Jones III, who was president of the university and arrange to get her into the school that following year after graduating from Nassau Christian Academy. I was able to do that and Jennifer went on to do four years of study at BJU. It is interesting to note here that in her fourth year at BJU our granddaughter, Katherine Jean, Lily Ann's oldest child, entered the university for her first year of studies and Jennifer became Katherine's "big sister."

The following year, 2000, I returned to Guyana for another three months of ministry. By this time the Willovers had retired and John and Cindy had returned for another term of service. I stayed with them and, once again, preached out at #53 village and taught at the Bible college, as well as preached at Black Bush Village, which was reached by a half hour ride over a very bumpy and pothole filled paved road. The Burrows had electricity in the evenings by means of a kerosene generator they had installed in a small shed in their back yard. Also, John had a cell phone and I was able to call Wilma every Wednesday evening at about 5 p.m., which was four hours behind Guyanese time. There was a communications relay tower near Bush Lot Village and by dialing two numbers I was able to get hold of a telephone operator in Canada, who made contact with Wilma in just a few seconds. We enjoyed talking with each other for nearly half an hour every week.

The end of June we went over to Vancouver Island and spent a weekend with the folk at Grace Baptist Church in Courtenay. From there we drove up the Island to Port Hardy, where we stayed at a lovely bed and breakfast facility. We were on our way on a special trip through the Panhandle of Alaska. Wilma had received an inheritance from her father's estate and we were using part of the money to fulfill a dream Wilma had of one day going to Alaska. We arranged to stay at a hotel in Juneau for six days, while Phyllis and Mark flew up to Juneau and spent five of those days with us. The four of us split the cost of chartering a 45-foot boat and went out for two days of deep-sea fishing off the coast of Juneau. We enjoyed that time and each of us caught our limit of salmon. We had taken British Columbia's large ferry, Queen of the North, on a 14-hour trip up to Prince Rupert, BC from Port Hardy. There we stayed in a bed and breakfast home and the next morning, the lady, who operated the bed and breakfast facility, took us down to catch an Alaskan ferry to Ketchikan. While we were on that trip up through the Panhandle of Alaska, our car was kept for us there in Prince Rupert and when we returned there we stayed again at that lovely bed and breakfast. We felt as though we were being treated like a king and queen.

During our two-day stay in Ketchikan, which extended to two more days, we were informed that our ferry from Ketchikan to farther up the island had been cancelled. We had arranged to stay at Blue Berry Hill Bed and Breakfast for two days, but couldn't stay there longer. The woman who ran that bed and breakfast arranged for us to stay at another one on the southern edge of Ketchikan. It was a beautiful home and the gentleman of the house happened to be the district attorney for that part of Alaska.

Leaving on an overnight ferry the evening of our fourth day in Ketchikan, we went on to Juneau and had those wonderful six days in Alaska's capital city. Our trip to Alaska was not finished yet, for we then traveled a short distance through the inland waterway to a small town called Haines on the southern tip of a peninsula. Knowing that we would be arriving there on Wilma's 75th birthday, and that we would be staying at a nice little motel in town, I arranged ahead of time to have a floral arrangement put into our room at the motel. What a shock it was for Wilma to find those flowers upon our walking into our room.; but was certainly a pleasant shock, to say the least. We enjoyed our brief stay in Haines, but looked forward to the final leg of our "cruise" through the inland waters of Alaska's panhandle. From Haines it was a short distance to Skagway. We were there for three days and enjoyed our time very much. One day we took a narrow gauge train up to and across into British Columbia to a ghost town called Kennedy. The train seemed to hug the side of the mountain, as it slowly wound its way up to the end of its line. The town had once been the jumping off point for men headed for the Klondike gold rush in Yukon Territory that began in 1897.

Our return by ferry to Prince Rupert was quite uneventful, for we returned without stopping anywhere along the way. Our trip to Alaska was over and after staying again at the bed and breakfast in Prince Rupert, we headed back home to Abbotsford in our car, a trip that took us about five days.

Scotland: Back To My Roots

At the end of December 2000, we flew to Glasgow, Scotland to serve at Troon Baptist Church. Our two months in Scotland were, without doubt, the most momentous time we had anywhere in special ministries since we went on retirement status with Baptist Mid-Missions. For one thing, Scotland is where part of my heritage is found. On my paternal side of the family, my people came from Scotland; you can tell that, of course, by my name. In recent years I have taken a great interest in tracing m family roots. Unfortunately, I have not been able to trace the history of my paternal side back beyond two or three generations. Hopefully, one day I shall find a good source for tracing that history farther back in time. As for my maternal side of the family, my maternal grandmother's father, James

McDermont, came from what is now Northern Ireland, in Country Tyrone. He had immigrated to America and settled in Lake City, Minnesota, married Emma Arnold, who were to become my grandmother Minnie McDermont Condon's parents. Going back much farther in my grandmother Condon's family, we find ourselves all the way back to 1640 to Plymouth Colony and to my ancestor William Sabin, who was born in England in 1609. The Sabins were Huguenots, who had fled from France because of their Protestant beliefs in the early part of the 17th century.

As for our ministry in Troon, Scotland during those two months at the beginning of 2001, I have added a report to the addenda, entitled, "Scotland Sojourn 2001." It gives a near full account of our time in Scotland and of our ministry at Troon Baptist Church. We left Scotland on February 28, flying into Heathrow Airport, where we had a layover that night, intending to fly the next morning from London, England to Seattle, Washington, nonstop. About 11 p.m. that night we were awakened out of a deep sleep at the hotel where we were staying. It was a call from Bob Vance; he was calling from their home in Aldergrove, British Columbia. What a surprise to hear from him. When I answered the phone his voice seemed to have an urgency in it, "Have you heard that there has been an earthquake in Seattle and much damage has taken place at SeaTac? All flights into that area have been canceled. There was no way we could make it the next day to Seattle." As soon as Bob hung up, I called the airline's 800 number and managed to make a change in our flight plans. We were to fly to Vancouver, BC, with a change of flights in Chicago. We contacted Gloria and Dave right away and let them know what our new flight plans were. They were living just an hour's drive from the airport. How wonderful it was to have Gloria, Dave and the boys meet us at O'Hare airport where we were able to spend time together until our flight from Chicago to Vancouver was due to board. We finally made it back home, relieved that with all this excitement we were home, safe and sound. I was thankful for the opportunity of returning for a time back to part of my family roots, back to Scotland. It is a memory that will last for the rest of my time here on earth.

In May of 2001 I went over to Victoria, capital city of British Columbia, which is located on the very southern tip of Vancouver Island. I had been invited by the pastor, Don Johnson, brother to Paul Johnson, to preach at Grace Baptist Church of Victoria. Don and his family were away for three weeks and he wanted me to preach for the three Sundays they were away. Again, it was an enjoyable time. The people were very warm-hearted and received me with open arms. It was as though I had known them for many years. I stayed in the home of the Johnsons and did much of my own cooking, though the members of the church brought in some meals for me already prepared; they also had me in their homes for a number of meals. After my ministry in Victory, I was home less than two weeks when I then flew up to Juneau, where I preached for three weeks at Bethany Baptist Church. The church is a ministry of Baptsit Mid-Missions and pastored by missionaries, John Bigelow; John and his wife, Judy, were the resident missionaries in Juneau. John had gone to Seattle for some tests regarding a possible kidney replacement and I asked if I could fill in for him.

A Call to Prince Edward Island

Just before I left for my three weeks of preaching in Victoria we received an urgent call from Rev. Steve Butler, our North America Field administrator. Could we go out to

Charlottetown, Prince Edward Island to fill in for Glenn and Sharon Gardiner for three months, from August through October? We prayed about the matter and had total peace of mind about accepting the request. We began almost immediately to make plans for yet another station supply ministry. We had always wanted to take a trip to PEI and especially visit the setting for that famous story, Anne of Green Gables. This was another dream Wilma had, which now seemed possible. We did make it to Charlottetown, but as for visiting the site of Anne of Green Gables, God had other plans for us, which would change our lives dramatically.

After a quick trip to California to help Kathy and Bruce celebrate their 25th wedding anniversary, we were back home and getting ready to leave on our trip to Charlottetown, capital city of PEI (Prince Edward Island), Canada's only island province. We had reservations on Canada's famous VIA train that crossed the country in five days. We had shipped our car ahead to Moncton, New Brunswick by freight train, with assurance that it would be there ahead of our arrival. We appreciated our former Canadian representative of Baptist Mid-Missions, Rev. Tim Friesen, parking our car in his garage until we arrived a few days later. Tim was pastor of Emmanuel Baptist Church in Moncton. His wife, Verna, was not there at the time, for she had gone down to the States to be with their daughter, who was to deliver her first baby. We arrived in Moncton on Sunday afternoon, July 29, in time to attend the evening service. The next morning Brother Friesen drove us over to the coast to the Bay of Fundy, which is known to have the highest tide in the world, when it is in. It is said to rise 53 feet at high tide. We enjoyed our time there and were able to walk all the way down to the beach below, for the tide was out. It was a difficult walk back up to where the car was parked and several times Wilma had to stop to rest; we thought it was simply because of the steepness of the path and that she was out of breath. Little did we know what was to happen to her the next morning in Charlottetown. Later that afternoon, we said goodbye to Tim and drove across the Confederation Bridge to PEI, a distance of about 8 miles across open water. The bridge connects the island to the mainland. We were to stay in the home of the Gardiners during those three months of our ministry. Their home was in the suburb of Stratford and about three miles from downtown Charlottetown.

Stroke!

Stroke! Something that no one wants to see happen to a loved one under any circumstances. Tuesday morning we had done a washing in the basement and as Wilma carried the basket of dried clothes upstairs, she struggled with the basket. We had taken a brisk walk earlier in the morning and Wilma seemed just fine. There was still no hint of what would happen within two minutes of leaving the house that Tuesday morning, on our way to the church. As we headed toward Charlottetown, Wilma's voice began slurring and she suddenly slumped over on me; she was experiencing a stroke. Realizing this I broke the speed limit as I drove ahead, not knowing where the hospital was, but knowing that I had to get her there quickly. Spying a gas station ahead of me a short distance I quickly stopped the car, leaving Wilma in a slumped over position and dashing into the gas station, cried out, "My wife's having a stroke; where's the hospital?" One man replied, pointing in the direction of the hospital, "There it is!" It was within view and hardly one minute later I pulled up to the emergency door to the hospital; again leaving Wilma in the car and dashing into the hospital I cried out the same thing, "My wife's having a stroke." Within seconds five medical personnel raced out to the car and began getting Wilma out of the car and onto a gurney. It was questionable over the next few hours as to what her survival chances would be. As soon as I gave the hospital the information they needed, I got on the telephone and began calling our family members to let them know what had happened. I contacted our mission home office and got word to all our supporters. Lily Ann got into her Internet connection and began sending word out to all on her mailing list. It was not long before people around the world began praying and God began answering prayer.

On the fourth day in emergency a specialist told Wilma, "As soon as a bed is available, we are moving you into rehab. I believe you are ready to begin therapy." And she did. It was slow going at first, but in time, she showed great progress. Near the end of the fourth week at Queen Elizabeth Memorial Hospital in Charlottetown PEI, the head nurse in the rehab section of the hospital made arrangements for us to fly back to Vancouver. Medical people would meet our flight and take her by ambulance to the general hospital in the town of Mission, near Abbotsford. In the meantime, our friend, Pastor Tim Friesen, arranged to ship our car back to Vancouver for us, where it would then be brought out to our home in Abbotsford shortly after we arrived home. God was certainly in all of this. Of course, it was the end of our ministry in Charlottetown before it even began. The people at the church were so good to me during those weeks Wilma was in the hospital. They prepared ready cooked meals for me and left them at the church every day, where I would pick them up. It meant a sudden change in plans for the Gardiners, for they had to return to PEI by the time Wilma and I flew back to Vancouver by commercial jet.

Why did God allow this to happen? We don't know, but we do know this, God never makes a mistake. It was our turn to trust Him and to rejoice in His plans, purposes and provision for our lives. This meant the end of our active ministry in retirement; no more would we be able to serve in a station supply ministry. Was this God's way of saying, "Now it is time to really retire."

We praise the Lord that our personal doctor in Abbotsford, had a doctor friend in the nearby town of Chilliwack, who was a specialist in the field of surgery that Wilma needed. We were told at the hospital in Charlottetown that her right carotid artery was approximately 80% blocked and needed to be cleaned out as soon as possible. Considering the long waiting time for a typical surgical procedure to take place in Canada, it was truly a miracle that within three weeks after our arrival back home from Charlottetown, Wilma had surgery on her right carotid artery. After the surgery was completed, I was able to see the doctor, who informed me that her artery was 100% blocked! There was no way he could clear out the artery because of her arteries being so small. As a result, he took out a vein from her right ankle and inserted it in place of the blocked part of the carotid artery in her neck. Now she has a vein that has been turned into an artery!

Yet Another Move

Near the end of 2001 we saw that it was time to make another move; this time, away from Abbotsford and to a place less stressful and with little, if any, pollution. It was because of the advice of our doctor that we made the decision to sell our home at 31539 Lombard Avenue. The house sold within a few weeks of putting it on the market, getting the price we asked for. We were able to pay off the mortgage on the house and have a sizeable amount left to put down as a down payment on our new home. We decided to move over to Vancouver Island and settle in the small town of Comox, which is not quite half way up the island from Victoria on the mainland side of the island. We bought into a twenty-four unit condominium complex, a two-bedroom apartment, which overlooked the harbor, with a nice view of the mountains to the west of us, which includes the Comox Glacier. We became part of a small, but loving congregation at Grace Baptist Church of the Comox Valley and had many opportunities to serve in the church.

By the year 2004 circumstances arose regarding family needs in the States and, once again, there were difficult decisions that had to be made. We finally made the decision to sell our condo, say goodbye to all our friends in Comox and Courtenay and move back to the States. That move took us to our Baptist Mid-Missions retirement village at Missionary Acres. The Acres, as it is commonly known, is located in the foothills of the Ozark Mountains in Southeast Missouri. We have been happy about the move, though we miss British Columbia, Canada, which had been our home for over 27 years. Opportunities to serve the Lord abound at the Acres, at our church, Evangel Baptist Church and in the surrounding communities. Is there a possibility that one day we may have to make yet another move? It's possible. By this time in our lives, we are quite used to moving and establishing ourselves in a new place. How many times have we moved in our lives? We've lost count. But until God tells us otherwise, we are contented to live out our days right here at #7 Missionary Acres, Silva, Missouri. Of course, our final move will be that day when God calls us to our eternal home in heaven. We look forward to that move in great anticipation.

While I filled in for John and Judy Bigelow in Juneau, Alaska in the spring of 2001, I read a quotation printed in a publication called, *A Lamp For My Feet*...It has been a great encouragement to me since then, especially as God took us through those deep waters of Wilma's stroke in Charlottetown, Prince Edward Island, Canada. I related, over the course of our lives, how God has given us assignments to carry out in different parts of the world, whether in the States, in India, in Canada, Scotland, Guyana, the Bahamas. I have noted that on more than one occasion doubts had arisen in our minds at first as to whether God really wanted us in a particular place of ministry, wondering how God would supply the finances, along with other basic needs. The following is the encouragement:

Fear Not
God's Assigned Task

Sometimes a task we have begun takes on a seemingly crushing size and we wonder what ever gave us the notion that we could accomplish it. There is no way out, any way around it and yet we cannot contemplate actually carrying it through. The rearing of children, or the writing of a book are illustrations that come to mind. Let us recall that the task is a divinely appointed one and divine aid is therefore to be expected. Expect it! Ask for it, wait for it, and believe that God gives it. Offer to Him the job itself, along with your fears and misgivings about it. He will not fail or be discouraged. Let His courage encourage you. The day will come when the task will be finished. Trust Him for it.

--- Source unknown.

+ Postlogue +

As I look back over the past sixty plus years of active and semi-active ministry that God gave Wilma and me, I marvel at God's grace in our lives. We have served Him in many places all over the world in different kinds of ministries. God used us to reach multitudes with the gospel of Christ and see many of them come to trust Christ as their own personal Savior. We enjoyed each and every ministry. While the moves were not always easy, we came to enjoy every place God took us.

God has blessed us with four daughters and, with their husbands, have produced for us thirteen grandchildren. Of those grandchildren we have thirteen great-grandchildren and certainly there will be more.

With the Apostle John, we can echo his words found in 3 John, verse 4, "(we) have no greater joy than to hear that (our) children walk in truth." May God keep them safe from Satan, who would seek to draw them away from the truths of God's Word. My heart's desire is that I might be found of my children, my grandchildren and my great-grandchildren, walking "worthy of the vocation" wherein God called me so many years ago. God has given me "only one life" and it is not mine to use as I see fit, for I have "been bought with a price," the blood of Christ, shed for me on Calvary's Cross.

Oh God, keep me faithful to Your Word. Whatever the price that I may have to pay, I am willing to pay it, to be faithful to You, Who has given me only one life on this earth.

ADDENDA

Addendum I. a

Minneapolis Morning Tribune's "6 A.M. Alarm Clock Edition" of Tuesday, Nov. 12, 1940 account of the Armistice Day Blizzard on November 11, 1940.

N.W. STORM RAGES ON
Forecast Gives No Hint of Letup;
7 Die as Zero Wave Rides Blizzard

Motor Traffic Paralyzed;
Scores of Towns Isolated

Gale Hits Hard at Telegraph and Telephone Services - Auto Mishaps Trap 100 Near New Brighton - Blocked Streets Sends Hundreds to Hotels

The Armistice day blizzard that virtually paralyzed transportation and crippled wire communications in Minneapolis and the northwest, roared into Tuesday with no sign of abating...The storm which passed through stages of rain and sleet to a blinding gale of snow, hit telegraph and telephone services hard. Most communities were isolated. Temperatures fell by the hour. At 4 a.m. it was 5 degrees above zero in Minneapolis.

The full extent of casualties will not be known until communications are opened up again, but deaths of six men, three of them hunters, and one woman, were reported last night...Meanwhile, they warned motorists not to venture forth unless they had specific and authentic information about road conditions. Those who had found shelter were urged to stay there until conditions improved...

Nearly 100 persons, a dozen of them cut by flying glass, were marooned near Brighton following a mass traffic accident in which 30 or more cars piled into each other on highway No. 8...The jam started when an automobile collided with a White Bear-Stillwater bus. Three more cars piled into the bus, and one of them sideswiped an oncoming car in the opposite traffic lane. Within a short time two dozen other motorists, blinded by the snow, slid into the pile of disabled machines.

Hundreds of Holiday duck hunters were marooned – 100 along the Mississippi river between Winona and Wabasha, and another 100 near Parkers Prairie, in addition to smaller parties in various sections. One group on an island near Winona was rescued by a government towboat.

(Note: on the same page that this article appeared in the Minneapolis Tribune on November 12, 1940 was the following ad: "Come FIRST to WARNER's for SNOW SHOVELS. You'll find your kind and size at the price you want to pay only 69 cents)

Addendum I.b:

My Letter to the then Editor of the Minneapolis Star Tribune, Scott Gillespie, dated, August 2, 2006:

"This article brings back many memories for me about the Armistice Day Blizzard of November 11, 1940. You see, I was not quite 15 years old at the time. Our family lived out on old D Street in Crystal Village. I had a Star Tribune paper route at the time, delivering papers out on D Street and roads that led off of that narrow two-lane road. We lived about 300 feet south of the Soo Rail line. That day I rode my blue-colored balloon tire bicycle into town (Robbinsdale) to pick up my newspapers. Mother was concerned for me, for by the time I left the rain had begun turning into snow. By the time I got to town the storm was raging in all its fury. Needless to say, the truck that usually brought the newspapers out there to Robbinsdale to deposit in the galvanized shed on Broadway never arrived. What was I to do? I knew that I couldn't stay in that unheated shed and all the stores in town were closed because of the holiday. Then I thought of our friends, the Sipes, who lived just beyond Robbinsdale High School where I was a student in the 9th grade. Mr. Sipe ran the Texaco gas station just down the street a very short distance, less than a block away. Leaving my bike inside the newspaper shed, I struggled through the deep snow, now up to my knees. Walking against the howling wind, I headed for the Sipes' house about half a mile away; it took me at least half an hour to reach their house. When they saw me they took me in and insisted that I stay at their place until the storm subsided and I could get back home. Well, I was there for three days. In the meantime, my parents were worried sick, not knowing at the first as to where I was. While I am aware that many of the phone lines were down, I do remember that I was eventually able to call them on the phone and let them know where I was and that I was safe. Yes, that experience has been burned deep into my mind that I will remember the rest of my life, if I live to be a hundred."

(Note: My letter to the editor contained a request for permission to include the article in this story of my life and ministry. Mr. Gillespie graciously granted that permission in a reply to my letter.)

Addendum II

India Comes to Canada - article by Mrs. Merle Richardson in the Spring 1974 issue of Baptist Mid-Missions' Quarterly "The Harvest"

Have you ever lived where you were surrounded by a people of foreign descent and culture? No, I don't mean in France, Germany or Mexico. I mean right here in Hometown, USA or Canada.

In Merritt, British Columbia, you may hear the strange sounds of a foreign language, high-pitched and rapid, and look out the window to see a group of East Indian ladies walking to town, East Indian children playing hockey in the street, or some of the East Indian men coming from the mills for lunch...

Right now in the province of British Columbia there are over 12,000 East Indians from the Punjab region of northwest India. In the capital city of Victoria there are about 400 families; in the city of Vancouver there are at least 1,000 families, many in Abbotsford and throughout the Fraser Valley, also interior in the smaller towns like Merritt and Quesnel. There are more coming into Canada each year...

These people speak their own Punjabi language in their homes but the men soon learn English in their work and their children in school. The women are slower to learn it. Many times they will accept a Scripture portion in Punjabi and the same in English to help them learn English. Sometimes they will also attend English classes.

What is their religion and what does it teach?

These people belong to the Sikh religion, founded in the 15th century by Guru Nanak, who is sometimes called the Martin Luther of the East because he sought reformation of his Hindu faith. He denied the existence of Jesus Christ, the prophets and the apostles. "Salvation," he said, "lies in realizing the god within one's soul (man has a spark of god; is a part of god), and dedicating oneself to him – that is, leading a clean, brotherly life as he would."

He taught only one simple belief: the oneness of god, and one simple religious practice: the constant remembrance of his name. The practice of remembering his name is done through constant repetition of his name, one of which is Waheeguru, meaning "Wonderful Lord."

What can we do to help these people from India?

First of all, let's pray for them. May we never underestimate the power of prayer. Pray that they will seek the truth and recognize the inadequacy and failure of their own religion to meet their eternal needs. And pray that the Lord will send laborers among these people, to show them THE WAY, THE TRUTH and THE LIFE
(John 14:6)

Jehovah Witnesses are taking advantage of the Indian desire to learn English by getting their false propaganda into their homes. But they will accept Christian literature and read it, too, especially if they are given a copy in Punjabi and the same in English so they can compare the two.

Some have observed that the Sikhs display a dedication and

fervor not found in Christian, Muslim or Hindu faiths. Isn't it time to change this picture?

Addendum III:

The following strategy paper was sent to the consular officer at the Canadian Consulate in Detroit, Michigan after our meeting with him in February 1977.

Subject:

A proposed strategy for establishing a new ministry of Baptist Mid-Missions of Canada in the Province of British Columbia.

Concentration of Ministry:

Mainly amongst the East Indian population, though available for all communities

Purpose of Ministry:

To minister the Christian gospel to the total man, mainly amongst the East Indian population and the establishing of orthodox Baptist churches in the communities where there is presently no such church.

Proposed Strategy for Establishing Ministry:

In order to establish a ministry amongst a given people, it is necessary to, firs of all, determine their particular needs. It will be necessary for us, therefore, to establish contact with the people amongst whom we expect to minister. This we plan on doing by means of a thorough survey in the community to determine those needs. It is interesting to note that with our East Indian population, simply by knowing a person's family name, we can generally know the following: the part of India from which he has come, his religious background and his mother tongue (language).

We shall make ourselves known to the East Indian population in that area where we shall eventually establish a work for Baptist Mid-Missions of Canada, to establish that needed rapport with them and make ourselves available to them for whatever area of service might be needed.

We shall eventually establish what we refer to as "back yard" Bible clubs for the children, as well as to organize Sunday School classes for all ages. In addition, adult home Bible study groups will be started, which will lead to the eventual organization of Baptist Church in those communities where such a Baptist testimony is not presently available. Any organized spiritual ministry of this type must begin, of course, in a well-planned home visitation program, involving many hours of visiting in the homes of interested people, as is done by any faithful pastor.

It is to be expected that in carrying out our full ministerial responsibilities, we shall be available for the total community, even beyond the East Indian ethnic group. As we determine that community, or those communities where there seems to be a need for establishing a Baptsit church, we shall seek at the earliest time possible to establish that work as an indigenous work, such that the church congregation would call its own pastor and freeing us to go on to a new area to begin a new work.

While we have been appointed by Baptist Mid-Missions of Canada to establish a spiritual ministry, primarily amongst the East Indian ethnic group now living in the Fraser Valley in the Province of British Columbia, we recognize our responsibility of ministering to the total man; i.e., to minister to both body and soul. It is our desire to be of assistance in any way possible to the newly arrived immigrant from India. They come to a land whose culture is strange to them. We believe that by our long association with them in their own homeland, we can help them in many ways to become a part of the total community.

Many of them have little or no knowledge of English, or else do not have confidence in what English they may have to actually use it. By our help, they will be able to develop a good working knowledge of English and gain full confidence in its use in the community.

--- Kenneth N. Steward
February 19, 1977

Addendum IV -

Scotland Sojourn 2001 - Special Report

<u>A Call From Cleveland, Ohio</u>

It began in early September last year, when the phone rang with a call from Rev. Bill Mosher, Field Administrator for Scotland, one among many of our Baptist Mid-Missions fields of service for which he is responsible. "Would it be possible for you to go to Scotland for two months?"

Rev. Mosher briefly outlined the situation for us. Jim and Becky Storey, who are in church planting ministry in Troon, Scotland, needed to take an emergency five-month furlough. Becky was already in the States, taking care of some important matters concerning her mother, who had recently had the second of two amputations; there was further surgery to follow. Another of our retired missionary couples, Verne and Helen Kirby, who had served for many years in Alaska and Hawaii, would be able to go for the months of October and November. If someone else could fill in for December, we could go for January and February.

We prayed about the matter and God gave us complete peace about it. As soon as we contacted Brother Mosher with an affirmative answer, things began to move swiftly. We contacted our supporters and let our church here know. We needed to have others in the church take on our responsibilities for the time we would be in Scotland. By faith we made flight arrangements and purchased tickets. The Lord provided and funds were soon in hand to pay for our air tickets to Scotland and return. In the meantime, we needed to study and make preparations for our ministries at Troon Baptist Church. Wilma would be teaching the children's Sunday school and I needed to prepare messages and Bible studies for nine weeks of service. We soon came to know that in Scotland it is the custom to have Sunday school classes for children only, which follows the morning worship service.

Travel To Scotland

Our travel to Scotland was quite uneventful, as far as to London, England. We flew from Seattle to San Francisco on December 27 with a brief stop before boarding our plane for London. It would be a tiring ten-hour flight, taking us across the northern tip of Canada, south of Greenland and Iceland and then cross over Scotland, nearly right over where we would be serving for the next nine weeks. During those ten hours we lost eight hours of time. There had been a heavy snowstorm, blanketing all of the United Kingdom. Our flight to Glasgow would be delayed by three hours. Only one runway in Glasgow was open. But we finally made it, tired and glad to be on the ground for a while. Our single missionary, Fern Kruse, was at the airport to meet us, along with one of the ladies in the church. By 11:30 pm we finally reached what would be our home during the time we served at Troon Baptist Church. W had only one desire at that time and that was to just get to bed; unpacking could wait until the next day. It had been nearly thirty-six hours since we had left our home in Canada.

Life In Scotland

Life in Scotland is decidedly different than what it is in Canada or the United States. For one thing, driving is on the left side of the road. I had no problem getting used to this change, though the problem lay with driving a left-hand drive American van on the left side of the road; in such circumstances it is not always easy to judge distances between your vehicle and the ones coming from the opposite direction, especially on narrow roads.

One word can be used to describe much of Scotland; that is "wee" (little). People drive "wee" cars on "wee" roads and live in "wee" houses. There are very few crossroads controlled either by traffic lights, or stop signs; but rather, there are 'roundabouts' requiring you to give way to the left. Even motorways (divided highways) are controlled by roundabouts when other roads make contact with the motorways. While metric measure should rule in Scotland, one sees very little evidence of it, in that speeds are given in miles per hour and weights in supermarkets seem to always be in pounds and ounces.

We had the use of the Storeys' American Dodge Caravan, which gave only about 16 mpg, or even less in stop and go traffic. Petrol (gasoline) cost nearly 80 pence per liter, or about $4.50 US per American gallon. We did very little pleasure driving, except to go to the next town, about five miles away, on Wednesday mornings to do our weekly grocery shopping.

The cost of living in Scotland is very high with the VAT (Value Added Tax – sales tax) being at 17.5%. That is how the Government in the U.K. pays for its social programs.

Struggle For National Identity

Scotland's history is one of struggle for both political and religious freedom. Scotland had fought over several centuries for independence from England, having their own kings and queens. It eventually became a part of the United Kingdom, along with England, Wales and Northern Ireland

(Ulster). Scotland enjoys home rule and has its own parliament, which was instituted in 1999. It has its own banking system and bank notes. It should be noted that her three main banks print their own currency, which is on part with the English pound and is used interchangeably.

The most interesting part of Scotland's history was its struggle for religious rights. Its people hated the Roman Church, which had great political power in the United Kingdom. But when the Catholics were replaced by the Church of England (Anglican), they were hated just as much by the Scots. Much could be written about Scotland's struggle for its religious rights, but I will comment upon just three situations.

One person who played an important part in Scotland's struggle for religious rights was John Knox. Knox, who came to be known as the "Fiery Scot," lived in the 16th century and was ordained to the Catholic priesthood. Knox broke with the Church when he came to know of its false teaching and corruption within the Church. He became convinced that the Presbyterian form of church government and doctrine was correct and, in time, was appointed as minister of the famous St. Giles (pronounced as 'Jiles') Cathedral, near to Edinburgh Castle on High Street (known more popularly as the "Royal Mile").

John Knox eventually became a bitter opponent of Mary, Queen of Scots. This cruel queen of Scotland once remarked, "I fear the prayers of John Knox more than all the assembled armies of Europe." Mary fell out with the people and soon fled to England, seeking the protection of her cousin Queen Elizabeth I. But, in the end, Queen Elizabeth, ordered the execution of Mary, Queen of Scots when it was learned that Mary had sought the overthrow of the English throne. John Knox continued his fiery preaching, but because of much illness and weakness of body, he died in 1572. He was buried behind the cathedral and now his gravesite is actually parking spot number 44 in a public parking lot. There is but a small flat stone, which identifies the place where Knox is buried.

On Wednesday, February 28, 1638 a gathering of nobles signed a National Covenant in Greyfriars Kirk and stood against Charles I, who was the ruling monarch of Scotland at the time. Those who signed the Covenant became known as the Covenanters. We were deeply moved as we visited the church and wandered through the churchyard filled with the graves of many who were killed because of their faith. At the far end of the kirk yard is located the Covenanters' Prison, where some 6,000 were kept prisoners, many of them dying there in inhumane conditions. But the most moving experience we had at the time was to view the Martyrs Memorial, a large stone, which tells the story of the 18,000 who died, many of them by hanging in nearby Grassmarket.

Another moving experience we had was our visit to Wigtown (pronounced as 'Wigton'), a small village in the southwest part of Scotland, about an hour's drive south of where we ministered in the small town of Troon. Wigtown is known as Scotland's "Book Town." It seemed to us that every other shop is a used bookshop. Just outside the village and down in what is now marshy land, there is a small monument that briefly tells the story of the two Margarets. The story in brief is this. Margaret Wilson, 18, and Margaret Lachlan, 63, both had refused to recant their faith in Christ. As a result they were both tied to a stake and left to die by drowning when the tide came in. As we visited their grave site in the nearby church yard, we tried to imagine the scene that day on May 11, 1685, when those two beautiful ladies stood firm in their faith and without a sound, entered the presence of their Lord, as the waters completely engulfed them.

The testimony of these and man thousands of others can be summed up in the words of the closing paragraph of that National Covenant signed in Greyfriars Kirk. The Covenanters did not oppose the king, but only the church that he stood for and the false doctrines it taught. "...we call the LIVING GOD, THE SEARCHER OF OUR HEARTS, to witness, who knoweth this to be our sincere desire and unfeigned resolution, as we shall answer to Jesus Christ in the great day and under the pain of God's everlasting wrath and of infamy and loss of all honour and respect in this world; most humbly beseeching the LORD to strengthen us by his HOLY SPIRIT for this end and to bless our desires and proceedings with a happy success; that religion and righteousness may flourish in the land to the glory of God..."

An Old Bible

While in Wigtown we walked into the Corner Book Shop and up to the first floor, into a small back room, where was located the theology section. There were numerous old books having to do with theology, most not very old and uninteresting. Btu sitting on a windowsill, along with several other books, was a small book. When I picked it up I found it to be part of the Bible, containing Genesis through the Psalms, along with the Psalms in metric form. This portion of the Bible was printed in the year 1823. When a find! When I opened the cover and looked at the price scrawled with a pencil, I read 3 pounds sterling (about $4.50 US). And so, I purchased that little Bible, which has found a special place in my library of numerous other Bibles, some of them nearly as old as that Bible portion. If the pages of that little Bible could speak, what stories it would have to tell, of the many hands which must have handled it, especially of one James Johnson, whose hand-penned signature, with the ear 1838, were written inside. Possibly he was the original owner of the Bible. But the pages of that little Bible do speak out, as they did on February 25, 2001, with that message from Psalm 63:

> LORD, thee my God I'll early seek;
> My soul doth thirst for thee,
> My flesh longs in a dry parch'd land,
> Wherein no waters be…

Our Ministry in Troon

Beyond all the moving experiences we had during those nine weeks, far more than we can relate in such a report as this, our ministry to the congregation of Troon Baptist Church was the most rewarding. We were greatly blessed for having had that experience. Troon lies right on the edge of the Irish Sea, about thirty miles south of Glasgow. Scots, as a whole, are some of the friendliest people on earth and especially the Christians, those who truly love the Lord. Talk about hugging people! It seems to be the custom that when you enter their homes they give a hug and again when you leave. We liked that custom.

Our ministry was not just teaching and preaching, as important as that was. We were very much involved in hospital visits, visiting in the homes of the people and seeking to meet their spiritual needs where ever and however we could. The adult daughter of one of the senior ladies lay desperately ill in a hospital in Glasgow with a seriously infected leg. One day we went with the mother by train to Glasgow to visit the daughter; it was an all day trip. Sometime later, one of the doctors on the case had suggested to the daughter the possibility of having to amputate the leg. The mother, in great despair, called us to let us know what was happening. Wilma prayed with her over the phone.

One of the men in the church had fallen from a ladder some eight feet and broke his leg so badly that several bones were sticking out of the leg. Two different surgeries, along with rods and pins, had repaired the leg; but the healing process promised to be a long one. That meant more than one visit to the hospital to see him.

Our 86-year-old neighbour across the street lived by herself, but was very weak in body and got around the house by using a "zinger" (walker). One evening she did not answer the call of another neighbour, who looked in on her every day. We supposedly had a key to the house, but it did not work, for sometime ago she had had new windows and doors installed in the house and the locks had been changed. We called 999, the emergency number in Scotland. When the police arrived, they too could not get into the house and they were not allowed to break down the door. Finally, a key was found and when we all entered, including the police, Cathy Newby, our 86-year old neighbour, was calmly sitting on the floor talking with a friend on her cell phone. So much for the emergency.

We would be amiss in this report if we did not make mention of the personal care Fern Kruse made for us. She had a ministry to university students in the nearby town of Ayr, where she had an upper two-bedroom flat in a housing development. Fern met with us every week, at which time we discussed ministry needs and prayed together. Whenever we had free days she would drive us to see the sights of Scotland. Fern was truly our able tour guide. On two occasions we had the opportunity to meet with a group of university students, share our testimony with them and also taking them briefly to the Word of God to see what God's Word had to say about the subject, "How can I know the will of God for my life?"

We left Scotland on Wednesday February 28, 2001, exactly 363 years to the day after the signing of the Scottish National Covenant at Greyfriars Kirk. Scotland is the land of my heritage and we left with mixed emotions. We had come to love Scotland, the people and the ministry at Troon. And yet, we knew our ministry there was complete. It was time to return to our home in British Columbia, Canada.

Printed in the United States
210581BV00003B/76-183/P